For my daughter Jennifer and my son
Andrew, who may be as surprised as I am
pleased that this project has come to a
successful conclusion.

Second Lieutenant Alexander Rule in 1917
(image courtesy of The Gordon Highlanders Museum)

Yet Another Glorious Day

The 1915 World War I Diary

of

Alexander Rule

D Company, 4th Battalion,
The Gordon Highlanders

Graham J Shanks

Published by Graham J Shanks
Printed and bound by The Gatehouse, Robert Gordon University

Yet Another Glorious Day

First published in 2015 by

Graham J Shanks
24 Glenury Crescent
Stonehaven
Aberdeenshire
Scotland
AB39 3LF
Copyright © Graham J Shanks

ISBN: 978-0-9934415-0-9

British Library Cataloguing-in-Publication Data

A catalogue record for this book is available from the British Library

Printed and Bound in Great Britain

by

The Gatehouse – Design and Print Consultancy
Robert Gordon University
www.rgu.ac.uk/gandp

CONTENTS

PREFACE

Alexander Rule was born in Huntly, Aberdeenshire, Scotland on the 21st of September 1895. He died, aged 87, at the Cottage Hospital, Meigle, Perthshire, Scotland on the 4th of July 1983. That he lived to such a grand age – and experienced so much on the way (as seen in his diary and in the chapter later that bears his name) – is little short of miraculous as this book, the transcript of his 1915 diary, shows.

In 1913 Alexander, aged 17, progressed from school in Huntly to matriculate as an Arts student at the University of Aberdeen, where he joined the University Company (U Company) of the 4th Battalion, The Gordon Highlanders. This unit was part of the volunteer Territorial Force that came into being in 1908, although U Company, 1st Volunteer Battalion, The Gordon Highlanders, had been established on 10th November 1898. Additionally, University students had helped swell the ranks of other local military units for many years previously.

(The rich history of volunteers in and around Aberdeen is laid out elsewhere, most recently and clearly by JB Duffus in his very readable *Town, Gown and Gun – A Centennial History of Aberdeen Universities Officers Training Corps 1912-2012'*.)

Young Rule joined U Company for a number of reasons. He says, in his 1934 book *Students Under Arms'*, that *"the kilt in itself is sufficiently attractive – provided one's legs are reasonably proportionate – and, even with the lowly status of a private of the line, one can bask fully in the reflected glory of regimental traditions. The kilted recruit enters into a particularly colourful inheritance, that dates from "battles long ago".*" (For various reasons, not all of them admirable, the kilt features on several occasions in Rule's diary, but that is yet to come.)

However, the main attraction for him to join was the *"good fellowship in U Company's ranks. Friendly senior privates, several of whom were leaders in the social and corporate life of the university, gave me helpful hints. ...I was expected to walk humbly and bare-headed, to wear no unseemly raiment and to refrain from carrying a walking stick. So ran the unwritten law."*

The highlight of the training year for U Company members was the two-week annual camp held every summer at various locations around Scotland. In 1914, summer camp was held at Tain in Ross-shire and commenced on the 17th of July.

The movement northward to Tain was by troop train, the journey hastened by inter-compartmental singing loud enough to be appreciated by bemused passengers waiting on the platform at Inverness.

Having settled into their tents and pushing thoughts of recent exams to the backs of their minds, the student soldiers, many in their late teens, enthusiastically tackled their military training, sporting activities and the local social scene.

Rule tells us in his book that the instructors "*did their damnedest to lick us into shape on parade, but ... frequently some luckless sergeant had to serve as the main butt of an officer's wrath for our shortcomings in the military art*".

Relaxing beside their tents at Tain. Alexander Rule is on the right.

Few would argue that the balance between 'studenting' and soldiering during this camp was much more in favour of the former than the latter. How that was to change.

U Company rests on a route march near Chapel Road, Tain.

U Company bathing parade, shores of Dornoch Firth, July 1914

This photograph (with Alexander Rule on the extreme right) was probably the last one taken of U Company all together. It was early on the morning of 30th July 1914. On their return to camp, they learned of the coming war with Germany and the resultant mobilisation. Territorial Force soldiers were not obliged to serve overseas, but most readily volunteered to serve King and Country and experience what then was called 'the great adventure'.

The War Office decreed that Bedford would be the best place for many of the Highland Regiments to undertake their pre-deployment training. Some 18,000 men descended on the town during autumn, 1914, to prepare themselves for war. Included in this number were the members of U Company, now designated D Company (the original name of the Aberdeen Grammar School and Robert Gordon's College contingents of 4th Gordons with whom U Company was now merged). Additionally, many former members of U Company had re-enlisted upon the outbreak of war.

The change of unit name – almost always a thorny issue in military circles – was met with little enthusiasm or, initially, compliance by those ex-U Company students who remained in the 'new' D Company. However, members being transferred to, or commissioned into, other units during the long tedious spell at Bedford hastened the dilution of the usage of the title 'U'. Many of these transferees were anxious not to miss active service, due to the widespread belief that the war would be "over by Christmas".

Although it was helping to prepare them for their service overseas, Rule and his colleagues took badly to the level of military discipline imposed at Bedford, which was far in excess of anything they had encountered before. These bright young minds did not take well to what they saw as the pettiness of army regulations covering, for example, the exact placement of spare laces during a kit inspection, or the awarding of extra duties for a piece of fluff found on a uniform jacket. There were also frequent spells of inactivity, when a natural inclination to learning helped fill in the time.

Whiling away the hours at Bedford

When D Company 4th Gordons was finally ready to go to war in 1915, Alexander Rule was one of some 120 'former' U Company soldiers who were included, many of whom were still disinclined to embrace the change in title foisted upon them by officialdom. They cherished the camaraderie that had bonded them during their pre-war service with U Company, even to the extent in several cases of declining the opportunity of a commission so that they might continue to serve with their fellow Aberdeen University students.

Coming from an environment that involved much study and writing, it is not surprising that many of the members of U Company kept diaries and wrote many letters. In John McConachie's 1995 book *'The Student Soldiers'*, which is a comprehensive history of U Company, he draws heavily on the diary of John F Knowles M.A. and includes extracts from several others, Alexander Rule's being one of them.

'The Student Soldiers' provides much fascinating detail about the months spent in Bedford and provides a great deal of interesting background to the context of Rule's 1915 diary transcript contained in this book.

In his diary, Rule frequently gives us a daily weather report. More information on the weather is to be found in Annex B – Diary Data, but as winter turned to spring and spring turned to summer in 1915, he often described the weather in Belgium as 'glorious', hence the title of this book –

'Yet Another Glorious Day'

THE DIARY

Alexander Rule's 1915 diary formed part of the research material collected by John McConachie for his book '*The Student Soldiers*' from Rule's nephew, John Rule Philip. McConachie subsequently passed the diary on to Aberdeen Universities' Officers Training Corps who made it available for the transcript in this book.

The Diary is a fascinating artefact. It is, literally, what it says on the cover – a Collins Pocket Diary. However, inside that cover is found a rich mix of original pages in chronological order, pages in their correct chronological context but which have been re-dated and re-ordered, as well as memorandum pages removed from their original place at the end of the diary and used to supplement lengthy entries.

In addition, there are some completely 'new' pages that have been made from what appears to be sheets taken from a lined exercise book and cut to size. To add to the challenge of reading Rule's very small handwriting and making sense of his unique abbreviations, most of the original script has been overwritten. (Rule comments appropriately in his 1967 book '*Forests of Australia*' where, in his acknowledgements, he says, "*The typing services coped equally efficiently with foul handwriting and with much unfamiliar jargon.*")

To be borne in mind, however, is the very difficult environment that any paperwork faced during this conflict. Given even the number of occasions on which Private Rule and his comrades were soaked to the skin it may be incredible that this diary survived at all. Or is it? Did Rule carry his diary with him at all times?

There is evidence to suggest he did not. He makes reference to writing up "*back numbers*" of his diary on 24th April; to "*writing up diary – completed portion on France right up to date*" on 7th May; and he refers to writing in his "*dry diary*" on 7th September. There are also passages in the diary that summarise several days or weeks at a time, although some of these are on the 'new' pages described earlier.

He may well have decided that, along with other kit, it would be safer to leave his diary behind when his unit went for a spell in the front line.

Additionally, for reasons of security, it made sense for soldiers not to have personal diaries that might fall into the hands of the enemy. Information on people, units, locations and equipment would all contribute to German intelligence, albeit that they might have expended a disproportionate amount of resource determining the meaning of, for example, *Turra*, *neeps* and *a thrashin'*.

A likely explanation for much of the re-working of the diary is linked to Alexander Rule having written a book, mentioned earlier, based on his 1915 wartime experiences – '*Students Under Arms – Being the War Adventures of the Aberdeen University Company of the Gordon Highlanders*' (Aberdeen University Press, 1934).

He obviously and understandably draws heavily on his diary as the foundation for his 1934 book yet, whilst writing an excellent and structured volume, he does, with the passage of time and an almost doubling of his age, leave behind some of the spontaneity, excitement and emotion that characterise the original work transcribed here.

Whether Rule made the supplements and amendments found in his diary specifically for – and in the run-up to – his '*Students Under Arms*' book of 1934, or immediately after the war, or perhaps even whilst recovering from his wounds, we shall never know – but does it really matter?

Does the diary absolutely accurately reflect all the situations through which, for much of 1915, this teenager lived such a hugely demanding existence? Possibly not, but who would argue that every published diary has been one hundred per cent representative of the facts. As a very experienced police sergeant once said of road traffic collisions, "When you read the variations in witness statements, you can't help but wonder about history".

Without any doubt whatsoever is that what we read in Alexander Rule's 1915 diary is an extraordinary insight into a unique unit and how these very bright, capable, fun-loving students developed into battle-hardened soldiers, overcoming deprivation and hardships with a spirit and determination that brought enduring credit to them, The Gordon Highlanders and The University of Aberdeen.

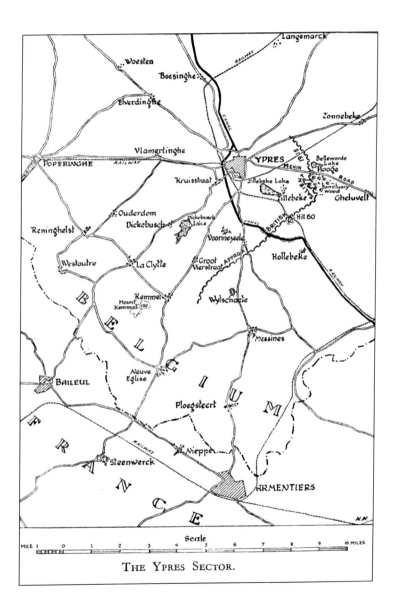

THE YPRES SECTOR.

THE TRANSCRIPT

It became clear quite early on in the work of transcribing the diary that there was a need for notes, illustrations and other information to put some of the places and events described into context, to explain military terms, to give meaning to some of Rule's own abbreviations and contemporary language, as well as to give a little background to many of the individuals mentioned.

These notes, photographs and diagrams provide as much content as the diary entries and, consequently, in the next section they have been placed on the left-hand pages, with the diary entries on the right-hand pages.

Additional details of many of the individuals mentioned in the diary are to be found in Annex A.

NOTES ON THE TRANSCRIPT

[2.1] BEF – British Expeditionary Force. The British Army force that was sent to the Western Front. In 1914, the German Army opened the Western Front by first invading Luxembourg and Belgium, then gaining military control of important industrial regions in France. The tide of the advance was dramatically turned with the Battle of the Marne. Following the race to the sea, both sides dug in along a meandering line of fortified trenches, stretching from the North Sea to the Swiss frontier with France. This line remained essentially unchanged - but fiercely fought over - for much of the war.

[2.2] Leave – It was - and remains - standard practice for troops to be given home leave prior to a planned period of service overseas.

[2.3] Cat's wash – Face and hands only.

[2.4] Tay Bridge Disaster – The Tay Bridge Disaster (1879). The bridge collapsed during a storm whilst a train was crossing carrying some 75 passengers, all of whom were lost. Remains of piers from the old bridge are still visible.

[2.5] Charles Rule – See Annex A - People in the Diary

[2.6] Mons – The Battle of Mons took place in late August 1914. It was the BEF's first major action of the War and was a subsidiary action of the Battle of the Frontiers, in which the Allies clashed with Germany on the French borders. The British Army attempted to hold the line of the Mons-Condé Canal against the advancing Germans. Although the British fought well and inflicted disproportionate casualties on the numerically superior enemy, they were eventually forced to withdraw due to both the greater strength of the Germans and the sudden retreat of the French Fifth Army, which exposed the British right flank. Though initially planned as a simple tactical withdrawal and executed in good order, the British retreat from Mons lasted for two weeks and took the BEF to the outskirts of Paris before it successfully counter-attacked, along with the French, at the Battle of the Marne.

BEDFORD

January 19th-24th BEF[2.1] Leave[2.2]

Tuesday 19th January
Bedford → Huntly

Left Bedford 8pm on special train on "BEF leave". Very cheery crowd including Gordons, Camerons, Argylls, etc. Blazing light in Midlands and North - steel production for implements of war.

Wednesday 20th January

Dawn at Carlisle: Cat's wash[2.3] and leg stretch on platform.

First sight of Edinburgh Castle, Scott Monument, Calton Hill, Firth of Forth, etc. Impressive show of cruisers and destroyers etc.

Tay Bridge[2.4]. Stubs of old piers from 1870 (?) disaster visible.

Aberdeen 12.30 to 2.30. Met brother Charlie.[2.5] First-hand accounts of Mons,[2.6] etc. from a Cameron Highlander (Regulars) - a fellow passenger to Huntly.

Huntly - round of calls at Lodge, a very late sitting.

[4.1] Huntly Lodge – Now the Castle Hotel, The Lodge was built as a family home for the Dukes of Gordon during the 18th century. It was refurbished and extended with stone from the old Huntly Castle in 1769 and renamed Huntly Lodge. The 5th and final Duke of Gordon enlisted Archibald Simpson - the celebrated Aberdeen architect - to help with its design. After the Duchess of Gordon died in 1864, it was occupied by a series of tenants, normally estate workers from Richmond and Gordon estates. Alexander Rule's father was Estate Forester and the family lived in the Lodge. His sister Jane (Jeannie) married a neighbour who also lived in the spacious Lodge (Michael Philip, Domestic Gardener, who lived with his widowed mother and sisters). Huntly Lodge was sold from the estate in 1924, the Army used it as a hospital during World War II and, in 1946, it was sold once more and became the Castle Hotel.

[4.2] Shanks, [4.3] C Reid, [4.4] Middleton – See Annex A - People in the Diary

[4.5] Coy – Company. In early 1915, the organisation of the Army's units was: 12 men in a section with a Corporal in charge, 4 sections in a platoon with a Lieutenant or Second Lieutenant in command, 4 platoons in a company with a Major or Captain in command, 4 companies in a battalion with a Lieutenant Colonel in command and 2 or more regular battalions in an infantry regiment with a Colonel in command. However, this was frequently subject to change as the fortunes of war - not least of which casualties on one hand, yet massive recruitment on the other, as well as development of new tactics - required differing setups in different units.

[4.6] r&rm – Running and rapid marching.

[4.7] 2Lt Ian Clarke, [4.8] Sgt Sandy Skinner – See Annex A - People in the Diary

[4.9] Route marches – Marches of many miles, in formation, designed to improve soldiers' stamina and endurance as well as camaraderie.

[4.10] Clapham and Oakley – notwithstanding these being names of areas in London, in this context they are villages near Bedford.

Thursday 21st & Friday 22nd January
Huntly Lodge[4.1]

Hard frosts. Made a round of old haunts also cemetery to visit mother's grave.

Old "work gang" with James Wilson, foreman, at their accustomed tasks - pruning hedges, etc.

Saturday 23rd January

Left Huntly for Aberdeen.

Sunday 24th January Aberdeen → Bedford

Left Aberdeen by special train for Bedford in compartment with Shanks,[4.2] C Reid,[4.3] Middleton[4.4] 'U' Coy[4.5] - a wearisome trip.

(John Shanks and Hugh Middleton both killed at Ypres in 1915)

Monday 1st - Thursday 18th February
Bedford

Routine training exercises from early morning "r&rm[4.6]" onwards. Under 2Lt Ian Clarke[4.7] (Champion Scottish Hurdler) very strenuous for most of us but Sgt. Sandy Skinner[4.8] easily kept pace. Extended order drill, bayonet fighting, musketry, Company and Battalion drill in Area "A". Route Marches,[4.9] e.g. via Clapham & Oakley[4.10] - attack formations ("blobs") to dodge artillery fire - sandwiched into a march of about 12 miles.

AT BEDFORD

Colour Sergeant J D Pratt

Two members of U Company

4th Gordons crossing Bromham Bridge, some 2.5 miles from Bedford

AT BEDFORD

Relaxing in the garden of billets at Landsdowne Road, Bedford

Soldiers of U Company at Bedford

[8.1] Mounted Officers – So many Volunteer officers were injured due to having little or no riding experience that many Commanding Officers banned the practice. Trench warfare finally did away with the need within most infantry units.

[8.2] Lachie MacKinnon – Captain Lachlan MacKinnon - See Annex A - People in the Diary

[8.3] O.C. – Officer Commanding.

[8.4] O.R.s – Other Ranks – the rank and file soldiers.

[8.5] Pack Drill – Marching whilst wearing heavy pack of equipment – sometimes used as a punishment.

[8.6] picket – properly 'picquet' or 'piquet' – in this context, guard duties.

[8.7] fatigues – non-combat, but essential, duties. A unit had to be self reliant in many ways, e.g. it often had to dig its own trenches and cook its own food. On the Western Front, fatigues included carrying food, water and ammunition, erecting barbed wire obstacles, acting as guides or guards and filling sandbags.

[8.8] N.C.O.s – Non-commissioned Officers. In the WWI Gordon Highlanders, these would be soldiers promoted from the rank of Private to Lance Corporal, Corporal, Sergeant and Colour Sergeant. Above NCOs were Warrant Officers Class I and II. Other regiments have different names for equivalent non-commissioned ranks.

[8.9] Major General Bannatyne-Allasan – Properly Bannatine-Allason – See Annex A - People in the Diary

[8.10] Silver – See Annex A - People in the Diary

[8.11] Spud Thomson – See Annex A - People in the Diary

Coy. Officers were mounted by now.[8.1] Several of them, including Lachie McKinnon,[8.2] O.C.[8.3] U Company, were no horsemen.

O.R.s[8.4] got extra items of equipment issued for overseas use and there were regular occasional "night operations" of digging trenches in rear of Biddenham Village.

For various army 'crimes' e.g. dodging early morning 'r&rm' parade or faults in turnout (Uniform, equipment, etc.) at daily inspection, we were given pack drill[8.5] or extra picket[8.6] fatigues.[8.7] Railway Station picket duty, in lieu of routine parades, was popular under easy going NCOs[8.8] meeting girl friends on London trains.

The weather varied from Spring-like days to winter conditions but affected routine very little.

On the eve of our departure for France (18 Feby) we were inspected on Area 'A' by Major General Bannatyne Allasan.[8.9] Later by Brigadier General Campbell, both in complimentary mood.

Wild celebrations marked the final night especially amongst U Coy cooks, with Silver[8.10] beseeching Spud Thomson[8.11] to "peuk out of the window like a gentleman".

[10.1] Lieutenant Jimmie Watson – See Annex A - People in the Diary

[10.2] Glengarry – The first use of the classic, military glengarry, capable of being folded flat, may have been around 1841. In the 1850s, its use spread to other Highland Regiments. It continues to be worn by The Royal Regiment of Scotland to the present day.

Glengarry with Gordon Highlanders cap badge and check pattern

[10.3] SS 'Archimedes' – A transport ship that was used as a troop carrier for much of the War.

Friday 19th February - Bedford →
Southampton. Boat

Wild rush to get on parade first thing. U Coy
overslept almost to a man.

Lieutenant Jimmie Watson[10.1] last on parade
with a mighty 'hangover'.

Lachie: a recent bridegroom, almost in tears.

Spud Thompson with crossed ladles strapped
on his pack & minus his Glengarry[10.2] bonnet.
Lachie asked him why and got a feisty answer.

Crowds along the route to Bedford Railway
Station from the 'house'.

U Coy loaded Battalion transport in style.
Leisurely trip. Reading. Winchester - Oxford
(college rowers in barges on the river).

"Archimedes"[10.3] old cattle boat: ORs packed
like sardines in a filthy hold - horses & mules
on deck above.

Heavy rain dripping down hatches.

Picket duty on deck. Occasional glimpse of
destroyer escort & hospital ships all lit up.

[12.1] Presenting/Sloping arms – Different forms of rifle drill, awkward when carrying lots of other kit.

[12.2] La Marseillaise – The French National Anthem.

[12.3] Knox – See Annex A - People in the Diary

[12.4] Goatskins – Additional outer clothing, made of animal hides, was issued to soldiers on the Western Front during the winter of 1914-1915. Some were made of sheepskin, some of goatskin. Whilst effective in having good insulation properties, the men often referred to them as 'Bunnies', 'Woolly Bears', or 'Stinkers'. By the second winter, the serge-lined leather jerkin superseded animal skins and continued to be seen in one form or other throughout much of the Twentieth Century.

[12.5] Estaminets – small, no-frills cafés that served beer and wine.

[12.6] Bell tents – Conical shape, sleeping around 15 men. Large enough to hold a section and their kit – at a push.

[12.7] Gamins – Street urchins.

[12.8] Lachlan McLean Watt (Padre) – See Annex A - People in the Diary

[12.9] Padre – In the Gordon Highlanders' case, a serving officer who was an ordained minister, providing for the troops' spiritual welfare.

[12.10] Turra – Turriff, an Aberdeenshire town.

[12.11] Roy – Robert Topping – See Annex A - People in the Diary

FRANCE & ONWARD TO BELGIUM

Saturday 20th February - Le Havre

Hove to outside Le Havre 4am. Sunken transport at entrance to harbour. Casino high on cliffs - our first sight of France. March to Bleville Camp led by our pipers.
French sentries presenting arms brought us frequently to attention (arms sloped)[12.1] to our annoyance.
U Coy sang La Marseilles[12.2] in French to joy of locals. Steepish climb & sweat. Cold breeze at top. Eddie Knox[12.3] to goatskin-coated[12.4] train Conductor - "Comment se porte votre Teddy Bear M'sieur?" Everything new and strange not least the language. Beer at estaminets[12.5] cheap and nasty. Comfy enough in bell tents.[12.6]

Sunday 21st February - Le Havre - Bleville

"La Dimanche"! Could scarcely believe it was Sunday. Tried to shave. Those d-d army razors. Rifle & med. inspect. in forenoon. Ration of dates! Trying out "French"? on Fr. gamins[12.7] (advertising wares & sisters!).
Pretty scenery & mild weather. Met Lachlan McLean Watt[12.8] (padre[12.9] & poet) in YMCA - ideal padre (full of fun) asking me if I knew "Turra". [12.10]
Nice looking M'selle in estaminet, full of joie de vivre (fond of Jocks too). Roy[12.11] & Knox on diagnostic expedition.

[14.1] Billy A – Billy Anderson - See Annex A - People in the Diary

[14.2] Knockando – Robert Smith - See Annex A - People in the Diary

[14.3] MP – Military Police. In WWI, there were Military Mounted and Military Foot Police. They were responsible not only for aspects of discipline and investigation involving more serious offences, but also route control, host-nation liaison and straggler control.

[14.4] Piled arms – Rifles stacked in pyramids.

4th Gordons, 1914 (Courtesy of The Gordon Highlanders Museum)

[14.5] Full equipment – For the Highland Regiments, this was:

Clothing worn		18lb 12oz	8.50kg
Arms		10lb 9oz	4.78kg
Ammunition		9lb 0oz	4.08kg
Tools		2lb 9oz	1.15kg
Accoutrements		8lb 4oz	3.81kg
Articles in pack		10lb 2oz	4.58kg
Rations and Water		5lb 14oz	2.65kg
	TOTAL	**65lb 2oz**	**29.55g**

[14.6] Souvenirs – French and Belgian civilians craved souvenirs early in the war, often swapping dubious-quality alcohol for regimental buttons and badges.

Sunday 21st February - Le Havre - Bleville
(Continued)

Goatskins issued - made us look like teddy bears - mittens too!
Billy A.[14.1] & Knockando[14.2] got their names taken by MP[14.3] for being in billet "Out of Bounds" to troops. "Knock" of all people. We just escaped.
Very chilly in evening - had to close up tent flies.

Monday 22nd February - Le Havre - Train

Hoar frost. Up at 2.15am. Rolled blankets, packed & left Camp about 3am. Silent march through dark dreary streets of Havre - stillness made us enter into the spirit of things. Long wait at Station - piled arms[14.4] & lay in gutter (hard cobble stones) then into Station open platform to wait till daylight - hoar frost outside. Sleep mere pretence.
"All Aboard". Horse boxes (8 cheval en longue 40 hommes) 30 of us with full equip[14.5] and rifles.
Bales of straw welcome on floor.
Horrible jolting & funereal pace.
Eternal cry of "souvenirs"[14.6] at all towns in exchange for "vin" (sometimes).
Only once allowed to get out to stretch aching limbs. Scenery monotonous. As viewed from between slats of horsebox windows (just like cattle).
Thro' Dieppe -

[16.1] Lord Roberts – See Annex A - People in the Diary

[16.2] Bully (Beef) – Tinned corned beef, a hugely important mainstay of army rations. Could be eaten cold, straight from the tin, or in sandwiches, or heated with vegetables.

[16.3] Contemptibles – Emperor Wilhelm II of Germany was very dismissive of the BEF. He reportedly issued an order in August 1914 to "exterminate... the treacherous English and walk over General French's contemptible little army". Hence the survivors of the regular army dubbed themselves "The Old Contemptibles".

No evidence of any such order being issued by the Kaiser has ever been found. It was probably a British propaganda invention, albeit one often repeated as fact and the name certainly stuck.

[16.4] Travailleurs – Manual workers.

[16.5] Horse box – See right. The image is of U Company members.

[16.6] Firing Line – The forward-most line of trenches from which an infantry unit would direct fire onto the enemy.

[16.7] "4s" – Marching four men abreast was the normal formation at the time.

A break on the journey to Bailleul

Tuesday 23rd February - Train → Bailleul

Rain, sleet and <u>snow</u> during night.

Through Boulogne, Calais, St. Omer (where Lord Roberts[16.1] died). Sleet made snowy landscape look bleak & uninviting. "Is that Calais - the place the Germans wanted?" "Then why the hell didn't we let them have it?" Succession of halts in fields - jam & bully[16.2] - evidence of past halts (following in footsteps of Contemptibles).[16.3] Cheerier aspect by day.

French "travailleurs"[16.4] in evidence. Trains crawled along - ample time to pick flowers <u>or</u> <u>grow</u> <u>them</u>. Never forget frightful nightmare of cramp, lying partly under & partly <u>over</u> <u>bed</u>mates.

Bailleul at last - pessimist suggested we might be glad of horse box[16.5] sometime! Hosp. train with patients in Stn. Billeted at "Grapperies du Nord" - huge glass houses. Canadians & Cheshires staggering back fr firing line[16.6] - some ghastly & at last gasp (no attempt at 4s).[16.7]

Proper atmosph. of firing line - guns booming. Short walk thro' streets & good sleep in strange surroundings.

[18.1] Foot inspections – Preventing Trench Foot, caused when feet suffer prolonged exposure to damp, dirt and cold. Untreated, it often results in gangrene, which can require amputation. It is still found – cases were reported in soaked music festival-goers in recent years.

[18.2] Lime juice – A source of citric acid; preventing scurvy, a disease with symptoms of malaise and lethargy, followed by spots on the skin, spongy gums, and bleeding from the mucous membranes. Scurvy was prevalent amongst sailors and others who lacked a regular supply of fresh fruit and vegetables on long voyages. Limes, not as effective as lemons, were easily come by in the British West Indies, leading to UK sailors being called "Limeys".

[18.3] Funk – Could mean someone who shirks, is hesitant, or even cowardly. Most soldiers feel some fear but, as has been said, *"Courage isn't freedom from fear, it's being afraid and going on"*.

[18.4] Grappery – Les Grapperies du Nord – glasshouse-grown vines.

Arrowed, Left-Right; DD Booth, Charlie Reid, 'Gamin' Anderson, Sandy Gunn, WR Kennedy, R Davidson, AP Spark, RB Topping.

[18.5] Crichty – Sergeant Arthur Crichton - See Annex A - People in the Diary

Wednesday 24th February - Bailleul

Rain & snow. Quagmire at entrance gate. Cold wash in hot? house. Rifle & foot inspct.[18.1] Rush on grapes & French rolls (on sale by women vendors). "Parade for lime juice!"[18.2] Entirely bad - very bitter. 3rd blanket taken away but not without argument. Out with Billy A on pass. Saw few of Artists Rifles. Beer, coffee & convict haircut from Froggie. Wouldn't stop jawing French at me. Cheshires appeared to be mob of funks.[18.3] Wondered as I sat x leg on Grappery[18.4] floor & the guns roared, will I be a funk or not? - but didn't seem possible to get to grips with question - going up to line - just in natural order of things. Peculiar feeling to pass hand over my head & not encounter any 'resistance'.

Thursday 25th February - Bailleul - Orders to move on Saturday

Not a bad day on whole. Heavy snow-fall in morning. Feet washing (for feet inspection) delicate operation these mornings (with sponge) - too d-d cold at outside pond. On pass in forenoon with Crichty[18.5] & Billy A - inspect. of Bailleul Grand Place etc. transport all over place. Roar of big guns shaking the windows - prospect of knowing gunfire at close qrs. didn't seem to worry us.
Hair cutting craze (convict style). Little Coy drummer got his Regt No branded on his head (Lachie didn't quite appreciate the joke!) Good few 'planes around. Incessant rumble of guns. Issue of hot rum in evening.

[20.1] Kilt braces – Kilts often required the extra security of braces to prevent their unwanted descent. This was brought about by the wearer becoming slimmer due to regular exercise and often-spartan meals and/or by the kilt becoming much heavier due to being soaked or caked in heavy mud.

[20.2] Put in Pass – Soldiers normally required written permission to be 'off camp' when not on duty.

[20.3] Northum Fus – Northumberland Fusiliers.

[20.4] Granadine – Properly Grenadine, a non-alcoholic cordial often made from pomegranate.

[20.5] Indians – The Indian Army contributed a large number of divisions and independent brigades to the European, Mediterranean and the Middle East theatres in World War I. Over one million Indian troops served overseas, of whom 62,000 died and another 67,000 were wounded. In total over 74,187 Indian soldiers died during the war.

Friday 26th February – Bailleul – Great many aeroplanes

(Glorious day) Doing bit of 'needlework' in the button line (for kilt braces).[20.1] Put in pass[20.2] in afternoon – no need to – whole Bn 'let loose' for afternoon & evening. Out with Billy. Inspected Cathedral interior – very ancient – fine carving – altogether deeply impressive effect.

"Café du Canard?" afterwards. Roy, Knoxie there too – gt. fun. Madame made everybody pay twice (once at table & once again going out) – except us – we waited until we were leaving! Pretty well painted place red aftrd. Knoxie airing his French? in shops with devastating results. Made round of estaminets – struck decent one at last. Met some Northumb Fus[20.3] with extensive vocabulary of swear words. Hot "Granadine"[20.4] then hot rum on return.

Saturday 27th February – Bailleul → La Clytte

Snow on ground in morning & bitterly cold all evening. On loading fatigue (blankets). Packed up then weary wait.

Left Bailleul 9.30am – march through streets headed by pipers (D Coy leading). Pack felt like ton weight. Passed aerodrome, a few Indians,[20.5] a dog team in harness (weird sight) & some very fine Country Chateaus. Halts very acceptable (2 only to La Clytte). Hard pavé roads – but very muddy.

[22.1] 8th Bde (III Div) – The 8th Brigade of 3 Division.

[22.2] R Scots – Royal Scots.

[22.3] Middsex – Middlesex Regiment.

[22.4] "Saw shell bursting for 1st time!" – This one sentence gives an insight into the commonly-held feelings of excitement that so many soldiers, new to the front and often in their teens, held prior to their exposure to the horrors of war. Especially in the trenches, war could, in an instant, be all at once shocking, deafening, brutal, violent, gory and deadly butchery – but that was still to come.

"Bursting Shell" by Christopher RW Nevinson

[22.5] Father – John Rule – See Annex A - People in the Diary

[22.6] Verey lights – Flares, often brilliant white, used to illuminate the battlefield for a short time, thus seeing whether the enemy were moving about, for example in working parties or patrolling. Named after their American inventor, Edward Very, a naval officer.

Saturday 27th February - Bailleul → La Clytte (Continued)

2nd halt just over frontier between France and Belgium (1st Frontier I've seen & nothing wonderful).
Passed good few troops Scot. English. Arrived at huts pretty well done (long inactivity & cold). 23 in hut (miserable affairs) & sea of mud around. Remainder of 8th Bde (III Div)[22.1] - 1st Gordons, R Scots,[22.2] Suffolks & Middsex[22.3] all around La Clytte.

Saw shell bursting for 1st time![22.4]

Braziers in huts - kippering effect but comfy. Wrote Father.[22.5]

Sunday 28th February - La Clytte - Billets

Pleasant day. Drying wind & sun. Inspected by Brig. Gen in forenoon. Little man with gentle face. 15 Platoon on fatigue in afternoon. Bitterly cold washing & shaving these mornings in "burn". Couldn't realize it was Sunday.
Guns shelling trenches quite near rattling corrugated iron roofs of huts.
Suffolks' transport "damaged" by shellfire on way back from trenches last night.

Curious place this 'town' of huts. Watching verey[22.6] lights in evening.

[24.1] Monkey Motions – Physical exercises (called 'p jerks' later).

[24.2] Wattles – A wattle is a woven lattice of wooden strips. It can be used as fencing, to make gates or, as here in Rule's diary, to improvise a track over muddy ground.

[24.3] Gen Sir Horace Smith-Dorrien – See Annex A - People in the Diary

[24.4] Maj Gen Fergusson – See Annex A - People in the Diary

[24.5] Sgt Calder – See Annex A - People in the Diary

[24.6] 1st Jocks – 1st Battalion Gordon Highlanders.

[24.7] Camerons – The Cameron Highlanders.

[24.8] Pratt – See Annex A - People in the Diary

[24.9] Dickebush – Properly 'Dickebusch' or 'Dikkebuss'.

[24.10] Pete – Private J.H.S Peterkin – See Annex A - People in the Diary

Monday 1st March - La Clytte - Billets

Thunder, rain & snow! March came in "like a lion" all right. "Monkey Motions" [24.1] in morning in cold & mud. Clearing away mud (or trying to) in forenoon laying "wattles".[24.2] Inspection in afternoon by Gen Sir Horace Smith Dorrien.[24.3] Very strong face and piercing eyes, square jaw very picturesque figure and like in photos. Maj Gen Fergusson[24.4] there too besides usual crowd of staff officers. Had almost given up hope of their arrival (d - d long wait).

At La Clytte with Billy Anderson evening. Coffee etc. Nice looking M'selle in shop (buxom type). Present of 'baccy' & 'fags' to 1st Gs. Sgt Calder[24.5] left for Bailleul (Commission) without firing a shot! Lucky or unlucky?

Tuesday 2nd March - La Clytte - Billets

No rain! R&rm then "p jerks" before breakfast (or "monkey motions") as the "1st Jocks"[24.6] call them. Cutting down trees in wood near R Scots HQrs - gathering brushwood in wagon loads. Camerons[24.7] there too. (Rotten job - hot & cold alternately) Pratt[24.8] working like a Trojan - wielding the axe! "Camp Improvement" in the afternoon.

'A' Coy went into trenches in evening - wonder it wasn't 'D' (leading the way as of yore). So this is the real thing at last! Good few Regular Battalions passed - going towards Dickebush.[24.9]

Visited La Clytte in evening with Pete.[24.10]

[26.1] Baths – A hot bath had to be used for a number of soldiers consecutively which, although not always desirable, was far better than no hot bath at all.

Another member of U Company describes the process in his diary – "*Two men in a tub and a bucket of dirty water is taken out and a bucket of clean water substituted after each platoon. There was plenty of disinfectant in the water otherwise it would not be safe. It was quite a treat to get clean again*".

Tin bath, similar to those used by Rule and his compatriots

[26.2] "greasy slime of every hue" – Many roads had become coated with the remnants of all manner of substances; spillages of oil and other chemicals, horse manure, food and animal and human remains.

[26.3] Huts – Billets were supposed to be handed over, from one unit to the next, clean and tidy. However, as we see here from Rule's obvious annoyance, that was not always the case.

Wednesday 3rd March - La Clytte - Billets

Wet and cold. No rifle inspection. Miserable job in forenoon. Making hurdles (wattles) in mud and rain. Feet & hands frozen.

Finally gave it up but sitting in huts with cold feet not much better.

Remainder of Bn at baths.[26.1] Short route march in afternoon (3 mls or so) - better idea even if roads like nothing on earth - greasy slime of every hue[26.2] - reached outskirts of Reninghelst.

Concert by 'D' Coy 1st Gordons in evening. Our 'D' Coy invited. Attempted to find our way to their lines but hopeless in mud and darkness. Rum very acceptable (and potent).

Thursday 4th March - La Clytte - Billets

Much milder. Hard run with Clarke in morning. A few fell out. On fatigue in forenoon making road in front of huts to washing burn. Made sort of "jetty" and place for towels. Rifle inspection & platoon drill in aftnoon then Coy drill - rotten. Lachie in true "Lachie mood" eg "take that man's name" etc. Proper mess coming home. Some of 15 & 16 Platoons digging trench near front line.
Still another mire in the lines. Vacated our huts in favour of Suffolks and shifted to 'A' Coys huts[26.3] - filthy places - just like their own homes.

[28.1] Taylor – John William – See Annex A - People in the Diary

[28.2] Commission – This promotion from the ranks to become an Officer was a feature of life in the Army and particularly amongst Rule's very able fellow students.

[28.3] just like at rifle butts – Similar to the experience of seeing his first shell explode, Rule's first encounter with bullets in close proximity could well have been strangely exciting. The similarity to rifle butts is that, on a shooting range, whilst working there to raise and lower targets, rifle shots pass a few feet overhead and the distinctive 'crack' of a high velocity bullet is clearly heard - and seldom forgotten.

[28.4] Wee sma' oors – Wee small hours – Very early in the morning.

[28.5] "Slough of Dispond" – (properly Despond) This "Swamp of Despair" is a deep bog in John Bunyan's *The Pilgrim's Progress*, into which the character Christian sinks under the weight of his sins and his sense of guilt for them. Cecil Sommers (Capt. Down) writes in similar vein in his 4th March letter in his book *Temporary Heroes* – perhaps he and Rule shared a conversation on the topic.

[28.6] Alma Mater – from the Latin *alma* "nourishing/kind", *mater* "mother". From 1883 for some 80 years, it was the title of the University of Aberdeen weekly magazine. This was a very welcome link to student life and an excellent channel for University news.

[28.7] Pay – Soldiers were paid once a week, usually on a Friday afternoon. Where conditions permitted, troops attended a Pay Parade, often with a lieutenant or captain in charge, assisted by one or two NCOs of the unit. Each soldier's name would be called out in alphabetical order along with the last three digits of his regimental number - "Maclean, 299!". The soldier would come to attention and shout back, "Sir!" or "Present!" then march smartly forward to the pay-table, salute, have his pay-book marked with the correct amount, receive his pay in cash counted out by the NCO, confirm "Pay correct, Sir!" salute again, turn and march back to his place.

Friday 5th March - La Clytte - Billets

Taylor[28.1] left for his commission.[28.2] Cold in forenoon but no rain. Pltn Exercises. Cleaning up lines (vacated by 'A' Coy). Objected to doing their 'dirty work' but had to 'carry on'. Drill in field close by. Volunteered for trench digging & got off drill. At La Clytte with Billy Anderson. Left for trenches at 10pm (very dark and muddy). Hefty load of sandbags + shovel & rifle. Tiring load - sand bags being silently 'shed' all along road. Stopped smoking & speaking! About turn near Kemmel. Discovered new way to carry sandbags - happy. Lovely night but roads awful. First impression of verey lights & rattle of 'angry' musketry at close qrs (just like at rifle butts).[28.3] Heard 1st bullet as left main road. Some felt much closer after that. Fm houses in ruins everywhere - some boarded up (felt sentimental). Man wounded. Hard work.

Sat 6th March - La Clytte - Billets

Home in wee sma' oors[28.4] - soup & rum a great reviver for tired 'sojers'. Raining heavily. Perfect sea of mud around huts. "Slough of Dispond".[28.5] Lay in bed till dinner! Rifle inspection in bed! Great argument as to whether we should get out. The more faint hearted got up - and received nasty drop (not recommended). Heel badly skinned from wet boots. "Alma Mater"[28.6] - quite interesting. Pay.[28.7] Party off to finish trench - can't be much to do but I don't envy the poor b - rs! (miserably wet night and dark).

[30.1] Bomb throwers – Unlike nowadays, when most soldiers carry 'bombs' (now 'grenades') in combat, in the early days of WWI, bomb throwing was seen as a specialised skill for a few infantrymen. Volunteers were trained specially and the main use of these bombs was in attacking and clearing enemy trenches.

[30.2] Waddell – See Annex A - People in the Diary

[30.3] Vic Macrae – Sgt Victor C J MacRae – See Annex A - People in the Diary

[30.4] Parade to hear death sentences – Between August 1914 and 31 March 1920, just over 3,000 men were sentenced to death in British Army courts martial. Offences included desertion (by far the most common capital crime), cowardice, murder, espionage, mutiny and striking a superior officer. (In roughly 90% of cases, the sentence was commuted to hard labour or penal servitude.) It was quite common for these sentences – and the fact of them having been carried out – to be communicated to soldiers at unit parades, a very British version of '*pour encourager les autres*'.

[30.5] Wattie Gray – See Annex A - People in the Diary

[30.6] Billets ➔ *Trenches* – The march from La Clytte to the trenches near Vierstraat was approximately three miles.

[30.7] Anti-frostbite – Used to help keep the feet warm and dry, anti-frostbite cream or lotion often contained a high percentage of animal fat or whale oil (although the latter was unpopular due to its smell). As can be seen later in the same day's entry, creative Jocks found other uses for it.

[30.8] K Mckay – Cpl Keith Mackay – See Annex A - People in the Diary

Sunday 7th March - La Clytte - Billets

Reveillé later. Raining most of day. Church service put off owing to rain but the good? old fatigues carried on (dodged them wonderfully). Lecture on bombing (for intending bomb throwers).[30.1] Volunteers called for to attend practice afterwards in bomb throwing - didn't assist. Saw few 'A' Coy men (unshaven but soldier like). Waddell[30.2] & Vic Macrae[30.3] telling us yarns of life in the trenches. Parade to hear "death sentences" etc. read out[30.4] ("The sentence was duly carried out") Stale day. Issue of free tobacco (Martin's Mixture) Heard of Wattie Gray's[30.5] death with 6th Gordons. Terrible shock.

Monday 8th March - La Clytte - Billets → Trenches[30.6]

Bitterly cold. Rush for morning sprint (quite 'blown). Usual inspections. Applied "anti-frostbite"[30.7] to feet. Blankets - rolled in 10s handed in - great excitement! Parade to hear death sentences read out again. Joined Suffolks at 5pm. Split up into '2s' & '3s' to get "leavening" effect to the full?! With K McKay[30.8] & Billy Anderson, Suffolks seemed "windy" going in but own feelings indefinable. Exciting going across the open (hail of bullets) - didn't quite appreciate gravity of situation I 'spose. Man hit right in front of me. Narrowly dodged shell holes (pure luck) until very last (then thoroughly soaked). Very cold. Brazier started at long last with help of anti-frostbite.

[32.1] "Caught us all asleep" – The Suffolk Sergeant was very forgiving. A sentry discovered asleep normally received severe punishment as he placed his comrades in danger by not watching for the enemy. Almost 400 men were sentenced to death for sleeping on sentry duty in WWI, but only 2 were executed (sentries were usually posted in pairs to keep one another awake; these two, in Mesopotamia, were made examples of because they were found sitting asleep together, suggesting that they had colluded).

[32.2] stand-to – The most likely time for an enemy attack would be early in the morning or evening so, to be ready, all soldiers would 'stand to arms' for half an hour, i.e. adopt a high level of alert with weapons ready to repulse an attack.

[32.3] Grouse Butt – Sometimes, when digging deep trenches proved very difficult, cover was provided using concentric rings of sandbags, several feet high, to provide shelter. Leaving these 'Grouse Butts' to enjoy the sunshine was not recommended!

Left-Right: AF Fowlie, Dan Walker, Eddie Knox, R Davidson
(Tam O'Shanters being worn before the issue of steel helmets.)

[32.4] Coal Boxes – The nickname for high explosive German 5.9inch howitzer shells, which emitted a heavy black smoke.

31

FIRST TASTE OF THE TRENCHES

<u>Tuesday 9th March</u> – Vierstraat – Trenches "Ls"

<u>1st day in trenches</u> – Suffolk Sgt caught us all asleep[32.1] at stand-to.[32.2] Bitterly cold night – peculiar sensation to doze & wake up with start as if heart missed 'beat' – everybody the same. Feet amongst water & huddling round brazier. Spells of sentry broke the night but glad to see dawn break (tea brought up by ration party – awful). Bullets whistling & cracking overhead by night. Sunny day – tempted out to back of 'grouse-butt'[32.3] – driven in by shrapnel & 'coal boxes'[32.4] – didn't realise danger at first. Got breakfast spoiled by snipers (showers of muck from sandbags). Some of Brit shells very low. Few planes overhead (wings glistening in the sunlight). Plenty to eat if unusual food. Felt confinement irksome. Sing song "When this b–y war is over" "He was mentioned in despatches & gained the DCM" Few, if any, of trench mates (old militia) had been other than poachers or burglars in civvy life – great experience – very decent fellows. Pte Seeley a philosopher – no wash etc.

<u>Wednesday 10th March</u> – Vierstraat – Trenches "Ls"

"Souveniring" hop poles for brazier. Got 2 hens (I got into No Mans Land – & Seeley fell amongst pigs.) Not so sunny. Rum in tea – tasted like "Cat's piss and pepper"

[34.1] McC – Meat & Vegetable Ration (M and V Ration), aka Maconochie's Stew, 1900-1918.

[34.2] French '75 – 75mm artillery shell nose cap similar to the one shown below;

Wednesday 10th March – Vierstraat – Trenches "Ls" (Continued)

Not much rifle or artillery fire in forenoon but "hotter" in afternoon – 2 planes on patrol & getting badly shelled. Experiment in cooking line – McC[34.1] & pea soup (powder) for stew – rather successful. Word passed along that we'd taken 5 miles of trenches? Sentry work not much more exciting than at Bedford so far! Shivering with cold when relieved. Left trenches by very decent track – very different from coming in. Into 'lousy' byre – same stall as Scott (Suffolks) Dog tired. Tea with rum in it. Didn't like taste but it made me sleepy.

Thursday 11th March – Vierstraat – Trenches "Ls"

Misty in forenoon but cleared up.
Bombardment feared. Shifted at 5 am to a small barn further back. Split up into small parties.
Wonderful sight to see Belgian kiddies playing about quite unconcerned while shells were falling not too far away. Too misty for much shelling (visibility poor). More or less of a picnic except for 'food'. Coffee from nice looking wenches at farm house.
Back to 'lousy byre' at dark. Met Scott again (in the same stall in fact not in the 'pit'). Plenty of cigarettes. Picked up nose cap of a French '75.[34.2] Suffolks good company – quite a jolly evening. Rum issued in tea – sickly but very soporific effect.

[36.1] Revetting fatigue – An element of trench construction. The revetment here is the part forward of the standing soldier.

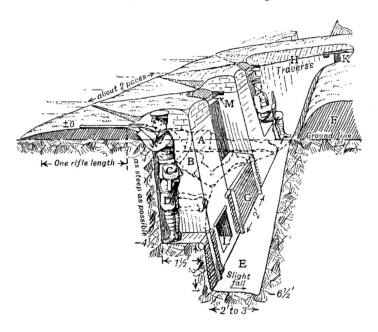

[36.2] "clicked" – was killed. Often reluctant to actually say 'killed' or had 'died', troops used a number of words or phrases instead, e.g. becoming a landowner, going home, being buzzed or huffed, drawing your full issue, being topped off.

[36.3] Midsex – Rule's abbreviation for the Middlesex Regiment.

[36.4] Sgt tried to bag a hare (missed). – It was not unusual for soldiers to try and supplement both the quantity and the variety of their rations by having a shot at the local wildlife. However, attempting to 'bag' a running hare with a rifle was both highly optimistic and potentially dangerous for the shooter in terms of exposure to sniper fire, as well as for fellow soldiers.

Friday 12th March - Vierstraat - Trenches
"Ls" → Rest Barn

Much less misty. Shifted to furthest 'barn' at 5 am. Great fun. Seeley (Suffs) lay on pile of discarded lousy pants. Language fitting occasion. Revetting fatigue.[36.1] Seeley "clicked" [36.2] as he knew in his bones he would (fatalist!).
Washed as much of body as possible in tin! Lice? - false alarm. Cooking slow business. Great sleep in afternoon - didn't know they were shelling us (never heard a sound). Midsex[36.3] Sgt tried to bag a hare (missed).[36.4] Got French bullets from Scott (very generous). Left with Suffolks at dusk but had d- d long wait on the road - bullets flying around. Through Vierstraate again - another long delay. Suffolks grousing in style but felt in great good humour personally. Pipers met us. "Muckin' O Geordie's Byre" - Suffolks transformed. I never appreciated the pipes so much - wonderful how they made us lift our heads and lengthen our stride! Thoughts of warm huts speedily shattered - Bn standing by - no blankets issued!

Saturday 13th March - La Clytte - Trenches - Rest Billets

(Glorious day.) Not much sleep in night (standing by) - bit rough just after first spell in line. Hut littered with papers and rubbish (just my luck to be room orderly!) everybody deluged with parcels from home.

4th in
Lent.

Sunday 14

(Glorious day) Rush to get on parade.
Cross country run - one of Clarke's patent
felt rotten till got "2nd wind. Over all sorts of
ground - one big marsh — where good few stopped
to consider! Felt in gt form when reached wood - Clarke
pretty fagged - beaten by Skinner. Row for
being late for breakfast. Church service afterwards. No sloppy
sentimentality - plain straight talk. good
hymns. Guns roared while we stood with
bowed heads in prayer? All very impressive
Packed & paraded in full m. order
& then dismissed. "C.Coy attempted to get thro'
to line + shelling on rds too fierce: retd for
make attempt at dawn. Horizon continually
lit up by the flashes of the guns —
bombardme bombs always & standing by.

Diary page (enlarged)

Saturday 13th March - La Clytte - Trenches - Rest Billets (Continued)

Rifle inspection etc. at noon and Coy drill in afternoon - thought we had finished with that sort of thing. At La Clytte with Billy. Corner shop crowded - our comely wench appeals to others also apparently. Tried "In Transvaal" and "Au Chasseur" - both closed - tired and sleepy - so to bed!

Sunday 14th March - La Clytte - Billets

(Glorious day) Rush to get on parade. Cross-country run - one of Clarke's patent ideas. I felt rotten till got "2nd" wind. Over all sorts of ground - one big marsh where good few stopped to consider! Felt in great form when reached wood - Clarke pretty fagged - beaten by Skinner. Row for being late for breakfast.

Church service afterwards. No sloppy sentimentality - plain straight talk - good hymns. Guns roared their hymn while we stood with bowed heads in prayer! All very impressive. Packed and paraded in full marching order - then dismissed.

"C" company attempted to get through to line - shelling on roads too fierce - returned to make attempt at dawn. Horizon continually lit up by the flashes of the guns - terrific bombardment. Standing by.

[40.1] "Drawer of water" – Menial drudges; labourer. [From Joshua.9:21 – "The leaders said to them, "Let them live." So they became hewers of wood and drawers of water for the whole congregation, just as the leaders had spoken to them."]

[40.2] Dixies – Large metal pots (often 12 gallon camp kettle), used for cooking.

[40.3] La Clytte to Kemmel trenches was a two-mile march.

[40.4] Hawes – See Annex A - People in the Diary

[40.5] 7th RFs – 7th Royal Fusiliers.

[40.6] Kemmel – Rule notes a 'very fine church' but by the end of the war this, plus most of the village, had been blasted to rubble. The image below was taken shortly after the end of the war.

Monday 15th March - La Clytte - Billets

"Standing by" all night (Glorious day) "Drawer of water"[40.1] (without the "hewing of wood" part). Long trek to "burn" with dixies.[40.2] Few of us had sponge baths in burn to great & unconcealed delight of Belgian women on the road about 50 yds away! Showed no inclination to move away. Just finished (and a fairly heroic stunt too) when told about a real bath parade! Still very welcome. Hot water gets at some of the dirt cold water cannot remove!

Tuesday 16th March - La Clytte - Billets → Trenches[40.3]

Lovely day. Cold & misty in evening. Running & physical exercises. Coy drill in field "far away". Platoon races "13" won. Shanks ran like an ostrich (long legs & head down) & Hawes[40.4] like a duck (splay feet). Covered with mud on way home. Prepared for guard mounting - cancelled. Orders to move up to trenches. 7th RFs[40.5] (newly out) "jumped" our hut - weary march to Kemmel.[40.6] Bn split up there, one half put up at deserted school. K fairly big village with very fine church & some fair sized buildings. Our Ptn on fatigue - carrying water jars from 'dump' to firing line. Pretty hot cross-fire. Appropriately termed "Hellgate". Utterly played out, sweat pouring off me. Didn't care if hit. Knoxie d - d nuisance losing touch. Trying to get past him, fell into disused? latrine head first: filed down trench - through big water hole - waist deep then back again (too far!!)

[42.1] Crichton – Sgt Arthur – See Annex A - People in the Diary

[42.2] MGs – Machine Guns – The Germans were particularly adept at preparing defensive positions that relied on the use of belt-fed machine guns, deadly against the Allied tactic of advancing in line across open ground.

[42.3] Charger – British Army .303 ammunition was distributed to infantry riflemen in chargers of five rounds, suitable for loading directly into the rifle's magazine. It was a habit of the time for a fresh-in-the-line soldier to keep his first charger. (The image is of a Mark IV (Type 2) introduced later in WWI.)

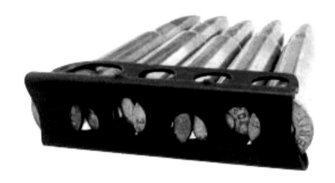

[42.4] L/Cpl Scott – See Annex A - People in the Diary. Whilst casualties were inevitable, the first loss of a member of U Company would have impacted greatly on them all. At this time, the Gordons took their dead some way back from the trenches and gave them a Christian burial. As the fighting became heavier, burials were carried out where the soldier died – if that were possible.

[42.5] 'Cooshie' – A wound or injury, not necessarily life-changing, but sufficiently serious to require the soldier to be repatriated to the UK for a period of treatment and recuperation. The word possibly originated with the British Army in India, being a corruption of the Hindi word 'khus', meaning 'pleasant'.

U COMPANY'S FIRST FATALITY

Wednesday 17th March - Kemmel Trenches

Cold during night. Tot of rum very welcome at "stand-to". NO sleep through the night. 1hr on & 1hr off sentry. Crichton[42.1] 'off' colour and didn't take his turn at sentry (like other NCOs). Eyes sore & bloodshot. Face filthy black with sweat marks (no wash). Stink awful – rotten potatoes and dead cow! Dead Gordons in front (memories of Charge of 4th Dec (fiasco) – Germans waiting for them with MGs).[42.2] Fired a few rounds but forgot to keep 1st charger[42.3] as souvenir. 1st rounds fired in anger, possible victims? L/Cpl Scott[42.4] killed (1st of 'U' Coy!) Pete got greatcoat ripped to pieces on parapet (by snipers).

Slow day. Relieved by Royal Irish Rifles – could hear them for mile back (celebrating St Pat's Day). One got nice 'cooshie'[42.5] as he hopped into our traverse. Too drunk to realise good fortune. Relief very late & gen mix up going out. Rapid fire made us hit the trail "at a rate of knots". Mix up in billets (barns full up) Lying about – everybody utterly fagged & wearily slept where we fell.

Thursday 18th March - Kemmel - Trenches

On fatigue during night. Rations to K2 (from HQrs) - Shower of bullets made us all lie flat in mud at back of trench. Digging new trenches afterwards with full pyrotechnical display of German 'Verey lights'.

[44.1] Poilus – French infantryman.

[44.2] CSM (or C.S.M.) – Company Sergeant Major. The senior warrant officer in a company.

[44.3] Knoxie, Spud & Gamin – Eddie Knox, Spud Thomson and Gamin Anderson – See Annex A - People in the Diary

[44.4] Grierson – Professor Sir Herbert John Clifford Grierson (1866–1960; often referred to as Herbert J. C. Grierson) was a Scottish literary scholar, editor and literary critic. He was educated at King's College, University of Aberdeen and Christ Church, Oxford. On graduating from the latter he was appointed Professor of English Literature at his Aberdeen alma mater, where he taught from 1894 to 1915, and subsequently became Knight Professor of English Literature at the University of Edinburgh (1915–1935).

[44.5] Low – See Annex A - People in the Diary

[44.6] Mess tin – Used by soldiers both for eating from and cooking in.

[44.7] H Corner – See Annex A - People in the Diary

[44.8] Middleton – See Annex A - People in the Diary

Thursday 18th March - Kemmel - Trenches
(Continued)

Easy digging (like cheese) - great sensation to
go down into 'safety' (from bullets). Allowed
to sleep till about 12 noon! Pleasant sunshine
all day. Found French cap (poilus')[44.1] &
German bullet. Left for reserve barn under
Pratt with last effort as CSM[44.2] (Gazetted to
4th as 2/Lt). Felt as if walking down Union St
(as safe).
Sandy Skinner pinched whole jar of rum from
'16' with disastrous effects. Knoxie, Spud &
Gamin[44.3] tight - Sandy 'happy'. Knox gave
longest and best sustained impression of
Grierson[44.4] to date. Officers had at last to
intervene.

Friday 19th March - Kemmel - Billets →
Trenches

Snowing at intervals - Snowflakes filtering in
through chinks? (gaps) in roof - woke me up
falling on my face! Lay till 9am. Shanks
couldn't get up (sick during night too much
rum). (Low[44.5] C.S.M.) Lost mess tin[44.6] down
well - minor tragedy of war.
Coy lined up for rifle inspection looking the
dirtiest in its career. Unshaved and unwashed
& gen unkempt, some half shot! H Corner[44.7]
like a black-face ewe - extremely funny -
appealed to Pratt who got his 1st salute under
these circumstances. A change from spick &
span Bedford days. Middleton[44.8] forgot his
rifle & explained it was "in oil" (like Shanks!).

Diary page (enlarged)

Friday 19th March - Kemmel - Billets →
Trenches (Continued)

On guard but designated to go to trenches
(K2C) - general mix up for trenches.
Roy T let loose on Sgt Buchan (C Coy).
Attached to 15 Ptn. Wakened (completely
snowed up in corner of traverse) by Dan W.[46.1]
calling for "volunteers". Jumped at the offer.
Pleasant surprise - return to HQ. Verey lights
very pretty against snow.

Saturday 20th March - Kemmel - Billets →
Trenches

Lovely day. Great to wake up with roof above
one's head. Pretty cold during the night,
though. Rose about 11am. Old frau nosing
around - a nuisance. Greatly scared about
personal belongings. Perhaps she has reason to
- the old dame.
Tried sleep in afternoon with indifferent
success. Brazier in outhouse.
Left for trenches at dusk. Adjt "decent".
Passed thro' Verstraat. Lost! Got Maj Smith's
HQrs! Acted as guide himself to "dump". Passed
dead Ger(man) en route. Taken to HQrs of "B"
Coy (behind wood) by circuitous route. Reserve
trenches very full. Usual general mix up -
lying about on frosty ground.
Into barn at last then cart shed (open both
ends). Very strict orders 'V' smoking etc
(ruins).

[48.1] German planes – One possible type was the Aviatik B.1 two-seat reconnaissance biplane.

[48.2] 'Malice in Kultureland' – Author Horace Wyatt. A parody on Alice in Wonderland, poking much fun at the Central Powers and especially the German Kaiser.

[48.3] "Jack Johnson" crater – Jack Johnson, nicknamed "The Galveston Giant," was the first African-American world heavyweight boxing champion. His name was used as a nickname to describe the impact of heavy German artillery shells that produced black smoke.

[48.4] Filling sandbags with all <u>sorts</u> of muck. – There was little opportunity, or inclination, to sift through what a shovel turned up (often from within a trench) when it came to filling urgently-needed sandbags.

[48.5] "And singing, still dost soar" – From 'To a Skylark', by Percy Bysshe Shelley (1792–1822).

[48.6] enfiladed – when an enemy fires along a line of troops rather than at them from their front.

[48.7] Grassick – William James – See Annex A - People in the Diary

47

Sunday 21st March - Vierstraat - Trenches

Very sunny. Frosty in morning. The first time
I've spent a night in a cart shed open at both
ends! Still - pretty comfy amongst straw.
German planes[48.1] around - whistle
continually going - d-d silly not to allow us
even to dodge across courtyard. (dry bully for
dinner). Reading "Malice in Kulturland"[48.2] -
clever in parts. Magnificent spring evn. Songs
of birds like in shrubberies at home. Glorious
sunset. Huge "Jack Johnson"[48.3] crater in field
nearby. Left for trenches at dusk with biggest
bag of coke I ever carried - took wind out of
me when stumbling. Shock when (after a "flop"
to dodge rifle bullets) I told a dead Ger. to
move on. N2 (Capt H.) - real boss. Filling
sandbags with all sorts of muck.[48.4]

Monday 22nd March - Vierstraat - Trenches

Cold night but glorious day. Basked in sun.
Lark began its song quite near "And singing,
still dost soar"[48.5] etc. (In reminiscent
mood.) Scanning country with field glasses.
Long now dead Frenchies at regular intervals
(enfiladed).[48.6] Few bodies (men, horses, cows
etc. behind) - utterly out of place in
sunbathed landscape. 'Plane getting shelled
vigorously. Young "Hoppy" a damned nuisance
- always on prowl. Great difficulty in keeping
awake during night - lucky to be awake when
Capt "Hoppy" came along - all next traverse
caught (Grassick[48.7] sentry) Dan W asleep but
I managed to lead Hoppy past him - then kick
him awake afterwards. Heavy Shelling.

[50.1] "Grey Backs" – One of many nicknames for lice, a scourge of life in the trenches, who found kilt pleats especially attractive.

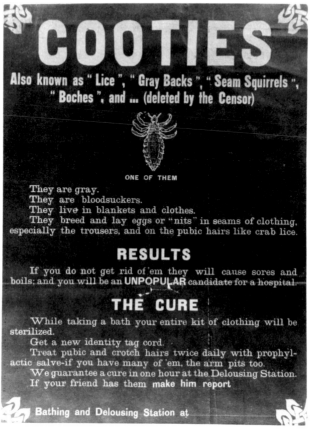

[50.2] "sair fecht" – It's a "hard life."

[50.3] N Chapelle – Neuve Chapelle was the first large scale attack undertaken by the British army during the war following the miserable winter operations of 1914-15. It demonstrated that it was quite possible to break *into* the enemy positions - but also showed that this success was not easily turned into breaking *through* them.

[50.4] Col McLean, [50.5] Capt Smith, [50.6] Lt Welch, [50.7] Lt Bisset – See Annex A - People in the Diary

Tuesday 23rd March – Vierstraat – Trenches "Ns"

Rain during night – but didn't mind – took chill off the air a bit. Colder during day. Discovered one louse & changed shirt immediately – haven't quite developed the philosophical attitude of my Suffolk sponsors to the little "Grey backs"[50.1] yet! Had to improvise filter for water – very dirty in shell holes. Relieved by 'A' & 'B' Coy at 10pm. General mix up – went to support trench led by a d – d fool of a guide? who didn't know the first thing about his job – lost 5 times & pack kept getting heavier. All parched when we reached 'dump'. Home & escort to water cart (empty) – half the lame riding on it by turns. Felt hill before La Clytte – a "sair fecht".[50.2] 30 per hut!!

Wednesday 24th March – La Clytte – Billets

Raining but sunny at times. Baths first parade – very enjoyable. Day seemed full of inspections with no time in between (incl CO's inspection). Re-arrangement of huts – with less overcrowding. Deluge of parcels incl socks from Old Abd Ladies Assoc (Varsity) with note about "Old Crown of Kings". Heard 6th Gordons casualties at N Chapelle.[50.3] Col McLean[50.4] (CO), Capt Smith[50.5] (Pittodrie) killed. Lt Welch[50.6] (Science Master at G Schools) & Lt Bisset[50.7] (ex 'U' Coy) wounded – must have struck a pretty "hot shop"!

[52.1] "In Transvaal" – If it was possible to 'sneak across' to this estaminet twice during a day, it must have been very close to the huts in La Clytte used by Rule and his compatriots.

[52.2] Billy – Billy Anderson.

[52.3] Home mail – It was a boost to troops' morale if they were able to receive letters and parcels from home regularly. The system worked well because mail was given as much priority in getting to the front as food and ammunition and the Ministry of War constantly updated the GPO on the whereabouts of units. Through these measures, mail was usually delivered, in either direction, within a few days of posting. At its peak, the service handled 12 million letters and parcels being sent to soldiers each week.

Sorting mail in the Home Depot at Regents Park, London

[52.4] John Rule – See Annex A - People in the Diary

[52.5] Nettie (Jane) Rule – See Annex A - People in the Diary

[52.6] Dan – Daniel I Walker.

[52.7] adjt's "bird" – Slang for punishment, for example extra duties, parades or detention.

[52.8] Scherpenberg Rifle Range – Regular practice allowed soldiers to improve their marksmanship and their rate of fire. It also ensured their rifles were in good working order despite the ravages of trench life.

Thursday 25th March - La Clytte - Billets

Raining and cold. Usual parades except r&rm. Sneaked across to "In Transvaal"[52.1] with Billy[52.2] in between forenoon and afternoon parades and again in evening. Usual sort of day. Home mail[52.3] interesting. Description by John (brother)[52.4] - (on leave) of new minister's appearance in pulpit. Nettie[52.5] giving me amusing extracts of Country School from school marm's point of view.

Friday 26th March - La Clytte - Billets

Bitterly cold. Threatening to snow. Running in morning. Great fun at Dan's[52.6] "Buchan Trot" (easy going canter characteristic of him). Pratt in officer's uniform. Extended order rapid fire in forenoon under Spark! Washed kilt aprons in response to Lachie in "mood". Good deal of swearing but great improvement. Playing footer. Minute rifle inspection in afternoon - breech action etc. Another at 5pm - adjt's "bird".[52.7] Extended order drill.

Saturday 27th March - La Clytte - Billets → Line (Verstraat)

Bitterly cold. Threatening to snow. On fatigue early with Pete. Parade as usual then to Scherpenberg Rifle Range[52.8] (quarry hole at foot of hill with windmill on it) - Lt Down in charge. My d - d rifle persisting in jamming - most useless thing I've ever seen.

[54.1] Knife rest – a defensive barbed wire construction.

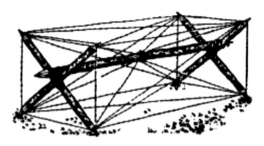

[54.2] "Sunny Jim" – McLellan – See Annex A - People in the Diary

[54.3] "Lead Thou Me On" – From "Lead, Kindly Light", a hymn with words written in 1833 by John Henry Newman as a poem titled "The Pillar of Cloud". The largest mining disaster in the Durham coalfield in England, was at West Stanley Colliery, known locally as "The Burns Pit", when 168 men and boys lost their lives as the result of two underground explosions at 3:45pm on Tuesday 16 February 1909. Incredibly, there was still a group of men and boys alive underground having found a pocket of clean air. They sat in almost total darkness, when one of them began humming the Hymn "Lead Kindly Light". In no time at all, the rest of the miners joined in with the words, "Lead kindly light amidst the encircling gloom, lead thou me on, the night is dark, and I am far away from home". These 26 men were rescued after 14 hours, four others being rescued later.

[54.4] "Recessional" – A poem by Rudyard Kipling, which he composed for the occasion of Queen Victoria's Diamond Jubilee in 1897. The phrase "lest we forget" forms the refrain of "Recessional." It introduces the reason for the entreaty expressed in the poem: that God might spare England from oblivion or profanity "lest we forget" the sacrifice of Christ ("Thine ancient sacrifice"). The phrase later passed into common usage after World War I across the British Commonwealth especially, becoming linked with Remembrance Day observances; it came to be a plea to not forget past sacrifices and is often found as the only wording on war memorials, or used as an epitaph.

Saturday 27th March - La Clytte - Billets →
Line (Verstraat) (Continued)

On fatigue afterwards to "dump" near
Vierstraat (firing line side). Carried knife
rest[54.1] with "Sunny Jim" (McLellan)[54.2] - pole
broke - devil of a job. Acute diarrhoea
coming home (bad water perhaps?) - simply
staggered along for 1st half of return journey
but finished up chirpier. Rain welcome in night.

Sunday 28th March - La Clytte - Billets

Sun pleasant but wind bitterly cold. Usual
inspections then Church parade - same padre.
Drum Major like to burst playing instrument
(very comic figure). "Lead Thou Me on"[54.3]
very fine, also Kipling's "Recessional".[54.4]
Drill in aftnoon - fell foul of Lachie thro not
ordering arms correctly - detached off for
further instruction under Topping - discovered
I'd never done it correctly before! (after all
these months & never detected before!)
"In Transvaal" in evening with Roy & Billy
there. "Father" Noble (old ex regular) there &
managing to get partly "shot".

Monday 29th March - La Clytte - Billets →
Trenches

Bitterly cold. Early morning run (good pace)
to La Clytte (Skinner) - felt "winded".
Inspects (including feet) in forenoon - then
drill in extended order. Enjoyed "firing
positions" best (flat on our respective
tummies).

[56.1] Down – Captain Norman Cecil Sommers Down – See Annex A - People in the Diary

[56.2] 'drum ups' – making a meal or, more likely here, a brew-up of tea.

[56.3] 'Sketches' & 'Punches' – Daily Sketch newspapers and Punch magazines.

[56.4] Jimmie Th – James G Thomson – See Annex A - People in the Diary

[56.5] Rumour of Italy declaring war – Italy joined the war, on 26th March 1915, on the side of the Triple Entente - Britain, France and Russia.

The Italian government decided to go to war because, in 1915, Italy had signed the secret Treaty of London. In this treaty Britain had offered Italy large sections of territory in the Adriatic Sea region – Tyrol, Dalmatia and Istria. Such an offer was too tempting for Italy to refuse.

Britain and France wanted Italy to join in on their side so that a new front could open up to the south of the Western Front. The plan was to split still further the Central Powers so that their power on the Western and Eastern Fronts was weakened. The plan was logical, but the part Italy had to play in it required military success. This was never forthcoming.

Between 1915 and 1917, Italian troops only got 10 miles inside Austrian territory. But in October 1917 came the disaster of Caporetto. In this battle, in fact a series of battles, the Italians had to fight the whole Austrian Army and 7 divisions of German troops. The Italian Army lost 300,000 men.

Though the Italians had a victory at Vittorio Veneto in 1918, the psychological impact of Caporetto was huge. The retreat brought shame and humiliation to Italy, as well as taking reinforcing British divisions from the Western Front.

Monday 29th March - La Clytte - Billets →
Trenches 'Ns' (Continued)

Bath parade very enjoyable - last Coy as usual
(must think we are naturally cleaner?)
Drill in afternoon - then cleaning up in prep
for going into trenches. Left early & no halts
on way - getting seasoned - even if packs
still feel heavy. In "support barn" (Clarke
strangely childish in some things) very
crowded. Digging new reserve trenches -
struck good job after a bit - holding
flashlight for Down! [56.1]

Tuesday 30th March - Vierstraat - Trenches

Splendid day. Sunlight in forbidden courtyard
reminiscent of days spent loitering about
"fairm toons" while father was away seein'
aboot drains & levels & things. Like caged
animals but necessary I spose - right on
skyline. Good brazier - plenty of 'drum
ups'[56.2] welcome after fatigue.
Oddy (Band Master) bit of nuisance. 'Sketches'
& 'Punches'[56.3] for reading material. Tried to
sleep - too cold. Big 'steading' - fine trees in
front of dwelling house. Substantial roofs.
Volunteered for guard. Turned out to be
permanent. 1st on - two hour spell. Knoxie &
Jimmie Th.[56.4] with me. 15 Platoon in from
Support trenches. 1hr spell in morning. All the
rest on fatigue party to firing line. Rumour of
Italy declaring war?[56.5]
PC from Charlie from Moffat.

[58.1] Like a lamb – as per the saying 'In like a lion, out like a lamb', March ended with good weather.

[58.2] McLellan – Private Duncan T H McLellan – See Annex A - People in the Diary

[58.3] Henderson – Lieutenant A R Henderson – See Annex A - People in the Diary

[58.4] gapin' up – looking upwards to see what was happening above the trench. A natural reaction to noise above a soldier's head but one which, with the ever-present danger from shell splinters and fragments, could lead to catastrophic facial wounds, especially at this stage in the war before the general issue of steel helmets.

Wednesday 31st March - Vierstraat - Trenches 'Ns'

Like a lamb[58.1]. Even better day. Night guard dismounted at 4.30am for all practical purposes. 1st on "door sentry". Oddy's (Bandmaster) lot never told us when they finished. Braziers all allowed to go out. Slow day. Crichton in my place - ill & snappy. I "drum up". 1st attempt spoiled by McLellan[58.2] who got mercilessly ragged from Skinner. Bit of concert before leaving "Little Tailor Boy" etc. Appreciated by Oddy. Left at dusk lovely sunset. Went by outskirts of wood. Exaggerated feeling of safety. Henny (Lt Henderson)[58.3] in charge of support trench "N9". Tree knocked over not 6ft behind our traverse! day before. Casualties fr splinters. CO on warpath about braziers drawing fire. Digging Communication trench (outline) greatly exposed. Dead Frenchies being callously rifled.

Thursday 1st April - Vierstraat - Trenches 'Ns'

"All Fools Day". Caught Roy — effort not fully appreciated. Feet d — d cold during night — glad when day broke — sunshine a cure for all ills. Roaming about wood — good few 'planes droning overhead like white moths. Narrow squeak from falling shrapnel. One man wounded in firing line (gapin' up).[58.4]

[60.1] C.T. Communication Trench – A trench used to link the front line fire trenches, support trenches and the rear area and providing cover whilst moving between these.

*[60.2]   Bombardier Wells   –   Bombardier Billy Wells was an English heavyweight boxer. Wells was the British and British Empire Champion from 1911 until 1919, defending his title fourteen times. The bout to which Rule refers (against Frank Moran in the Royal Opera House, Covent Garden) took place on the evening of Monday 29th March and coverage of it would have appeared in the following day's newspapers. It was quite a logistical accomplishment to have these and other newspapers delivered regularly to the front line trenches only some 72 hours after they were published.

Thursday 1st April - Vierstraat - Trenches 'Ns' (Continued)

Man killed just behind our trench (shell) - asleep when happened - no sign of wound (concussion?).
Left for firing line about 9.30 pm - by C.T.[60.1] part of way. Lachie in our trench but shifted (Praise be to Allah). Revetting & deepening trench - driest I've been in so far. Mail arrived & everybody happy.

Friday 2nd April - Vierstraat - Trenches 'Ns'

(Glorious day) "Cat's wash" in cigarette tin. Very sleepy after strenuous night work. Writing home in "idyllic" vein (result of sunlight on the fields) but inspiration spasmodic. Sardines & oatcakes! for breakfast - getting back my liking for sardines! Practically no shelling. Sun seemed to "go down" early. Work on C.T. (during night) got circulation going nicely. Putting out knife rests afterwards under Pratt (keen as mustard). Felt strangely itchy. Saw by papers that Bombdr Wells[60.2] knocked out.

Saturday 3rd April - Vierstraat - Trenches 'Ns'

Not nearly so "balmy" (weather). Chilly in afternoon. Felt "itchy" (could it be lice?) Applied benzene with dire results to very tender part of anatomy (pain luckily fleeting).

[62.1] 'Ns' – The trench system was sometimes annotated with names that would be familiar to the troops who first dig them, or by letters and numbers to assist with administration, navigation and command and control.

[62.2] Sleep, for the night cometh – probably from John 9:4 "...the night cometh, when no man can work".

[62.3] "Archies" – Anti-aircraft fire, or artillery pieces, or units of these.

[62.4] Barbed wire (knife rests) blown right on top of parapet! – Another lucky escape for Rule, also evidenced by Topping's reaction to Rule's apparent nonchalance concerning the proximity of the shelling.

Saturday 3rd April - Vierstraat - Trenches 'Ns'[62.1] (Continued)

Slept on fire step & felt greatly refreshed and on form for labours of the night (Sleep, for the night cometh).[62.2] New system / sentry / rest / fatigue covering most of the night.
On carrying fatigue - trenches full of liquid mud. Bivvy collapsed 4 times under weight of water - 4 cold douches.
Cooking hopeless for long time - wet wood but perseverance won.
Fixing up trench (parapet) - eternal job & putting out barbed wire (knife rests). Man killed. German 'planes droning overhead in darkness. Wonderful display of searchlights from our "Archies"[62.3]

Sunday 4th April - Vierstraat - Trenches 'Ns'

1st complete Sunday in trenches! Heavy shelling (usual thing for Sunday). Barbed wire (knife rests) blown right on top of parapet! [62.4] Close shave 5th shot (the closest) luckily the last. Heavy showers of mud falling on everything and everybody.
Don't think I quite realised the danger. Topping seemed aghast at my pleasantries when barbed wire was deposited practically on top of us. Not much sleep in forenoon.
(Mails opened - Easter Greeting fr Winnie Horne (Bedford)). Rifle in shocking condition. Attempts to "drum up" as follows: (1) Knox (2) Grassick (3) Success.

[64.1] relief (Worcesters) – The 4th Gordons' War Diary gives the relieving unit as 1st East Surreys.

[64.2]Relief at last – With the need to cross terrain without the use of light, plus the difficulty of trying to avoid shell holes and other obstacles, added to the maze of trenches, it was a quite common occurrence for groups of men to become lost on their way to relieve other troops.

[64.3] Begg – See Annex A - People in the Diary

[64.4] S Mirrlees – Stewart Mirrlees – See Annex A - People in the Diary

[64.5] Ch Donald – Charles ("Chatty") Donald – See Annex A - People in the Diary

[64.6] Bert Murray – Private Herbert Murray – See Annex A - People in the Diary

[64.7] Jock Thomson – See Annex A - People in the Diary

Sunday 4th April - Vierstraat - Trenches "Ns" (Continued)

Weary wait for relief (Worcesters). [64.1] Silly order to "Cease fire" (wind up). Relief at last[64.2] - had been lost.
Almost asleep on march out. Begg[64.3] put faith in <u>short?</u> cut - tangled up in network of trenches & fell in with water jar on top of me. Kemmel at last.
Blankets in hopeless confusion.

Monday 5th - Saturday 10th April - La Clytte - Billets

Pouring practically all day. Usual clean up after trenches & inspections of clothing, equip, arms etc. Some job too - scraping mud off puttees & gt coat - hard caked.
New 'draft' arrived containing kent faces - S. Mirrlees,[64.4] Ch Donald,[64.5] Bert Murray,[64.6] Jock Thomson[64.7] etc (latter to 'B' Coy)
Belgian peasant farmers busy cultivating and manuring land. Women on all sorts of chores also lace making on bobbins.
Mix here of weather - cold rain mostly.
Brewery baths & clean up after trenches.
Routine parades & inspections.
Sporting events: cross country runs.
Practice attacks. Sgt Dan Walker leading with great dash tripped & fell!
Fatigue party to front line one night.

[66.1] On way to bomb London – Alexander Rule is slightly ahead of himself here. The Germans had certainly begun to use Zeppelins for bombing purposes, their first successful raid having taken place on the night of 19–20 January 1915. Two Zeppelins targeted Humberside but were diverted by strong winds, and dropped their bombs on Great Yarmouth, Sheringham, King's Lynn and the surrounding villages. Paris was also bombed, but the first successful raid on London was on 30th May 1915, when 7 people were killed and 35 injured.

[66.2] J O Cruickshank – Private James Orr Cruickshank – See Annex A - People in the Diary. Rule seems quite matter of fact about this death.

[66.3] Boche – derogatory slang for German from the French 'alboche', itself taken from two words – 'Allemande' (German) and 'caboche' (head).

[66.4] Jim Leslie – James Dawson Leslie – See Annex A - People in the Diary

[66.5] A Duthie – Andrew May Duthie – See Annex A - People in the Diary

Saturday 10th – Thursday 16th April –
In Kemmel Trenches

Returned after bare 5/days rest at La Clytte on 10 Apr.

First 3 days in K3 (support) trench nicknamed 'The Hydropathic' partly in dead ground as regards rifle fire. Salvage from ruined cottages – chairs, crockery, etc and 'Spuds' made trench life homelier.

Some sport too, shooting at rabbits & pheasants in rear. Frosty nights, occl sun by day.

Silhouette of Zeppelin low on evening sky on 12th Apl. Prbl on way to bomb London.[66.1] Engine drone audible too.

J O Cruickshank[66.2] mortally wounded by Boche[66.3] sniper soon after we took over K2 front line on 13th Apl. Rather foolhardy in his eagerness to get a shot at the Boche who had already sent a bullet thro' C's Tam o Shanter! Clear view of Wytchaete village on low ridge behind German line.

Wiring parties with "knife rests": excitement. Caught in limelight of Boche flares (so superior to our own verey lights).

No mans land seamed with drainage ditches made treacherous going when man at front end of 'knife rest" support slips suddenly without warning.

Rumours of attack North of Ypres. U Coy had 2 casualties as we left front line on our relief – Jim Leslie[66.4] & A Duthie[66.5]

Found a rusty bayonet ("sword" type) without scabbard as a souvenir.

[68.1] drawing the bayonet clean through my right hand. – Rule writes a kinder version of this incident in his own 1934 book, where he notes, *"While returning from the trenches one night, I received a nasty wound in the hand, through falling on top of a rusty old French bayonet stuck in a shell-hole. This put me out of action for a time, in so far as front-line duties were concerned, and I replaced another member of U Company as chief trench guide."*

The trench system was so complex that the use of guides was essential to prevent, for example, relieving units and even *in situ* units' senior officers from becoming hopelessly lost.

[68.2] Red Iodine – A glass ampoule of red iodine was carried in troops' field dressing pockets. Iodine has been used for cleaning wounds, sterilizing skin before surgery and similar for many years. Antibiotics were not discovered until 1928, so a disinfectant such as iodine was the primary line of defence against infection from many wounds and injuries and was widely used.

[68.3] Pipe tobacco and cigarettes (Kitchener) – Amongst the most successful fund-raising efforts of the war was 'Smokes for the Troops'. On 29th October 1914, *The Times* announced that, at Lord Kitchener's request, a *Smokes for Soldiers and Sailors Fund* had been formed *"to provide our wounded…with tobacco and cigarettes in hospitals here and at the front…and is currently sending regular supplies to over 200 hospitals and convalescent homes."*

Those who were serving at the front were not forgotten either. To make it easier for the public to send these items, the Post Office allowed such 'comforts' to be mailed by the cheaper letter post instead of parcel post. The French Government also waived customs duty on tobacco and cigarettes addressed to British troops serving abroad.

[68.4] puttees – From the Hindi for bandage *(patti),* puttees are strips of khaki cloth that were wrapped round the lower leg to give some protection from mud and minor abrasions.

[68.5] A.A. fire – Anti-aircraft fire.

Saturday 10th – Thursday 16th April –
In Kemmel Trenches (Continued)

Just as we reached La Clytte huts Roy Topping
slid backwards on a wet muddy slope and I
fell forward drawing the bayonet clean
through my right hand.[68.1] Immediately
applied red iodine[68.2] (next day got M&D –
"Medicine & Duty" from the 1st Gordons' MO,
although incapable of arms drill pro tem.
One man in the long sick parade had a tummy
"Paint his belly with iodine"

Friday 17th – Tuesday 21st April – La
Clytte (Rest Billets)

Welcome brewery baths and change of
underclothing.
Simple joy of being at local estaminets – "In
Chausseur", "In Transvaal" with or without
extra meals – fried eggs with chips & mealy
puddings, bread & butter & coffee for a few
pence.
Issue of pipe tobacco and cigarettes
(Kitchener).[68.3] Judging by quality of such
issue tobacco, the manufacturers were
profiteering on a big scale.
Scraping mud off puttees,[68.4] greatcoat,
uniform a lengthy job. Laundry done locally
(privately) Some primitive RFC planes around.
One crashed in field nearby Boche trenches
drew A.A. fire.[68.5]
Gun Flashes VIVID in evening sky.

[70.1] Field punishment No. 1 – Field Punishment, introduced in 1881 following the abolition of flogging, was common during WWI, either as Field Punishment Number One or as Field Punishment Number Two.

Field Punishment Number One, often abbreviated to "F.P. No. 1" or "No. 1", saw the convicted man being attached to a fixed object, such as a gun wheel or a post, for up to two hours per day. Early in the War, this was often done with the arms stretched out and the legs tied together, giving rise to the nickname "crucifixion". (Due to its humiliating nature, many Tommies viewed it as very unfair.)

This was applied for up to three days out of four, up to 21 days total. It was usually applied in field punishment camps set up for this purpose a few miles behind the front line, but when the unit was on the move the unit itself would carry it out. It has been alleged that this punishment was sometimes applied within range of enemy fire. (During the War, F.P. No. 1 was issued by the British Army on 60,210 occasions.)

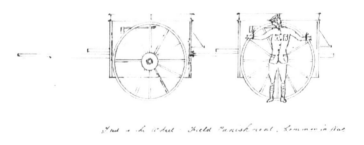

Tied to the wheel · Field Punishment, Somme in the War

Field Punishment Number Two was similar, except the man was shackled but not fixed to anything.

[70.2] Joe Reid, [70.3] Douglas McLaggan, [70.4] Tommy Cranston – See Annex A - People in the Diary

[70.5] Maxim – The first successful recoil-operated machine gun, invented in 1883 by Sir Hiram Maxim.

[70.6] Macaulay – See Annex A - People in the Diary

Friday 17th – Tuesday 21st April – La Clytte (Rest Billets) (Continued)

Unholy episode in which 'Gamin' Anderson of U Coy tied to a wheel on 19th April – Field punishment N°1[70.1] for sleeping in the trenches. On the way out he had stayed for hours with wounded Cpl Hawes, but Lachie omitted to mention this to CO in extenuation! On 16th June Gamin was mentioned in despatches.(Joe Reid[70.2] of U Coy wounded trying to rescue wounded man from shell hole, after Victor Macrae already killed in similar attempt.) Promotions in U Coy included Douglas McLaggan[70.3] as L/Cpl. Arrivals in new draft – Cpl Stewart Mirrlees to L/C. Tommy Cranston[70.4] from L/C to Pte
Local peasants 'nettoyage' system hive of activity in smallish plots. Cultv by bullock or one-horse plough – work from early morn till late.

Thursday 22nd April – La Clytte Billets → Trenches

(Glorious day) No r&rm. Didn't attend sick parade. Blankets rolled in bundles of '10' (good old army style). Hedges in blossom. Country very spring like.
At Scherpenberg Range. Saw 4 light Vicker's Maxims[70.5] (Midsex) in action (terrific hail of bullets). Hand grenade explosion at 1st Gordons camp. One man blown to atoms (saw stretcher with remains aftwds) Macaulay[70.6] hit.

[72.1] 15 inch gun – This very large howitzer was, unusually, operated by the Royal Marines as part of the Naval Brigade.

[72.2] Grotto – At the Western edge of Kemmel Chateau's grounds was a grotto, a shrine built out of rocks and stones. This was quite a common feature at the time and would have contained emblems of Catholicism, such as a statue of the Virgin Mary.

[72.3] Gas attack – On 22 April, the Germans launched the first large-scale poison gas attack ever, in direct breach of the 1907 Hague Convention on Land Warfare, which forbad the use of "poison or poisoned weapons" in warfare.

[72.4] Sandy Skinner – Sgt Alexander Skinner. Sandy was a very popular and well-respected senior NCO. A native highlander, he was very able at cross-country running and had an excellent tenor voice that, as Rule notes, was sadly missed after his death.

[72.5] Stewart Paterson – Private John McLellan Stewart Paterson – See Annex A - People in the Diary

[72.6] "Tommy"(CO) – Lt. Col. T Ogilvie, Commanding Officer, 4th Gordons – See Annex A - People in the Diary

Thursday 22nd April - La Clytte Billets →
Trenches (Continued)

At Baths... filthy water. In "Den Engel' -
Knoxie's birthday. Saw JO Cruickshank's' grave.
Appointed guide in place of McLaggan
(promoted). Saw 15 inch gun[72.1] at La Clytte.
Left for trenches at 7pm. One of our planes
brought down. Saw Ger plane signalling.
Passed through very fine Grotto at Kemmel[72.2]
- pretty tired - remained at HQrs.

Friday 23rd April - Kemmel - Trenches 'Ks'

British driven back (gas attack).[72.3] Canadians
outflanked. Not so warm & sky overcast.
Sandy Skinner[72.4] & Stewart Paterson[72.5]
killed last night - great shock to me on
wakening (No more "Maid of Morven" in
Sandy's tenor voice) Easy day - reading papers
etc. & sleeping in aftnoon. Out with Webster
(guide) after tea scouring crest of hill for
"Tommy" [72.6] (C.O.) Awkward to get the
Colonel mislaid!
Farm houses burning here and there -
searched one or two. Some fairly "close uns".
Tommy turned up at HQ ok. Made round of
trenches with Tommy & Clarke in even. &
discovered new (dry) track. Clarke & I stayed
on in trenches for a bit. 'U' Coy very cut up
about Skinner. Home by circuitous route - a
bullet just cracked ahead of us as we struck
Kemmel Rd.

[74.1] Barron – Arthur M Barron – See Annex A - People in the Diary

[74.2] Lairdie Johnstone – See Annex A - People in the Diary

[74.3] Isaac MacIver – See Annex A - People in the Diary

[74.4] Asher – See Annex A - People in the Diary

[74.5] challenge – Part of the duties of a sentry was - and still is - to challenge anyone who approached the sentry's position. A set procedure firstly tries visual identification. If unsuccessful, an exchange of passwords is attempted. If that fails the intruder(s) would be detained if possible. If not, they would be shot.

Diary Page (enlarged)

Saturday 24th April - Kemmel - Trenches 'Ks'

Very sunny but not so warm in afternoon.
Broken sleep during night (lice active) & feet
cold (literally). Café au lait for brekker &
proper toilet (incl <u>shave</u>) but couldn't put a
parting in my hair! Inspected cemetery near
pond & wrote up back "numbers" of diary and
reading novels. Standing by at HQrs in case
reqd. 4 wounded by rifle grenade. (incl.
Barron[74.1] & Lairdie Johnstone[74.2] & Isaac
MacIver[74.3]). Visited Signallers (Asher)[74.4] in
shanty. Concerts over the phone (Man on the
engine turns the little handle etc) & escaped
duty - couldn't be found. Gt excitement over
supposed attack. Extra men & amm. sent up.
Spent spell of duty during night in front of
kitchen stove (lucky!)

Sunday 25th April - Kemmel - Trenches 'Ks'

Glorious day after rain in night. Felt sorry
for poor b - rs in trenches - all standing to
while I got my breakfast in comfort - even
though I <u>was</u> sleeping in a <u>disused</u> pig 'stye'.
Could scarcely believe it was Sunday somehow
till I saw all the peasants at their homes
(dressed).
Having a squint through Asher's telescope at
the 'lines'. Doing sentry go to relieve guards
for fatigues. My post very sloppy but managed
to improve it with sandbags. Had to
"challenge"[74.5] a lot. Some bullets pretty close.

[76.1] D D Booth – See Annex A - People in the Diary

[76.2] country 'thrashin' – Thrashing (or threshing) separated grain from stalks after harvesting. This disturbed rats' nests and they would scurry about, often chased by the farm children and dogs.

[76.3] F C Stephen – See Annex A - People in the Diary

[76.4] "Confusion Corner" – likely alternative for HellFire Corner.

[76.5] IIe – Parallel.

[76.6] 'ome John' – likely a corruption of '*Home James (and don't spare the horses)*' meaning '*let's get back as swiftly as possible*'.

[76.7] Letters sent – On some occasions, when there was no time to write a letter, a soldier could send a Field Service Post Card.

Monday 26th April - Kemmel - Trenches HQrs

(Glorious day) Easy forenoon - mainly reading & sleeping. Made officially O.C. guides for general discipline and routine - 16 Pln cleaning out niffy drain - horrible stench - seemed to be all pervading. "Gladys" the old dame objected strongly but her plaints fell on deaf ears - she probably never heard of hygiene before! In evening, discussing 'Spiritualism' & 'Darwinism' with Mac (another guide) till packed off on more material quest - with message to another HQrs - fine big farmhouse left abs untouched (a rather remarkable state of affairs in this area)

Tuesday 27th April - Kemmel - Trenches 'Ks'

D.D. Booth[76.1] wounded. Ripping day. Woke up after 9. Tea without milk for brekker. Round seeing Roy Topping & Coy (guard). Gt rat hunt outside. Removing muck at door. One lapping food. Rats too numerous - distracting attention. Gt congregation of males & females in billet like a country "thrashin" [76.2] Soup & potatoes, beef & coffee for dinner! Sleeping in aft. British got into Dardanelles - advancing on land! F.C. Stephen[76.3] gazetted 2/Lt. Pretty heavy shelling in evening at "Confusion Corner".[76.4] Visited Dressing Stn then out with Clarke & Pratt to examine Com trench. Route - along rd 11e[76.5] to "Ks" - up along Com. trench - back along hill in the line of trees then 'ome John'.[76.6] Got letters sent[76.7] off home.

[78.1] partic – particular.

[78.2] A Mitchell – Alexander Mitchell - See Annex A - People in the Diary

[78.3] M.Ps. – Military Police.

[78.4] K McKay (actually MacKay) – See Annex A - People in the Diary

Wednesday 28th April - Kemmel - Trenches (HQrs)

Best day yet. Rose about 10am. Tea for brekker. Bit of problem about the bread part – none. Easy forenoon – nothing in partic[78.1] 'on' – well chosen lunch with Knoxie & Middleton. Cognac to finish up. A. Mitchell died.[78.2] Spent aft shaving & cleaning rifle then down to Brig HQrs solo (before tea) Man in "G" Coy wounded. Accident at rifle inspection. Over past 1st Gordons HQrs – looking for shells (cases!) on way – land glorious in sunlight. Bit of a bombardment on. Packed up, weary wait for Clarke. Took him & Morrison up to trenches. Young McKinnon adj'ng left half! Left them in line & got back about 2.30 am.

Thursday 29th April - La Clytte - Billets

Glorious day. No real parades. Ordered to parade at Orderly Room before C.O. – wind up! Explained about telescope & map which I'd taken to Brigade HQrs (bit mysterious) Bath parade. Our Coy last as usual – hardly time for bath. In "Den Engel" (beer) Swamped with parcels from home. Heard Charlie (brother) joined up after taking diploma. Rifle, bayonet & ammunition inspect. in afternoon (Begg). Good fun. Found "Au Chausseur" out of bounds to troops – now I wonder why? – special preserve for M.Ps.[78.3] – managed to get washing sneaked out though. Heard K McKay[78.4] had died of wounds in Bailleul Hosp. Writing letters home (Fathers 59th birthday)

[80.1] La Clytte Billets – In his diary, J.K. Forbes (the Sniper Sergeant) recorded that a march of three miles from the French-Belgian border brought D Company to La Clytte, '*a town of huts set down in a wilderness of clay which the multitudes of men had converted into an unspeakable horror of sticky mud.*

The huts numbered some three score, low wooden erections, with corrugated iron roofs, painted earth colour to deceive aircraft, the floor sunk a foot, and banked all round with clods of earth. Each hut was about twenty feet long, fourteen broad, and seven high in the centre, and was destitute of windows and chimney.

There were two dozen men in each, so that the space per man was cramped, but not so much so as in the railway truck from Le Havre to Bailleul'.

The first evening there, J. K. was detailed for guard. He had the first duty at No. 2 post – an ancient, broken-down carriage set in a sea of mud surrounded by transport carts, sunk almost to the axles in mud.

[80.2] Lawson – See Annex A - People in the Diary

[80.3] Thank 'Eaven we've got a "naivy" – According to The Dictionary of Catch Phrases, this phrase - or a variation of it - "was called into use whenever the incompetence of military authority became more manifest than usual".

[80.4] Short rifle v long – 1st Gordons were equipped with Lee Enfield rifles that had a barrel five inches shorter than the Charger Loading Lee Enfields that the former U Company had held before the start of the war and had brought with them to Belgium.

[80.5] 15 per minute – This was, for many years, a standard test of musketry skills throughout the British Army. The requirement was to make at least 15 hits, on a 12 inch (30.5cm) round target, at 300 yards (270 metres) in 60 seconds. The record was set in 1914 at the Hythe School of Musketry by Sergeant Instructor Alfred Snoxall, who achieved an incredible 38 hits.

Friday 30th April - La Clytte - Billets[80.1]

Sweltering heat after thick mists at early morning parade (running & p jerks). Ptn drill (Begg) consisted mainly in largely piling and unpiling arms. Musketry practice – flat on respective tummies on grass and d – d nearly asleep in strong sun (allowed to take tunics off) Range practice at Scherpenberg in afternoon. Either my rifle magazine no d – d good or I'm not. (former I think) Heat distinctly unpleasant in thick clothing. Footer match in afternoon. D Coy v 1st Gordons – we won. Trench digging fatigue cancelled. Heard that Lawson[80.2] ("Spare Colonel") had got his Commission. Thank 'Eaven we've got a "naivy".[80.3]

Saturday 1st May - Billets - Siege Barn (Kemmel) Brig Res

Sweltering heat. Running & P jerks but easy forenoon till went to Scharpenberg Range. 1st Gordons there. Competed with them at rapid fire. Short rifle v long.[80.4] Long (ours) won but only one man did the test 15 per min.[80.5] (Topping). Brigadier made short speech. (I didn't get a single round off – magazine jammed) Bath parade in afternoon but a few of us preferred an inner wetting at "Den Engel" (bar) to incrustations with dirty water & soap! Beer tepid – took custom to cottage further down. Left for "line" at 7pm (after seeing very fine draft arr for 1st Gordons) Tiresome march. Billet in big farm (evidently dairy farm). (tobacco plant too!) Detailed for guard (1st spell)

MAY, 1915.

4th after Easter. Sunday 2 Peach & cherry blossom orchard very pretty

Not so hot. Sunnier. Horse a ??. Saw swallows. In continual dread of Brig ?? appearing. Inspected byres & steading generally (very substantial) — got real cow milk for change. Surprised to see farmer's wife (Brig ?? masculine woman) making sign of + & splashing holy water before each window first after dawn. Brig came galloping up & ?? time to ?? out the "guard". G? dismounted at 7 pm & excused from night fatigues. Couldn't find place to "lay our weary heads" in loft. Wash anyhow & anointed body with saffron oil — nipped like hell too! Found floor space for sleep at last. Tragedy when spark (14–15 ft) hopped over our ?? & ?? ?? wall ?? on "Uhlan Bull's" head. Got distinct sniff of gas ?? 7 ft.

Diary page (enlarged)

81

Sunday 2nd May - Billets - Siege Barn (Kemmel) Brig Res (Fatigues)

Not so hot. Rain shower in aft. Saw swallows. Peach & cherry blossom in orchard v pretty. In continual dread of Brigdr appearing. Insp byres & "steading" generally (very substantial) - got real cow milk for change. Surprised to see fmr's wife (big masculine woman) making sign of + & splashing holy? water before each window just after dawn. Brig. came galloping up & no time to "turn out the guard". Gd dismntd at 7pm & excused from night fatigues. Couldn't find places to "lay our weary heads" in loft. Wash anyhow and anointed body with saffron oil - nipped like hell too! Found floor space for sleep at last. Tragedy when Spark (14-15st) tripped over our legs & sat down wallop on "Uhlan Bill's" head. Got distinct sniff of gas. Found '75' shell case.

Monday 3rd May - Kemmel - Brig Res

Very sunny & not too hot. Breakfast at 4am then good sleep. Started work at 11am under RAMC L/cpl (specialist in hygiene apparently) - digging 2 huge filter beds. Pete & I began to open up very 'niffy' drains in courtyard & got polite 'oiseau' from farmer - told to go and "schlafen" (sleep I spose) & he would do it - quite angry about it! Transferred energies to other fields - damming channel to "moat" (little island). Managed to dodge 3hr night spell by lying low (like 'Brer Rabbit') & saying nothing.

[84.1] Hill 60 – Hill 60, located around 3 miles SE of Ypres, was made from the spoil removed during the construction of the nearby railway. Although quite small, it overlooks a flat landscape and had great strategic importance in the battles in the Salient. At huge cost in lives, it changed hands several times during the course of the War.

[84.2] Kemmel 'Ks' – Part of the trench system near Kemmel.

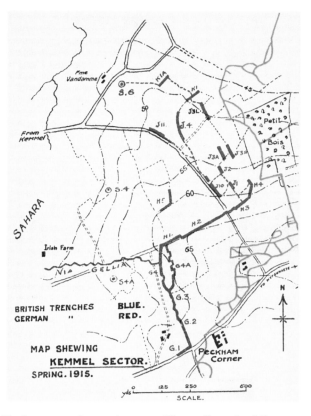

[84.3] obs. post – observation post. These allowed soldiers to watch the enemy's activity (for example trench digging, movement of transport and artillery, defensive works and general routine). They were also used to direct artillery fire, by observing the fall of shells and signalling adjustments back to the gunners so that following rounds would land on target.

83

Tuesday 4th May - Kemmel - Brig Res - fatigue

Miserable rain in morning. Sleep broken by being wakened for breakfast & couldn't resume. Heard that we'd lost "Hill 60"?[84.1] Reading "Waverly". On fatigue again at 11am. Carting bricks in wheelbarrow from ruin about half way to Kemmel. Gt expenditure of energy for little result until we found rubber tyred cart - carrying on in afternoon (very hot). Our batteries only 100 yds off rd - gun muzzles gleaming in sun. Felt quite brave strolling in front of them.
Visited "Madame" at partially wrecked "Chateau du Lievre" - voluble dame but beer very cool. Fatigues took some dodging. One at a time good enough.
Downpour in evening. "Tommy" (C.O.) up. Relieved by R Scots. Very sultry evening. Dan W & Spark wounded on way into trenches (Ks). Dan much worse but didn't make nearly so much noise about it. Down to dressing stn about 1am.

Wednesday 5th May - Kemmel - 'Ks'[84.2] Trenches (HQrs)

Glorious day. Lunch at Cottage as usual (but no orchestra). Lazed in afternoon at l'estaminet "Herbege den Mol" - getting quite blasé on the job. Good view of trench line through hole in roof of loft - good obs. Post.[84.3]

[86.1] KOSBs – Kings Own Scottish Borderers.

[86.2] Knowles – See Annex A - People in the Diary

[86.3] "at mine ease" – from '**A-Shelling Peas**' a poem by Harry ("Breaker") Morant, 1902. While commanding an elite British Army unit during the Second Boer War, Captain Morant was court-martialled for war crimes. According to military prosecutors, Morant had retaliated for the combat death of a fellow officer with the summary execution of nine Afrikaner POWs. He was found guilty and sentenced to death.

Morant was then court-martialled for the murder of a Lutheran, Rev. Daniel Heese. The German-born Heese had witnessed the POW massacre and vowed to tell Morant's commanding officer. He was shot to death on the way to the British Army HQ.

Morant was acquitted of the Heese murder, but his sentence for the POW massacre was carried out by a firing squad from the Queen's Own Cameron Highlanders on 27 February 1902.

Wednesday 5th May - Kemmel - 'Ks' Trenches (HQrs) (Continued)

Exploring old trenches behind hedge - bags of amn & some rifles lying about (battlefield must have had some funny changes).
Delightful evening - lay outside till dusk.
3hrs on guard at night but time passed ok.
Terrific gunfire - fainter in direction of 'Hill 60'. Heard counter attack on 'Hill 60' had failed. KOSBs.[86.1] driven back by gas Knowles[86.2] killed in trenches & Billy Anderson grazed by shell.

Thursday 6th May - Kemmel - 'Ks' Trenches (HQrs)

Ideal "growing" day for crops, with heavy rain in early afternoon - glorious evening after rain.
Effort to get up & make breakfast - scrounged bit off the "cooker".
Writing up diary in forenoon. Heard cuckoo for the first time. Pleasant toilet (incl shave) in afternoon.
KOSB transport kicked up frightful row on cobbled road (returning from 'Hill 60' to Dickebusch).
Row from CO. Sent to stop Suffolks from shooting at hares. Midges active in evening as I sat "at mine ease"[86.3] out of doors.
Knowles buried (little cemetery growing).

[88.1] Writing up diary – Here is an example of Rule carrying out some 'back-work' on his diary, probably firming up on those entries for which he may have had little time for writing during the days in question.

[88.2] D W Creighton – Properly 'Crichton' – See Annex A - People in the Diary

[88.3] Lice getting the upper hand – The ever-present irritation goes on.

[88.4] Major Baird – See Annex A - People in the Diary

[88.5] Respirator tank – Likely to be chemicals for use in the mouth-pad form of protection against gas attack used at this time.

[88.6] John Bull – In this context, Great Britain.

[88.7] World's News – The Signallers would likely have been members of the Telegraph units of the Royal Engineers who, in addition to their core function of providing military communications, also brought news to the front line troops.

[88.8] Lusitania –

Friday 7th May - Kemmel 'Ks' - Trenches

Glorious day - slight shower in evening. Very
comfy bed in straw - loath to get up.
Badly shelled in forenoon (small stuff) -
some very close. Men in reserve barn went into
trenches outside in case of accidents. Writing
up diary[88.1] - completed portion on France
right up to date. Various add. fatigues. D W
Creighton[88.2] - killed on fatigue party.
Another bright spirit gone west! Good deal of
gunfire in evening. Pleasant sound when not
in it & pretty to watch. Lice getting the upper
hand again.[88.3]

Saturday 8th May - Kemmel 'Ks' - Trenches

Glorious day. Over to HQrs of 1st Gordons -
Maj. Baird[88.4] C.O. Carried respirator tank[88.5]
from La Clytte - some job. Hot too but struck
cooling draught of beer at "Du Lievre".
Inspected chateau & church at Kemmel - La
Clytte seemed literally swarming with Belgian
"traveilleurs" but designation a misnomer.
Didn't catch one working! All loafing about -
mainly cutting one another's hair. Very
different to peasants on farms. I spose good
old John Bull[88.6] foots the bill. Can't be many
Belgians fighting!
Gun emplacements being put in all over place.
(Something doing soon?)
"World's News"[88.7] from Signallers.
"Lusitania"[88.8] sunk by German 'U'-boat with
all on board? Rumours of 'move'.

[90.1] "Spud Tamson" – By Capt R W Campbell. Published in 1915, it is a humorous tale of a fictitious unit of Scottish militia.

Private Spud Tamson.

The Glesca Mileeshy was a noble force, recruited from the Weary Willies and Never - works of the famous town of Glasgow. It was also a regiment with traditions, for in the dim and distant past it had been founded by 1000 heroic scally-wags from out of the city jails. These men were dressed in tartan breeks and red coats, given a gun and kit, shipped straight to the Peninsula, and on landing there were told to fight or starve.

"We'll fecht," was their unanimous reply, and fight they did. Inured to hardships, they quickly adapted themselves to the tented field, and early displayed a thirst

[90.2] German "taube" – Literally 'dove'.

Sunday 9th May – Kemmel 'Ks' – Trenches

Cold wind but pleasant during day. Chilly in
evening.
Warned about 'move'. Read "Spud Tamson"[90.1]
(RW Campbell) lying outside billet on grass.
Brigadier showed himself good sport. German
"taube" [90.2] brought down by British 'plane.
British mine fired in "Js" (trenches). "Hill 60"
retaken & everything in the garden lovely.
Went to Rossignol Farm after tea (HQrs of R
Scots) – long wait. 1st Gordons out of line –
general mix up. Took in relief (Border
Regiment?) & by very track I was supposed to
avoid (luckily snipers off duty) Rushed them
up at some pace too.
Sorry to leave HQrs when returned (place
looked deserted).
Home Rozenhill with McLaggan – seemed devil
of a long way – lost amongst trees for bit.

Monday 10th May – Rozenhill – billets

Glorious day. Deluge of parcels. Managed to
get coveted '75' shell case properly packed up
& dispatched home at last. 1st souvenir of the
Great war (Fr bayonet (of unhappy memory)
too dangerous to send without a scabbard).
Surprise parade at 2.15pm.
Practising 'Attack' – some wild rushes – quite
winded at times & digging trenches at edge of
wood. C.O. addressed Bn as a whole &
criticised the attack.

Rest Billets (Rozenhill)

MAY, 1915

Tuesday 11

Glorious day. B.O.S. had to come & chivy us out of bed (very sleepy – never heard the pipes at "Hey Johnnie Cope"). Rm. n...tb at skirts of Kennythorpe – lanes & hedges very picturesque. Had to be up for Comdt before breakfast (once one is up) Usual parade / then "attack" which meant 1 coy he at edge of wood – then parties advance on La C... he. Brig Gen watchd up. With ...s. Sneaked on to right flank & walked up "blind" side of a hedge. "Cease" "cease fire" at C..., then home by cross rds. So ended a strenuous day – reminiscent of Bedford days (which seem so far off!) ... likely ...

Diary page (enlarged)

91

Monday 10th May - Rozenhill - billets
(Continued)

Having quiet evening off with Jock Thomson & Jimmie - beer & lazing in transport field (on grass) when sudden Alarm - transport saddling up.
Rushed back to find everybody packing. My pack weighed a ton & felt like dropping but 2nd on parade.
Disillusioned by Tommy practice alarm - funny aftwds.

Tuesday 11th May - Rozenhill - rest billets

Glorious day. B.O.S.[92.1] had to come & chivvy us out of bed (very sleepy - never heard the pipers at "Hey Johnnie Cope"). R&rm - right to outskirts of Reninghelst - lanes & hedges very picturesque. Nice to be up for constit before breakfast (once one is up).
Usual parades then 'attack' which meant long lie at edge of wood - then spirited advance on La Clytte. Brig Gen watching.
Wild rushes. Sneaked on to right flank & walked up 'blind' side of a hedge. 'Closed' & 'cease fire' at La Clytte - then home by cross rds.
So ended a strenuous day - reminiscent of Bedford Days (which seem so far off!) - like by Oakley, Bromham etc but without the "brambles" on the hedgerows.
Knox & Shearer gt fun in evening.

[94.1] 'red tabs' – Officers of the rank of Colonel and higher (as well as by more junior officers in staff jobs in Headquarters) were signified by, amongst other things, red tabs on their lapels. This is demonstrated here in a portrait of Field Marshal Haig at General Headquarters, France, by Sir William Orpen, May 1917.

[94.2] 'Wipers' – It was commonplace for troops to substitute nicknames for place names, making them easier to pronounce. For example, Ypres became Wipers, Ploegsteert became Plugstreet and Poperinghe was shortened to Pop.

[94.3] S Lancs – The South Lancashire Regiment.

HILL 60

Wednesday 12th May - Rozenhill Billets - Trenches (Hill 60)

Glorious day. Prog. for day (incl footer matches) cancelled. Paraded 9.20am for address by Lt. Gen (Sir C Fergusson) - fine inspiring speech (good few 'red tabs'[94.1] around). Packing in earnest. Got away at 2.30pm in frightful heat and dust. Pack felt dead wt. Through Dickebusch & saw old friends in Suffolks (sponsors in trench warfare - Meade, Scott etc.) Belgians digging reserve trenches (working better than on roads - appeals to them more I spose). Halts enjoyable - one near 'Wipers'.[94.2]
Good few Indians (One Mountain Battery) - showed us their knives (after drawing blood) - also tasted their cakes.
Ypres magnificent sight - all ablaze - 2 slender ch spires standing out - belt of fir trees in foreground. Crossed Yser Canal & along rly line till ready to drop. Relieved KOSBs & S Lancs[94.3] on 'Hill 60'. Back to dugouts on rly. Continued procession of wounded all night long. Slept outside.

Thursday 13th May - Hill 60 - dugouts

One of wettest, most miserable days of campaign so far - steady downpour - vain search of dry places in dugout - finally flooded out & utterly soaked. Set to work again on it but energy lessened by want of food.

[96.1] Dugouts – Underground excavations, large enough for several people, here to provide shelter for a battalion headquarters.

[96.2] Cubby hole – here, a small one-man shelter dug into the side of the trench. In general, a small place of safety.

[96.3] so the poor dog had none – From the nursery rhyme 'Old Mother Hubbard'.

[96.4] Bedford House ("White Chateau") – This was the Chateau Rosendal, and, as well as Bedford House, it was sometimes known by the British as Woodcote House. During the war, it was used as a headquarters, for field ambulances and burial sites.

Before The War –

After the shelling –

" Bedford House ". Ypres . 1917.

Thursday 13th May - Hill 60 - dugouts
(Continued)

Got some dry biscuits & 'bully' aftwds - coy lines a quagmire. Heavy gunfire. Man hit by shrapnel on rly. Usual stream of wounded on stretchers (gunfire not for nothing) - some pretty bad (moaning).
Whole Bn on fatigue - called out to find some working parties that had got lost. Some job slipping & crawling along rly embankment - very dark. Dead bodies all along (fr gas attack). Forsaken cat rending the night with 'miaows'. Up into 1st Gordons dugouts.[96.1] Very interesting stories of campaign.

Friday 14th May - Hill 60 - dugouts

Miserable day, especially forenoon. Trying to dig sodden mud out of "cubby hole"[96.2] but had to give it up - rain coming right in. Race down to 'D' Coy's lines for tea to find it all gone (& so the poor dog had none)[96.3]
Reading of the sinking of the Lusitania - frightful atrocity.
Easy day as regards duty. Faired up in afternoon & so tackled dugout afresh & put in sandbags - but still very damp. Sleep impossible with damp feet on damp soil. Fine view of Ypres & of Bedford House[96.4] ("White Chateau") on opp side of rly line.
On duty 10-12 midnight - got well & truly soaked. Letters from home - heard John (Scottish Horse) was on the move.

[98.1] Stevenson – See Annex A - People in the Diary

[98.2] wrote letter of sympathy to Crichton's people. – Rule wrote quite a few such letters of sympathy to the families of his fallen comrades. Recognising that if he did not find it easy, it should be considered how demanding it must have been for the regimental officers who, whenever possible, wrote individual letters to the families of all their soldiers who died. Whilst mainly genuinely meant, these letters also often served to assure the family that their loved one had not suffered and that their sacrifice was not in vain, whether or not this had been the case.

[98.3] Sherwoods – Sherwood Foresters.

[98.4] L'Pool Regt – The King's (Liverpool Regiment).

[98.5] "Tommy" – 'Tommy Atkins', a general nickname for the British (mainly English) Soldier, with 'Jock' for Scots, 'Paddy' for Irish and 'Taff' for Welsh also commonly used.

One version of the origin of the name is that, when the Duke of Wellington, in the mid-nineteenth century, was asked if he had any views on a name that would be used as an example to assist in the completion of a range of new military forms, he picked 'Tommy Atkins'. Thomas Atkins was the name of a soldier he saw dying following a fierce engagement, but who had carried out his duty true to the standards and traditions Wellington admired. There is, however, evidence that the name was used much earlier in the eighteenth century.

Saturday 15th May – Hill 60 – dugouts

Lovely in morning but overcast later – with rain 'continually threatening'. Titivating 'cubby hole' – trying to make it habitable. Easy day (no 'calls'). Shed togs & had thorough 'hunt' with Great Slaughter amongst ranks of lice. C.O. out with party burying dead bodies (gassed). Met Stevenson[98.1] 1st Gordons (Huntly man) & had long chat. Wrote letter of sympathy to Crichton's people[98.2] – wonderful how difficult it is to express sympathy in words (seems so hypocritical somehow).

Sunday 16th May – Hill 60 – dugouts

Glorious day. Didn't remember it was Sunday until late in the day. No call for services of guides (easy day). Jerry 'planes getting shelled by 'Archie'. One nosecap fell quite close – row like motor car. Bits of shell cases falling everywhere (lucky – no casualties) "Feathered" my nest with dry grass & stuck newspapers on wall to keep off damp. Finally fell asleep in sun (strong too). Gt coat dry for once. Sherwoods[98.3] & L'pool Regt[98.4] around on fatigue – cheery mobs. "Tommy"[98.5] also sounds very much as at home.

Monday 17th May – Hill 60 – dugouts

Pouring practically whole day! Not so downhearted as might be expected however – learning to take things (incl weather) as they come.

[100.1] Q.M. – Quartermaster – the non-commissioned, warrant or commissioned officer (depending on the size of the formation) who had responsibility for the acquisition and supply of all of a unit's material requirements. From ammunition to bootlaces, sandbags to toilet paper, the quartermaster provided it all.

[100.2] 'Jupiter nods' – from Virgil's *'Aeneid'*.

[100.3] Tommy Cranston – Private Thomas Cranston - See Annex A - People in the Diary

[100.4] Jimmie Thomson –

Monday 17th May – Hill 60 – dugouts (Continued)

Missed breakfast thro' being wakened at 8 am.
Sponged some off signallers.
HQrs kept me pretty busy with messages. New
dugout on palatial lines being built for C.O.
Hadn't luck to strike a parcel from anywhere
so had to carry on with soldier's official diet
(Q.M.[100.1] not so 'flush' as usual either).
Brigadier challenged 'Tommy' to stone
throwing competition in evening. 'The Heads at
play' (& Jupiter nods)[100.2]
Very miserable evening in rain till finally told
to turn in for night (11.50pm).
Tommy Cranston[100.3] wounded.

Tuesday 18th May – Hill 60 – dugouts

Another miserable day. Dugout sopping wet
and sloppy outside but managed a non stop
run (sleep) 12 – 8am.
Welcome cigarettes in parcel. Parcels make a
wonderful difference to army life.
Calamity after tea – shell fell on Crichty's
dugout & buried everyone except Topping –
sitting chopping wood at door. Got them all
out alive though crushed a bit & suffering
from shock.
Jimmie Thomson[100.4] – last out and with shell
wound in addition – seemed freshest of the
lot!

[102.1] "only 2 left of old 13 Section" – A mistake on Rule's part as he refers to the number of the platoon (he correctly uses 'platoon' elsewhere) within D Company, 4ᵗʰ Battalion, Gordon Highlanders. This further illustrates how, from the move to Bedford onwards, the old U Company (where Rule had been a member of 13 Platoon) became diluted by changes in personnel. At first, these came about by transfers and commissioning then additionally, after deploying to Belgium, by changes due to serious wounds and deaths.

[102.2] "crumps" – loud thudding sounds, especially when made by exploding bombs or shells, or can refer to the shells themselves.

[102.3] R.A.M.C. – Royal Army Medical Corps. The RAMC itself lost 743 officers and 6130 soldiers in the war, of whom 470 officers and 3,669 other ranks were either killed in action or died of wounds. Corps members won:

- 1,111 Meritorious Service Medals, including one extra bar
- 3,002 Military Medals, including 95 with one extra bar, and 4 with 2 extra bars
- 395 Distinguished Conduct Medals, including 9 with one extra bar
- 3 Albert Medals
- 1,484 Military Crosses, including 61 with one extra bar, 22 with 2 extra bars and 1 with 3 extra bars
- 499 Distinguished Service Orders, including 25 with 1 extra bar
- 7 Victoria Crosses, one of which included 1 extra bar (Noel Chavasse) and another a second award (Arthur Martin-Leake, having won his first VC in 1902)

RAMC Badge

[102.4] Bedford – The Bedfordshire Regiment.

Tuesday 18th May - Hill 60 - dugouts (Continued)

Comedy when rescuers standing on head & trying to find it from position of arms & legs (spread out like a starfish). Roy & I only 2 left of old 13 Section[102.1] (except Silver - cook) Few casualties in fatigue parties.

Wednesday 19th May - Hill 60 - dugouts

Miserable day again. Heavy misty rain - hardened up in late evening.
Fearful shelling in afternoon. Terrific 'crumps'[102.2] landing all around us (very heavy stuff) Tree split in half & 2 R.A.M.C. [102.3] blown to atoms in dugout (direct hit) - burst inside - place like a shambles aftwds. Turned out that heavy German guns were searching for our batteries & these shells had fallen short.
Cooker out of action temporarily so no dinner but CO's dugout still carried on. Feet cold & wet.

Thursday 20th May - Hill 60 - dugouts

Glorious day. Peaceful forenoon disturbed by muffled explosion in RAMC dugout. RAMC Sgt blown to pieces by hand grenade (accident - thirst for knowledge). Refreshing toilet (head & feet only) in pond after haircut. Officers having celebration dinner (in new dugout) on cushioned chairs. Relief arrd 8pm (Bedford)[102.4]

[104.1] Very tired – Another former U Company member, James Fraser, had an altogether different experience on the same day, as he tells us in his own diary, *"Went to Zillebeke on a digging party to make some strong points, went into the village church with Cpls. Lamb and Burns. We tried the organ but it was too damp to work.*

Climbed the clock tower and moved the hands, some Germans must have seen the hands moving for we had only got to the church door when a blast of shrapnel swept over the church yard.

We ran to our trenches, but the Germans kept on shelling the village and our digging party went back to our lines. Were relieved and went back to the huts at Rosenhill."

[104.2] Boric Powder – Boric acid can be used as an antiseptic for minor burns or cuts and is sometimes used in dressings or salves. It is also used as prevention of athlete's foot, by inserting powder in the socks.

[104.3] photos taken by Crichty – See page 15.

[104.4] "seems a long time back! – only 3 months previously.

[104.5] Only man of original 13 Section – Interesting that Rule mentions this again (with the same use of 'section' instead of 'platoon') after only three days, perhaps reflecting on his possible longevity in this 'sole survivor' role.

It does, however, reinforce both the impact of deaths and serious wounds suffered by Alexander Rule's comrades, as well as their being posted to other units or commissioned to become officers. This combined attrition was indicative of U Company having effectively ceased to exist not only in name but in reality as well (See also [102.1]).

[104.6] Left marker – This is an important and responsible role when a unit is on parade. Other soldiers reference their position – 'take their dressing' – in relation to the marker, therefore he has to position himself exactly where the parade commander requires him to be.

Thursday 20th May - Hill 60 - dugouts (Continued)

Usual interchange of pleasantries - Left with Clarke after relief complete. Evening sultry but led out at cross country pace (C. ex Scottish Champion hurdler & x-country runner) Only one halt but "cracked hardy". Along rly line & thro' Dickebusch (lang toon) & La Clytte. Very tired[104.1] on last 'lap' & footsore. Cookhouse took some finding. Bedmates with Roy T.

Friday 21st May - Rozenhill

Pleasant weather - could do with it a bit warmer. Midsex in same encampment as us. Feet d - d sore after long spell without boots off. Boric powder[104.2] a healing "balm". 2 marvellous escapes at rifle inspection (Begg) Thought my rifle was one I'd newly picked up & inspected only those pouches of amn that weren't rusty! Saw photos taken by Crichty[104.3] at Le Havre & on troop trains - seems a long time back! [104.4] Only man (private) of original 13 Section on parade with 'U' Coy.[104.5]

Saturday 22nd May - Rozenhill

Glorious day. D - d hot in forenoon but chilly in evening (thundery). Right to outskirts of Reninghelst in early morning run. Left marker[104.6] for Ptn at Coy drill. Bit shaky especially when left marker for double Coy in line as my luck often had it.

[106.1] J Lamb – See Annex A - People in the Diary

[106.2] J K Forbes – Unusually, J K Forbes was promoted to Sergeant direct from Lance Corporal.

J. K. FORBES

[106.3] Allardyce, [106.4] Murdo MacIver, [106.5] Haig, [106.6] M McLeod, [106.7] Col Scott – See Annex A - People in the Diary

Saturday 22nd May - Rozenhill (Continued)

Relay races. Promotions out J Lamb[106.1] Sgt.
J.K.Forbes[106.2] & Allardyce[106.3] L/Sgts. Topping
& Murdo MacIver[106.4] Cpls. Haig[106.5], Gunn, M
McLeod[106.6] & Fowlie L/cpls. - usual ragging.
Strenuous bayonet practice in afternoon (Begg).
Mirrlees a failure.

Sunday 23rd May - Rozenhill - Rest Billets

Glorious day. No r&rm or rifle inspection!
Something wrong somewhere?
Bayonet pract. 10.30am (Begg). Pretty tiresome
(mentally & physically) till Begg got stuffed
bag & put in sentry box.
Then the fun began! Good practice too. Didn't
take long to rip the bags up.
Bathing parade. Long wait till 'C' Coy finished
& no money to buy beer! Rush for baths at
word 'go'. Change of underclothing very
welcome in this heat.
Church parade (W.O. dress) - Col Scott[106.7]
(old chaplain in Bedford) - drowsy as ever.
Luckily permitted to lie down during sermon -
drowsy lullaby (almost asleep). Communion
aftwds - not many there.
At Midsex concert in even - very enjoyable.
One fellow great on flute (acrobatically &
musically).
Writing letters.

[108.1] "Jam Pot" bombs – Sometimes called "Jam Tin" bombs. They were usually made from a used jam tin, filled with bits of scrap metal, a bit of explosive, and a fuse. They were also known as "Tickler's Artillery" after Tickler, a famous jam manufacturer, whose Plum and Apple Jam tins were often used as containers.

[108.2] Red + cars – Red Cross cars, for example this Crossley 15hp model.

Monday 24th May – Rozenhill (billets) –> Vlamertinge

Glorious day. Heavy gunfire during night. Gas sentries sick. Our eyes nipping at r&rm (gas in air) – got almost to Reninghelst.
Demonstr & practice in bayonet fighting (Topping). Forrest & W Donald provided fun. F. got the 'spirit' of it ok but not the accomplishment.
Lecture & demonstr on rifle & hand grenades (Watson – Lt) – very interesting. "Jam Pot" bombs[108.1] followed.
Crichty & Pete back – looking none the worse for being buried! Long lie after dinner waiting for orders – something in the wind?
Sudden orders to move. Usual rush & bulging packs.
Passed thro' Ouderdom (fair sized village) & Vlamertinge – cheery sight the eternal stream of Red + cars? [108.2] Some 'dust-up' on up in salient apparently.
Halted in field beyond Vlamertinge. Whole Brig in reserve to V Div. (Gen C Fergusson) Chilly after heat.

Tuesday 25th May – Vlamertinge – Brig Reserve (field) – trenches (fatigue) Salient

Glorious day. Shifted to further side of rly embankment about 4.30 am but sun made sleep impossible.
Sweating lying still!

[110.1] "Shall never forget Ypres" – This aerial photograph of Ypres in 1915, around the time of Rule's description, shows the devastation. The Church of St Martin is in the centre, with the Cloth Hall to its lower right. Things got worse as time went on.

[110.2] Sancty Wood – Sanctuary Wood. Given its name because, much earlier in the War, some soldiers had sheltered here (in effect were offered sanctuary) from a battle as they tried to return to their units. Following shelling in November 1914, the name could hardly be considered appropriate, but it stuck.

[110.3] "utterly dead beat" – This is no surprise, as the trip was over <u>seven</u> miles (11.25km) each way, marching over roads covered in mud, pitted with holes and with other soldiers, horses, guns, wagons and casualties trying to make their way at the same time as Rule and his fellow Gordon Highlanders.

Tuesday 25th May - Vlamertinge - Brig Reserve (field) - trenches (fatigue) Salient (Continued)

Too lazy to wash or read almost.
Writing letters an effort. Latrines too near.
Filthy looking sediment in 'tea' from cookers.
Rifle & respirator inspections.
Left camp abt 6.30pm for fatigue (fighting kit) & shovels.
Marched along rly line to Ypres passing magnificent chateaux.
Shall never forget Ypres[110.1] in its utter desolation (systematically wrecked) Walls brought down showing interiors of houses just as inhabitants had left them - like models with fronts removed. Cloth Hall & Ch of St Martin utterly wrecked. Comic site in statue of past civic dignitary with chains of office lying flat on "corporation" at base of pedestal.
Cemetery furrowed up by shell fire.
Crossed canal - collected sandbags - then on and on (like march of the dead) right to very tip of salient - got to work in Sancty Wd[110.2] abt 11pm with shells bursting on top of us almost: hottest corner we've yet seen.
Trenches littered with coats, equip & rifles of casualties. good deal of 'souveniring'.

Wednesday 26th May - Salient - Vlam

Got back fr Sancty Wood to field near Vlamertinge at 4am - utterly dead beat.[110.3]
Dawn came as we got back thro' Ypres which showed fresh aspects by daylight. Wrecked armoured cars etc.

[112.1] REs – Royal Engineers.

[112.2] "*Gaudeamus*" – The popular University song, *Gaudeamus Igitur*, was offered here in the hope of a response from within the "*Ladies Seminary*". Perhaps the translation of the first two verses would not bear too much reflection in wartime.

Gaudeamus igitur,	Let us therefore rejoice,
Juvenes dum sumus;	While we are young;
Post icundum iuventutem,	After our youth,
Post molestam senectutem	After a troublesome old age
Nos habebit humus.	The ground will hold us.
Vita nostra brevis est,	Our life is brief,
Brevi finietur;	It will shortly end;
Venit mors velociter,	Death comes quickly,
Rapit nos atrociter;	Cruelly snatches us;
Nemini parcetur.	No-one is spared.

[112.3] P de Lille – Port de Lille (The Lille Gate, one of the exits from Ypres.)

[112.4] C.T. – Communication Trench.

Wednesday 26th May - Salient - Vlam (Continued)

Fell asleep almost immedly on arrival & awoke with wrists badly sunburnt in strong sun without overhead cover of any sort. Throat parched with dust of "Wipers".

Wakened for bkfst and again (blaspheming) for respirator drill & lecture by REs[112.1] on new issue.

Then pay parade put final end to hopes of sleep. Refreshing dip in stream. Call for volunteers for 'outposts. Several of U Coy hit estaminets in Vlam for vin rouge etc.

Finally packed up and left for trenches in good voice. Thro Ypres by main road. "Gaudeamus"[112.2] as passed high wall of "Ladies Seminary" but no answering bar.

Out of Wipers by P de Lille,[112.3] along rly & packs feeling heavier & heavier.
Big 'crump' just missed us - spaces bet. platoons.

Filed into trenches on left of Menin Rd (converted C.T.)[112.4]

[114.1] Uhlans – German Light Cavalry

[116.1] Church of St Martin, Ypres –

<u>Undated May</u> – Notes on Ypres

Traces of barricades (echoes of street fighting
– Uhlans[114.1] I spose).
Barracks, huge red building on Vlam side,
badly shelled. Famous Yser Canal with locks.
Encirc. city wall or rampart on Menin Road
(Roulers side) – said to be family of swans –
still there – walls gtly pitted with shellfire.
Shops with wares still on counter. (Clearance
sales evidently didn't have suff. time or
customers.)

Wine saloons – wine glasses etc on counters –
some half filled (couldn't have been any
Scotsmen!)
Houses terribly shattered in many quarters.
Very few untouched.
Some with front wall cut clean off as tho' by
huge knife showing house in vertical elevation
"with one wall removed to show interior" –
bookcase with fine folios – pictures hanging
on walls – tables in some cases laid as for
breakfast – must have been wild scurry! Some
with fine fronts.

Place seemed full of cafes.
Prison! – ancient water tower – hit by shell
(wonder what became of prisoners).
Ladies seminary with high wall (Gaude' fr 'U'
Coy) – some very narrow streets leading off
main ones – all ankle deep in fine brick dust
(from ruins – silent eerie tread).

[116.2] Horses – Horses were widely used by both sides throughout the war.

Here, later in the war, a pair of horses struggles to pull a water trailer, with the one closer to the camera having slipped into the mud. If it could not be pulled free, it would almost certainly have been shot where it lay.

A mobile pigeon loft

Along with animals such as mules, donkeys, dogs and pigeons, horses made a huge contribution to the war. Without horses, supplies could not have been brought forward to the trenches and artillery guns could not have been moved around. However, this was achieved at a terrible price. Hundreds of thousands of animals died as a result of shelling, overwork, injuries or falling into mud or shell holes. In one day in 1916, 7,000 horses died during the battle of Verdun.

Undated May – Notes on Ypres (Continued)

Fine Flemish looking bldgs. still traceable
amid blackened ruins.
Frightful stench.

La Grande Place. Church of St Martin,[116.1] a
tangled wreckage of pews & bare walls.
Heavily shattered Rose Window. Altar so far
miraculously intact. Statue of some civic
dignitary in full regalia: corpulent figure
blown off pedestal by shell burst resting on his
tummy, still clasping official mace.
Cloth Hall – beautiful façade in ruins.
Carvings faintly traceable here and there. Old
State (ceremonial) Coach amid rubble. Clock
tower badly battered. Abandoned scaffolding
(for repairs). Clock dial still in position but
clock itself a tangled mess lying at the base
where it fell.

Town Hall – again with abandoned scaffolding.
Street trees – blasted & blighted by shellfire –
thoroughfares blocked in places by rubble.
Stench from broken sewers probably in park.
Also from swollen bodies of dead horses[116.2]
lying beside wrecked limbers.
Some attractive gardens still to be seen round
houses in outskirts.

Huge civilian cemetery with ambitious
mausoleums & monuments – large crucifix.
Chateaux in wooded grounds outside Ypres –
indications of affluence & leisure.

[118.1] Short Lee Enfield – Almost certainly the same type of rifle used by 1st Gordons in the 'short v long' competition held on 1st May. Rule may have felt that keeping his souvenir for his own use would have been acceptable, but reckoned without the Army's views on such matters.

[118.2] Dragoons – Dragoon Guards.

[118.3] KRRs – Kings Royal Rifles.

[118.4] Hell Fire Corner – The main easterly access to the Ypres Salient was via the Ypres-Menin road (the Menin Road). About a mile out of Ypres, the Ypres-Roulers railway crossed the road. This intersection provided a perfect target for German gunners. Because the spot was preregistered and under constant observation by the enemy, it was a place where troops, supply trains and artillery felt extremely vulnerable. Quickly nicknamed "Hell Fire Corner", it became standard practice for troops to transit the site only at a full run, for horses at a gallop and for lorries with the accelerator hard to the floor.

[118.5] Kitchener Divns – Kitchener Divisions. It was realised in late autumn 1914 that the opening weeks of the war had decimated what had been Great Britain's regular army. (Some 100,000 soldiers were deployed with the BEF in August. By the end of the year, 90% of those were killed, wounded or missing.) The Territorial Force had been mobilised, but that would not provide the numbers of soldiers required to sustain the losses that mechanised warfare was inflicting.

Kitchener fronted a recruiting campaign that sought 100,000 men to form a 'New Army'. By the end of September 1914 over 750,000 men had volunteered. Early in that month, over 30,000 men per day were enlisting. However, this influx almost overwhelmed the system in terms of the recruitment process – administration, medicals, etc. – let alone the capacity to then clothe, equip, train and lead such huge numbers, all of which took a great deal of time. The first New Army – or 'Kitchener Divisions' – volunteers to go into battle did so at Loos, on the 25th of September 1915...

MAMMOTH SPELL IN THE TRENCHES

Thurs 27th May – Ypres – Menin Rd
(Trenches)

Unpleasant change in weather: v chilly
morning. Cleaned up trench. Cleaned up Short
Lee-Enfield[118.1] for self & had to hand
blasted thing in, but found F pen, holdall &
contents (razors) new shirt towels etc. Miscell.
crests Dragoons,[118.2] KRRs[118.3] etc. must have
been badly shelled and/or gassed.
Burial fatigues & many others incl trip to Bde
HQrs (furnished w carpets); rations; ammn
boxes; water fr Hell Fire Corner.[118.4] Homeless
cat 'miaowing' amongst ruins. On trench
digging fatigue behind front line after dusk.
Completed job & planted cabbage to
camouflage earth. Back at dawn.

Fri 28th May – Ypres – Menin Rd (Trenches)

Slightly milder & sunnier. Trench in front
being heavily shelled; shrapnel bullet just
missed me. Discarded old (lousy) shirt &
underwear for new "finds". Our Cpl (J Lamb)
overslept so we dodged fatigues till late
aftnoon. Much milder: hot at times.
Heavy shelling before "stand-to" just as we got
back fr fatigue. Several landing in Ypres;
rumours of 2 new Kitchener Divns[118.5] there?
Lazier day – cleaning up, shaving etc. Reading.
Found several more dead behind trench.
After dusk marched up Menin Rd – scorning
the CT – and occupd trench on right. Orders
not to fire exc at planes.

[120.1] Niven – See Annex A - People in the Diary

[120.2] Periscopes – A high number of casualties came from the Germans' abilities at sniping. With a widespread fondness for hunting, coupled with the ability to produce first-class rifles as well as excellent optics to produce telescopic sights, the Germans had many snipers and used them to deadly effect. Observation of the enemy was essential but, increasingly, looking over the trench parapet became suicidal and periscopes were regularly used for observation. A few types are shown below.

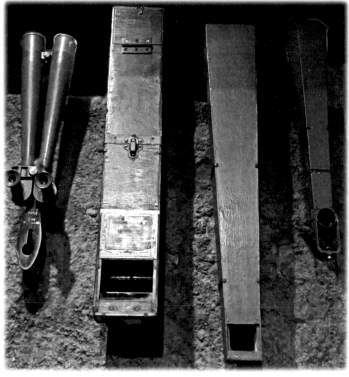

(Courtesy of The Imperial War Museum, London)

[120.3] 2Lt Hopkinson – See Annex A - People in the Diary

Saturday 29th May –

There is no entry in the diary for this day.

Sunday 30th May – Ypres – Menin Road
Trenches

Little sleep or rest possible.
Shellfire caused 13 casualties in 13 Ptn.
Wounded incl. Bert Murray, Stewart Mirrlees &
Niven.[120.1]
Dodging trench mortar bombs – good fun!
Periscopes[120.2] issued. Revetting party: under
Sgt J Lamb but no sandbags arrived for filling
so we slept for a time.
On burial party later – a grim job with bodies
on stretchers: limbs in rigor mortis: kept
catching on barbed wire entanglements on
jou'ny from outposts.
We buried all 4 of the dead in the abandoned
garden of a house in rear of our front line.
(We didn't realise it was Sunday)
2Lt Hopkinson[120.3] & Scott? fired on each other
on patrol in dark.

Monday 31st May – Ypres – Menin Road
Trenches

Sunny all day. Boche "taube" (dove-shaped)
'plane flew over us at morning stand-to. We
all fired at him with our rifles and got heavy
shelling later in reprisal(?) Little respite from
shelling all day.

[122.1] Lyditte – Properly Lyddite, after the placename Lydd, in SE England, where this explosive was developed for British use. It was based on picric acid, which formed the basis of the explosives used in shells by many countries, including Germany. It would have been the distinctive smell from that component that Rule noticed.

[122.2] R H Middleton – Private Robert H Middleton – See Annex A - People in the Diary

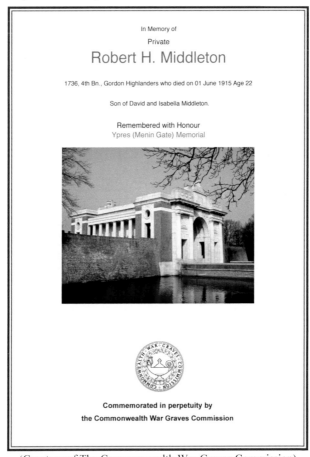

In Memory of
Private
Robert H. Middleton

1736, 4th Bn., Gordon Highlanders who died on 01 June 1915 Age 22

Son of David and Isabella Middleton.

Remembered with Honour
Ypres (Menin Gate) Memorial

**Commemorated in perpetuity by
the Commonwealth War Graves Commission**

(Courtesy of The Commonwealth War Graves Commission)

[122.3] Peterkin - See Annex A - People in the Diary

Monday 31st May – Ypres – Menin Road Trenches (Continued)

At one stage we were ordered to evacuate our front line for a support trench close behind. Out on patrol later. German patrol heard on opposite side of a hedge but no contact. Dug ourselves in when shelled later in new outpost line (under 2/Lt JD Pratt).

Welcome home mail arrived with rations despite heavy straffing of our Battn transport en route via Ypres.

Tuesday 1st June – Ypres – Menin Road Trenches

Returned to main front line at daybreak and struck heavy shellfire. Off & on all day. Tiredness plus lyditte[122.1] fumes from the Boche shells made it difficult to stay awake.

Amongst the killed was R H Middleton[122.2] of 'U' Coy – a promising writer and contributor to "Alma Mater".

A party of us returned to the outpost line at dusk: heavy shelling here also in our absence. Germans singing in their lines.
(A few days later, Peterkin[122.3] & I reached the 1st Gordons outposts on left of Menin Rd by daylight – crawling along the ditch for cover)

[124.1] Bengal Lancers – If Rule is correct in naming these Indian troops 'Bengal Lancers', they were probably the 18th King George's Own Lancers who arrived in France in 1914 with the Indian Cavalry Corps. This Regiment was a descendant of the original 'Bengal Lancers'. Life in the trenches would have been a particularly demanding experience for these soldiers, totally unaccustomed to the harsh European winter climate and usually deprived of the freedom of movement associated with cavalry operations.

[124.2] Murdo MacKenzie – See Annex A - People in the Diary

[124.3] S.M. – Sergeant Major.

[124.4] +s – Crosses. Unlike today, British policy in WWI was to bury those killed on, or close to, the battlefield in the land they had died to protect. Where possible, individual graves were marked with a wooden cross, but the ebb and flow of the conflict meant that many were lost during the four years of the war. Much care was taken after the 1918 Armistice to recover and properly bury those who had not been thus recognised. In the period up to September 1921, British Army exhumation units reburied 204,695 bodies.

The Imperial (now Commonwealth) War Graves Commission was founded by Fabian Ware and established by Royal Charter in 1917. It has responsibility for commemorating all Commonwealth war dead by name, on a headstone, at an identified site of a burial, or on a memorial. War dead are commemorated uniformly and equally, irrespective of military or civil rank, race or creed.

[124.5] ORs – Other Ranks.

Wednesday 2nd June - Ypres - Menin Rd Trenches

Warm June weather continuing. Good for sleep by day but for interruptions due to rifle & respirator inspections in the brief interludes between fatigues - trench digging, revetting etc - mostly at night. Heavy shelling and casualties - "side stepping" from one trench section to another actually increased casualties through bunching. Bengal Lancers[124.1] (with turbans) temporarily in support trenches.

Thursday 3rd - Tuesday 8th June - Ypres-Menin Rd Trenches

Fine weather, routine ± as usual, with occasional spasmodic reply by our field guns to German shelling. Murdo MacKenzie[124.2] in MG emplacement cynical about war in general. Good to be with stalwart like Sandy Gunn when digging in under fire on outpost duty.

Wednesday 9th June - Ypres - Menin Rd - Trenches

Very sultry. Enjoying perfect sleep when rudely awakened by S.M.[124.3] to go & fix up +s[124.4] on graves of 4 of 13 Ptn with Pioneer Sgt. Left Sgt at cottage behind supp tr & went on to fr line solo to see full effect of direct hit on trench (shell). 1 killed, Sgt badly wounded & 17 ORs[124.5] hit. Back to HQ for Dr & Adjt, then back again with stretcher. Fixed up crosses on return.

[126.1] Lt Simpson and *[126.2] Cook* – See Annex A - People in the Diary. Rule's account differs from the War Diary, which states 2/Lt Simpson was wounded during shelling on the 4th. Whilst Rule and the War Diary agree that on the 9th Lt Cook was wounded, the War Diary gives the second officer wounded that day as 2/Lt McKinnon. In any event, Lt Simpson died of his wounds on the 21st and now lies in the Military Cemetery named after Le Treport, a coastal town approximately 19 miles (30km) north-east of Dieppe. During the War, Le Treport was an important hospital centre with a capacity, by the summer of 1916, of nearly 10,000 beds.

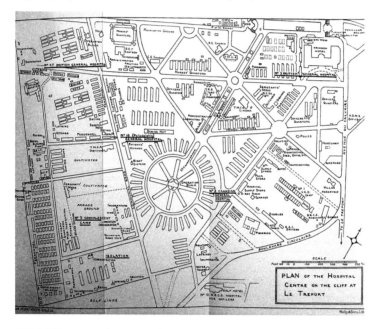

[126.3] bivvy – Bivouac – likely here to be a simple shelter under a piece of tarpaulin.

[126.4] Terrier Bns – Territorial Force Battalions, of which 4th Gordons was an example.

[126.5] hand (badly festered) – almost certainly related to the wound sustained in mid-April when Rule fell and badly cut his hand whilst carrying the French bayonet he had 'souvenired'.

Wednesday 9th June – Ypres – Menin Rd
Trenches (Continued)

Too late to have sleep. 'Relief off' – rotten!
On b. wire (knife rest) fatigue in front of new
trench. Shrapnel right amongst us. 2 trips to
HQrs.
A & B patrols got mixed up – d – d fools! Lt
Simpson[126.1] & Cook[126.2] both hit (Simpson
badly). Wind up about German patrols.

Thursday 10th June – Ypres – Menin Rd
Trenches

No sleep. Terrific thundershower. Woke up
under impression that someone was chucking
buckets of water on the bivvy[126.3] roof! Soaked
but snoozed off again till hauled out to bail
out trench.
Amn boxes floating. Dug 'sump' holes. Retreat
to bivvy cut off.
Pratt trying to put wind up us by telling us all
Terrier Bns[126.4] below 400 going home to
recruit. Felt lousy & couldn't wash because of
sore face & hand (badly festered) [126.5] –
spirits at low ebb.
Back to firing line again – heavy mist hanging
around. On extreme right next Suffolks –
trenches in awful mess – mud & water. 1st
sentry. Toothache, headache, feet sore & gen'
fed up & all alone. One bright spot in
otherwise drab evening when Suffolk on
fatigue party took header into shell hole (full
of water) at back of trench & said "Ain't it a
–––––– shame"?

[128.1] Joe Innes – See Annex A - People in the Diary

[128.2] heavy casualties in 6th Gordons – 6th Gordons were in action at Givenchy from 1st - 4th June, where they lost 1 officer and 27 ORs killed, 5 officers and 104 ORs wounded and 5 ORs missing.

[128.3] John Bull – The original **John Bull** was a Sunday newspaper established in London by Theodore Hook in 1820. Horatio Bottomley, an MP for the Liberal Party, became the publisher of the magazine on 12 May 1906. It continued production during the First World War and, off and on, until it closed in 1964.

[128.4] Brit. Art. – British Artillery.

[128.5] set snipers rifles – German sniping expertise was such that they could predict where British fatigue parties might work during the night. They would clamp rifles in place, having set the aiming points during the day, then fire random shots during the hours of darkness in the hope of causing casualties.

Friday 11th June – Ypres – Menin Rd Trenches

Nightmare of a night. Poured all night. Standing up to knees in water – soaked & miserable. Just rigged up waterproof sheet when M came along and knocked it down (accidentally I hope). Tried to drain trench when it faired up. Erected dam. Nearly flooded Suffolks. Baling continuously. Lit fire after great effort, lost knife then bully in water. Called on Suffolks (D Coy) & asked news of old bhoys!
Making supreme effort to build a bivouac when Lamb came & shifted me fr 'untenable' position. On fatigue in C.T. all evening (Joe Innes[128.1] there too) lengthening parapet. Heard fr home about heavy casualties in 6th Gordons.[128.2]

Saturday 12th June – Ypres – Menin Rd Trenches

(Glorious day) Decent sleep & breakfasted off "Maconochie". Germans shelling like hell. Some fine work by British batteries too. (We'll cop it for this?) – enjoying change in weather – made us feel sleepy. Reading 'John Bull'[128.3] slapping it across new Cabinet. Brit. Art. [128.4] plonking huge shells into corner of wood (some reason for it?) Went to work on C.T. at dusk – narrow squeaks from set snipers rifles[128.5] – while working in trench. Heightened parapet – laid duckboards etc – most of us half asleep.

[130.1] strawberry jam always fruitful source of squabbles! – As Rule explains in his book, "*squabbles ensued over the partition of rations. Strawberry jam was a case in point. The appearance of this rare delicacy was calculated to breed deadly enmity, often lasting for days, between otherwise inseparable pals*".

[130.2] Huge parcel sent to Billy Anderson (toasted him in absentia) – Again, as Rule describes later in his book, "*in the case of wounded men, enjoying hospital luxuries, their home parcels were seldom re-addressed and, in 'beanos' celebrated at their expense, the health of 'absent members' was gracefully toasted*".

[130.3] Cumming – See Annex A - People in the Diary

NB – James Fraser tells us in his diary for the 13th June that the Germans used a weapon that had not been seen in this sector before – the Minenwerfer. Fraser writes, "*This lady threw large bombs (about fifty pounds). One could see them coming and had sentries calling, bomb right, bomb left as the case may be. Thank goodness they were not very accurate but they made a mess of a strongpoint we had made at a farmhouse just ahead of our front line. Several men were killed there from 13 platoon.*"

German soldiers loading a 25cm Minenwerfer

Sunday 13th June - Ypres - Menin Rd
Trenches

(Glorious day) Expecting heavy shelling after yesterday's efforts by our artillery. (Sunday Jerry's 'field day' too!)
On ration fatigue - almost a free fight (strawberry jam always fruitful source of squabbles!).[130.1]
General toilet - even to putting parting in hair! Tooth brush a reviver. Pratt very decent.
On ration fatigue again:
1st trip - 15 or so sandbags (either a mistake or War Office getting soft?)
(2) heavy pole between 2 men - up to redoubt.
(3) water jars (rotten trip)
(4) Trench bd.
(5) Trench board again. Almost daylight before we finished & no rest - didn't get further than dump last trip.

(Monday morning.) Gt joy in the section. Huge parcel to Billy Anderson (toasted him in absentia).[130.2] Shell hit trench 3 killed (incl Cumming)[130.3] - 2 badly wounded.

Monday 14th June - Ypres - Menin Rd
Trenches

(Glorious day) Improving 'cubby hole' - sleep after 'stand to'. Whole Coy turned out to clean up trench (more of Adjt's cheek) - stinking holes full of water - built up parapet.

[132.1] Bobby W – Robert Wilson – See Annex A - People in the Diary

[132.2] Art F.O. Officer – Artillery Forward Observation Officer (FOO). The role of these officers – often an extremely dangerous one when it required them to go to the front line – was to observe the fall of artillery shells aimed at the enemy and then to pass sighting adjustments back to the gunners. To be effective, the FOO had to have sight of the British shells landing, either directly or via, for example, a periscope. Communication back to the guns was often by landline and handset, with all the issues involved in maintaining a thin cable, exposed in such difficult terrain.

[132.3] Tommy – On this occasion, given that it was the burial of an officer, this would almost certainly have been Lt. Col. T Ogilvie, Commanding Officer, 4th Gordons.

[132.4] C.T. (Union St.) – Communication Trench (Union Street) – As McConachie describes in his book, *"A long communication trench which U company helped to dig … was named 'Union Street' after the main street in Aberdeen. After the war, the 'Union Street Graveyards' No's 1 and 2, which contained the graves of men who fell in August and September 1915, were incorporated into the military cemetery at Zillebeke."*

It was quite common for units to name main trenches after home landmarks that were familiar to them, as it helped soldiers remember the trench layout, important when trying to find their way around, especially in the dark.

[132.5] i/c – in charge – here, Rule is being given some supervisory responsibility (but no promotion to go with it).

[132.6] Parados – The parados formed the side of the trench furthest away from the enemy line, i.e. the back of the trench. In order to protect the heads and shoulders of men manning the fire-step both the parapet at the front of the trench and the parados at the rear were lined with several feet of sandbags; in the latter case this was to protect men from fire from the rear.

Monday 14th June - Ypres - Menin Rd
Trenches (Continued)

Detailed with Roy, Pete & Bobby W[132.1] to bury
Art F.O. Officer.[132.2] Tommy[132.3] & Maj Smith
there. Smith read passage fr. Bible & Tommy
gave prayer - piece of shell just missed him as
he stood at head of grave! Middleton;
Cumming etc buried there too. Wonderful
reaction afterwards - laughing like anything
going back to trench! Working on C.T. (Union
St) [132.4] aftwds. i/c[132.5] one gang! - relaying
trench bds. Wind up at X rds - transport
getting hell - cd hear them quite plainly. A
few wk parties caught. On ration fatigue
aftwds - salvaging from xrds. 1st bag of bully
(2) huge ration box (3) with B Wilson (didn't
take a rest). Met Joe Innes - cheery soul -
never upset. Back to dump - shelled off it -
narrow squeaks - back again for amn.

Tues 15th June - Ypres - Menin Rd Trenches

(Glorious day) Glad to get into shelter of
trench again. Xrds littered with dead bodies
(men & horses) & limbers. Told of
approaching attack. Not much excitement
shown. Felt back bit stiff after last night.
Bombers detailed off. Trip fr. dump to support
trench w amm, then back for spades & packs.
Started to build up & strengthen the parapet.
In same traverse as Gamin, C Reid & Shanks.
Put in pretty solid graft. Had only started on
parados[132.6] when told to get into trench &
stand by for the attack (Got letter off - last
chance for day or two).

[134.1] Wilts – The Wiltshire Regiment.

[134.2] German prisoners – A German prisoner is offered water by a British soldier.

[134.3] fighting dress – Only the equipment required for actual combat, such as ammunition pouches, water bottle, entrenching tool and bayonet, leaving behind the non-essentials such as the greatcoat and personal items.

[134.4] Whizz bang – The term was originally used to describe the noise made by the German 77mm field guns, although it became more generally used to describe other similar high-velocity guns. Due to the speed of the shell, its 'whizz' was heard before the 'bang' of the gun that had fired it. Whizz bangs were feared because defending soldiers on the receiving end had virtually no warning of incoming high-velocity artillery fire, unlike when the fire came from enemy howitzers.

[134.5] MacSween, George – See Annex A - People in the Diary

[134.6] MacIver, Murdo – See Annex A - People in the Diary

Wednesday 16th June - Ypres - Menin Rd Trenches

Assembly positions in Suppt Trench. Barrage started 2.50am. Every sort & size of shell. Smaller fry grad. dropped out. Lark soared singing through hail of shells. Crow very funny - twisted all ways by draft of shells. Some rifle fire. Casualty in 13. Heard Wilts[134.1] had taken 3 lines of trenches with very few casualties. Great cheering. Saw wounded passing down Menin Rd then German prisoners! [134.2] (more cheers). Sudden order to put on fighting dress[134.3] & file out with spades - no definite news. Steady hail of bullets over M.G. barricade on M Rd. (not too healthy for our attack?) Through Midsex trenches (up to knees in liquid mud). Sniped at continually (attack disturbed hornets' nest). Pure hell on l. of Midsex trench. Dead & dying everywhere - moaning as we accidentally trod on them. Whizz bang[134.4] shrapnel - marvellous escapes. Over the top into C.T. 2ft deep. MacSween[134.5] & MacIver[134.6] hesitated & got killed stone dead just behind me. C.T. littered with dead. Choked up thro Tommies coming back. Staff officer with cane strolling in open as if on parade. Lines retiring & getting hvly cut up. One ptn formed up & got obliterated in one hit - dug ourselves in on edge of wood. Counter attacks beaten off by MGs. One MG kept going when by all laws of nature ought to have been blown to b - ry. Maj. Smith, Clark & Pratt wounded. 2 Brit planes going all the time! Buried twice. relieved at midnight.

[136.1] R P Gordon & *[136.2] D McLean* – See Annex A - People in the Diary

[136.3] Dr Stn – Dressing Station. Diagram shows the casualty clearing system in 1915 (RAP - Regimental Aid Post):

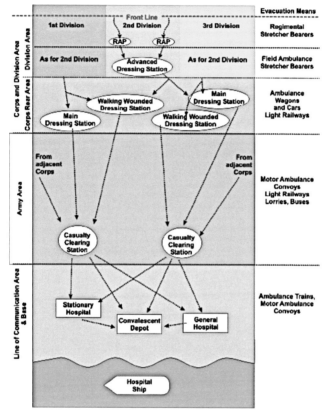

[136.4] S.A.A. – Small Arms Ammunition. One of the many items carried forward to the trenches at night by soldiers in fatigue parties.

[136.5] A Archibald, [136.6] J Berry & *[136.8] Whyte* – See Annex A - People in the Diary

[136.7] Waterloo Day – The anniversary of the Battle of Waterloo, remembering the role the Gordons' antecedent regiment (92nd Gordon Highlanders Regiment of Foot) played in Napoleon's defeat.

Thursday 17th June - Ypres - Menin Rd Trenches

Lovely day. Cold at "stand-to". Whole Bn in Suppt trench (slept on parados) Not much sleep Jerry got going on our C.T. - lovely shooting - 3 killed & few wounded right near HQ! Knoxie, RP Gordon,[136.1] D McLean,[136.2] W Donald back fr hosp at Rouen. Billy Anderson's name omitted fr draft by mistake - lucky Uhlan. Dr Stn[136.3] on fire. On amn fatigue. Box S.A.A.[136.4] each! Nearly decapitated myself jumping a trench - forgot about box which jumped up & caught me right across back of neck. One shell came over as we were walking along edge of trench & next moment everyone had disappeared. On souveniring hunt aftwds. Heard of casualties in 6th Gordons (A Archibald[136.5] & J Berry[136.6] killed).
Knoxie 'making' our mouths water with tales of Rouen.

Friday 18th June - Ypres - Menin Rd Trenches

Waterloo Day.[136.7] Rumour that 1st 'Jocks' had bombed Germans out of 3rd line! Forbidden to go out for water - rotten not having a wash. Very little shelling of any importance. Part of 'D' Coy working on CO's dugout. 'Tommy' hot stuff on dugouts. Whyte[136.8] reported to be dead (funny how we all had feeling that he'd peg out if hit at all (however slightly) - hadn't the 'guts' to hang on to life - poor chap.

[138.1] Salvo – A salvo is a number of rounds fired by different guns at the same time, designed to give a concentrated, or spread of, fire depending on the intended target.

[138.2] RPG at Huntly School with me – R P Gordon also attended The Gordon Schools, Huntly. As the North East was the Gordons' traditional recruiting area, it was unsurprising that many pupils, ex-pupils and staff joined the home regiment and Rule makes several references to his school friends in his diary. One hundred and forty four of those connected with the school were killed in WWI and a stained-glass window in the school commemorates them.

Excerpt on memorial window from Laurence Binyon's *'For the Fallen'*

Unveiled on August 24th, 1921, by ex-pupil Sir Edward Troup, this unique tribute was created by JAH Hector, art lecturer at Aberdeen Training Centre. In his address, Sir Edward said that the memorial *"was not erected because they who knew what those men did needed anything to keep their memory fresh – that would last while they lived – but in order that those who came after them, in days when the story of the great war had become a tradition and a thing to be read of in books, might know their names, might think of their deeds and their great sacrifice."*

[138.3] convalescent camp at Rouen – Rouen became the location for many hospitals (See note *[136.3]*) during the war. The aim was to restore a wounded soldier to fighting duty and this was done in Belgium and/or France wherever possible. Convalescence was the final part of recovery but it often lasted weeks or months. It was often, despite the preceeding trauma, an enjoyable experience, not least because of better conditions, food and female nursing company.

[138.4] On our relief – Rule's unit completed 24 continuous days in the trenches, much longer than the average time in the front line and particularly so in a sector as intensely active as the Ypres salient.

BACK FROM THE TRENCHES

Saturday 19th June - Ypres - Menin Rd Trenches

(Relieved in late evening) Warm sunshine and everyone relaxed at their ease when Boche shell dropped short in a salvo[138.1] aimed at Hellfire Corner (xrds just behind our trenches). It killed RP Gordon, & mortally wounded W. Donald (RPG at Huntly School with me)[138.2] & wounded D McLean & Eddie Knox - all 4 just back from convalescent camp at Rouen.[138.3] JK Forbes officiated at Gordon's burial - simple, impressive ceremony soon after. (Several others temporarily smothered in earth from shellburst.) House at X roads - collapsed like pack of cards. On our relief[138.4] we found Ypres Cloth Hall further demolished. All dog tired.

Sunday 20th June - Brandhoek (Rest Billets)

In hessian bivouacs abt 2 mls behind Vlamertinge. Warm sun after sleep in the nude under blankets (after weeks with all clothes on). Blissfully relaxed. Awakened by voice of Belgian woman selling "Chocolat". No guns heard. Later a civilian train with old type engine and a citizen with a white straw hat helped to banish wartime scenes pro tempore. Chaplain preached a thoughtful sermon. The CO paid tribute to 'D' Coy's part in "the recent show". 'Sunny Jim' of U Coy played his violin in the evening and so early to bed again for restorative sleep.

[140.1] parades – Jimmy Fraser recounts in his diary, *"Battalion parade, Col. Ogilvie had tears in his eyes as he looked at his battalion, now about half strength."*

[140.2] 4ᵗʰ GH – 4ᵗʰ Gordon Highlanders.

[140.3] 1Bn RS – 1ˢᵗ Battalion Royal Scots.

[140.4] W Inkster – See Annex A – People in the Diary

[140.5] Housey, housey – An alternative name for bingo.

[140.6] Pop – Poperinghe, 3 miles (nearly 5km) from the rest billets at Brandhoek.

[140.7] New boots – slang for fresh recruits.

[140.8] F Rose, [140.9] Sangster, [140.10] Tennant – See Annex A - People in the Diary

[140.11] King's – King's College, Old Aberdeen.

[140.12] Gibbon – See Annex A - People in the Diary

[140.13] Maj Gen Haldane – See Annex A - People in the Diary

[140.14] Sassenachs – Scots slang for their southern neighbours.

[140.15] L'pool Scottish –The Liverpool Scottish, an infantry battalion of the King's (Liverpool Regiment). Noel Godfrey Chavasse (one of only three men ever to be awarded the Victoria Cross twice) was a RAMC Captain attached to this unit. Of the other two double winners, New Zealander Capt. Charles Upham was related to Chavasse by marriage and Lt Col Arthur Martin-Leake treated Chavasse at Potijze in August 1917 after his fatal wounding. His two VC medals were bought for £1.5m by avid collector Lord Ashcroft in 2009 and are now amongst over 200 Victoria Cross medals on display at the Imperial War Museum.

[140.16] New subs – subalterns, newly commissioned junior officers.

Monday 21st June – Friday 16th July – Brandhoek (Rest Billets - bivouacs)

Mostly glorious weather, with usual parades,[140.1] regimental and inter-regimental games (4th GH[140.2] beating 1st Bn RS[140.3] at tug-of-war). 'U' Coy all comers x 4th Gordons. Ph. jerks early am (before bkfst) or pleasant strolls under W Inkster.[140.4] Toned us up for hard days to follow. Occ'y "practised the attack". Pratt v good. <u>Leave</u> began – names of lucky ones drawn from a hat (Gunn & Pete 1st fr 'U' Coy) Gambling (Housey housey[140.5] etc) of an odd evening added to the fun of the fair. Baths. Bathing parades at Ouderdom or Pop[140.6] (rare) and de-lousing still rarer, and we <u>were</u> lousy. New boots[140.7] arr'd – F Rose,[140.8] Sangster,[140.9] Tennant.[140.10] Sangster whom we'd left to carry on his studies at King's! [140.11] Bayonet fighting & bombing instruct (Gibbon)[140.12] One deluge (7th July) bivvies flooded out & ground sodden. Midsex & 1st GH left for trenches on 11th July – 1st Jocks at full strength: tough lot. Massed bands of 1st & 4th GH & RS made inspiring sight & sound at Bde sports with Maj Gen Haldane[140.13] OC Divn a spectator.

Concerts: Sassenachs[140.14] oprandos - Midsex & L'pool Scottish[140.15] fr 9th Bde seemed to have most of talent. As privates we occ'y had a tryout in taking command of the ptn: seemed less easy than we had supp'd! New subs[140.16] didn't app too happy either. Freddie Rose with Oxford 1st cl Hons. tongue-tied before guttersnipes.

[142.1] r march – route march.

[142.2] M Murray – See Annex A - People in the Diary

[142.3] J Forbes – See Annex A - People in the Diary

[142.4] J A MacLeod – See Annex A - People in the Diary

[142.5] Anniversary of going to Camp at Tain (complete year in khaki) – It is unlikely that Rule or any of the former U Company students would, in the summer of 1914, have expected to still be in uniform, still at war, a year later. Yet, despite this long absence from their studies and their families, in addition to the extreme conditions in which they found themselves, there is no indication of wanting to quit before the job is finished.

Members of U Company at Annual Camp at Tain in July 1914

[142.6] Woolmanhill – This was the location of the Gordon Highlanders (Territorial Force) drill hall in Aberdeen and where U Company undertook much of their training. It was a substantial two-storey building, built before the end of the 19th century, between Woolmanhill and Blackfriars Street. It was demolished to accommodate road realignment in the late 20th century.

Monday 21st June – Friday 16th July – Brandhoek (Rest Billets – bivouacs) (Cont.)

Boxing tournaments provided mixt of semi-skilled pugilism and street corner fights. Sing songs: Old King Cole, Little Tailor Boy. Occ' field day & r march[142.1] recalling Bedford. Promotions: Crichton L/Sgt, M Murray[142.2] Cpl, J Forbes[142.3] L/C, JA MacLeod[142.4] L/C etc.

Saturday 17th July – Brandhoek – Rest Billets

Pouring – most of night & gtr part of day. Officers off seeing trenches we're due to take over. R & rm in bet. showers! Parades a farce – slipping abt in mud & slush. High wind gave us an idea – pretended not to hear Sandy Gunn's Words of Command – kept on going & Sandy bellowing to beat the band! Thoroughly enjoyable parade. Offrs back with woeful tales of slush & mud in trenches. Anniversary of going to Camp at Tain (complete year in khaki).[142.5] Have packed good deal into 1 yr somehow. Little dreamt of it when "rookie" at Woolmanhill![142.6]

Sunday 18th July – Brandhoek → Trenches – Hooge

Ch. parade 9.30am at L'pool Scottish HQrs – nice service (new padre) – difficult to catch. Rolling blankets & cleaning amn. Seemed to have more 'goods' than ever to pack up. Left 4pm. Tea on way to "Hill 60" – hard marching.

[144.1] One of Duke of R&G's sons buried – The Duke of Richmond and Gordon in 1915 was Charles Henry Gordon-Lennox (Lord March), 7th Duke of Richmond and 2nd Duke of Gordon. His third and youngest son was Lord Bernard Charles Gordon-Lennox who was killed on 10/11/1914 whilst a Major in the Grenadier Guards. Lord Bernard's widow was killed on Sunday 18/06/1944 during morning service in the Guards Chapel in Wellington Barracks, London, after it was hit by a V1 flying bomb. One of Lord Bernard's sons, Lieutenant General Sir George Charles Gordon-Lennox, became Colonel of the Gordon Highlanders in 1965.

[144.2] Bayonet periscope – an arrangement of mirrors temporarily fixed to the end of a bayonet, allowing the viewer to see out of the trench without exposing his head to the enemy. (The example shown is from later in the war – and looks rather contrived.)

[144.3] Lt Erskine – See Annex A - People in the Diary

Sunday 18th July - Brandhoek → Trenches - Hooge (Continued)

Skirted Ypres - passed Zillebeke Lake & Zillibeke (where one of Duke of R&G's sons buried)[144.1] - Cheery march (singing). Ch at K Zillibeke still standing. Very fine C.T. for a bit - then had to leave it (too muddy). Trenches seemed a d - d long way off. Got one nasty fall. Relieved R Scots. Put i/c a 'traverse'.

Monday 19th July - Hooge Trenches

Bit too warm - "bluebottle" flies in 1000s. Souvenired a bayonet periscope.[144.2] Snipers & bombers conducting a little offensive on their own. Portion of brick wall (of Hooge Chateau) blown up by British mine at 7pm after short British bombard. Midsex rushed the position led by 1st Jocks bombers under Lt Erskine.[144.3] (E killed after capt. M.G. by himself!) Counter attack amidst shelling & bombing - beaten off. Breezy time. Sort of "No Man's Land" as usual. Allardyce killed. Parapet of our trench blown in (2 places). Midsex lost pretty heavily. Grad. quietened down exc. for bombing. (Pratt wounded (finger)

Tuesday 20th July - Hooge Trenches

Kept fair. Mails & rations up as usual (good old Falconer!)
'A' Coy in with Midsex in case of counter-attack. 'C' getting it hot. Inkster back.

[146.1] H.E. – High Explosive (shells).

[146.2] h. grenades – hand grenades.

[146.3] Sam McLintock – See Annex A - People in the Diary

[146.4] Huge TM menacing captd position – Huge trench mortar menacing the captured position. First developed by the Germans before the war with a view to attacking French forts, trench mortars fired at an angle of over 45°, thus dropping their projectiles into the trenches and making them a feared weapon.

[146.5] "9.2" – British 9.2-inch siege howitzer, capable of firing a 290 lb (130kg) high explosive shell 10,060yds (9,200m).

[146.6] wonderful Ger. Officers dugouts etc. – Jocks and Tommies were generally highly impressed by the quality of German trenches and dugouts compared to theirs. Not only were they more spacious and comfortable, they were often very much stronger, deeper and better able to withstand shelling better than the Allied trenches. This gave the German soldiers better protection so that, when the bombardment lifted and the Allied troops advanced to attack, the Germans were able to leave their shelters and quickly man their defences, including their machine guns, with devastating effect.

[146.7] DCM – Distinguished Conduct Medal. Awarded to other ranks, between 1854 and 1993, to recognise gallantry in the field.

Tuesday 20th July - Hooge Trenches

Ger' bombardment started just before evening "stand-to" - hefty shelling for a time. H.E.[146.1] in wood behind us but our suppt. line escaped. My traverse blown in but no casualties - got it fixed up as soon as it got dusk.
"Stand-to" all night - & shelled practically continuously. 2 nasty "Taubes" having it all their own way - flying right up & down our trench!
Good few casualties in 'C' thro h. grenades[146.2] etc.

Wednesday 21st July - Hooge Trenches

Weather fair. Lay down immed after "stand-to" - v. uncomfortable sleep (Heard Sam McLintock[146.3] of the cheery grin was back) 1st Jocks relieved Midsex overnight. 'Mids" recalled after being 2hrs at Vlamertinge (bet they swore!)
Huge TM[146.4] menacing captd position. Good view of aerial torpedoes - terrific crash. Wind up about mines owing to peculiar rumbling in ground.
"9.2" [146.5] opened on TM backed up by whizzbang fr Hill 60. Some of 9.2 shells scored direct hits on Gr. trenches. Jerry shut up. 'C' Coy getting it hot fr. hand grenades. Tales fr. bombers about captd trenches - wonderful Ger. officers dugouts[146.6] etc.
Allardyce (killed) was magnificent Cpl of bombers recommed for DCM.[146.7]

[148.1] OC traverse – Here, Rule is put in charge of a section of trench and a few men. Fire trenches were not dug in a straight line, otherwise it would be too easy for the enemy to fire along them if they attacked into them. The French army built zig-zag trenches, whereas the British preferred a system where each trench was dug with alternate fire-bays and traverses. Whereas fire-bays were straight sections of trenches, traverses were built at angles. This limited the effect of enfilade fire or shell-burst.

[148.2] KRR's MGs – King's Royal Rifles machine guns.

[148.3] arty formn – Artillery formation. A troop formation devised to give an amount of spacing between individuals that would lessen the effect of an artillery round landing in their midst. In his book, Rule says his unit was *'still in the danger zone when dawn broke. We were compelled to adopt artillery formation in crossing the exposed ground.'*

[148.4] Stooks – bundles of sheaves, often of corn, set up in a field to dry.

[148.5] mess orderly – Officers ate and socialised, separate from the other ranks, in the Officers' Mess. Where there were no permanent orderlies (servants) available, soldiers were allocated this set of duties, mainly serving meals and drinks.

[148.6] no rest! – Hooge trenches to Brandhoeke via Kruistraat and Vlamertinge was a distance of about 8 miles (13 km).

[148.7] Wrote letters of sympathy incl. RPG's father – On the website giving information about the village of Kennethmont, where R P Gordon was raised, it says *'His friend Pte (later Sgt) Alec Rule of Huntly wrote to his father on 21st June and confirms that Pat was killed by a shell which burst in the trench traverse where Pat was and that he believed he was nearest it. The others in the traverse were slightly wounded. This ties with the (4th Battalion Gordon Highlanders) War Diary entry of 19 June - 1 man killed, 5 wounded. Rule writes that Pat returned to the front a day or two earlier.'*

Thurs 22nd July - Hooge - Trenches (Relief)

Glorious day until evening (v. wet) Arguments over sentry duty. Some of drafts haven't got camaraderie spirit v well dev. yet! O.C. traverse[148.1] - not much sleep (sore tummy). Saw 1st of relief (KRR's MGs).[148.2] Our snipers doing great work. Saw Jock Thomson mins before sniped! (V hard luck). Heard relief (KRRs) had got lost. Waited & waited (couldn't get a meal - everything sopping wet) Finally filed out before relief in trench! Got it thick & heavy - shelled all the way. Could feel the vicious hot breath of the closer shell explosions. Falls into shell holes frequent. C.T.s knee deep in mud. At last gasp & d-d fool said "Double"!

Friday 23rd July - Left Trenches for Rest Billets - Brandhoek

Morning rain - faired up a bit later. Crossed open ground in arty formn[148.3] - just about all in, especly in Zilibeke Lake C.T. Staggered on to Kruistraat without a halt & pipers met us there. Parched inwardly - sucked coat lapel for moisture. First halt at Vlamertinge drink of water like nectar. Tried to race past C Coy by superhuman effort (stooks[148.4] in roadside fields - harvest goes on!) Arr'd in camp 6.30am to be promptly detailed as mess orderly[148.5] with Pete: no rest![148.6] Bivouaced on sodden ground without g'sheet or blanket on top. Almost shivered myself warm by time sun rose. Rifles like 'pig's bkfst'. Wrote letters of sympathy incl. RPG's father.[148.7]

148

[150.1] Whizzbang Wd. – Whizzbang Wood, a nickname for a wood, well known for being the target for German 'whizzbang' artillery fire (See *[134.4]*). The wood was some 100yds SW from Hill 60.

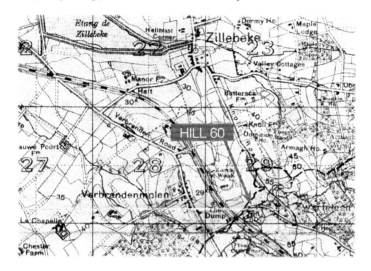

[150.2] In France – actually in Belgium.

[150.3] sylvan solitudes – Here, Rule gives an excellent example of the contrasts that could still be found despite the extreme conditions. To be able to comment so positively on the scenery and the views of Ypres in the distance, marred only by "a few bullets singing around (mainly ricochets)", might indicate an eagerness to hang onto any 'normal' things whilst surrounded by so much death and destruction. 'Sylvan' itself derives from the Latin *silva* (meaning "forest, woods"). This root is found in place names like Pennsylvania (Penn's woods), or forenames like Sylvester or Sylvia.

[150.4] only 15 yds apart – the British trenches were only 15 yds (13.7 metres) from the German trenches.

[150.5] Saxons – It was German soldiers from Saxony who had been involved in some instances of the 1914 Christmas truce. The appearance of a sign saying "*If you don't fire we won't*" showed, as McConachie puts it in his book, that "*their appetite for war did not seem to have developed greatly in the interim*".

WHIZZ BANG WOOD

Saturday 24th July – Brandhoek → Trenches at St Eloi ("Whizzbang Wd.")[150.1]

Lovely weather. better sleep tho with occ crack of Hun bullet. Orders out for trenches again – lying about most of day. Lazy to begin packing up. Packs v weighty. Sam McL, old adjutant back again. We looked v small battⁿ (under strength) as we filed out. Via Kruistraat – mainly same route as to Hill 60 then to left (Bd HQ. in 'cooshie' farm house) Quiet approach to Whizz Bang Wood – roomy dugout shelters, some with garden plots! Enjoyed delightful sleep after "stand-down".

Sunday 25th July – St Eloi – Trenches (Whizz Bang Wood)

(Saw Jerry plane falling) Heavy rain when I awoke. "Stand-to" at 2.30am! Had good look around "whizzbang wood" – scenery delightful in sunlight. Finest I've seen in France[150.2] Good view of Ypres – looks imposing fr distance. Few bullets singing around (mostly richochets) tended to mar sylvan solitudes.[150.3]
Putting in traverses in C.T. on edge of wd to prevent enfilade fire. Carrying fatigue in afternoon fr Bn HQrs – then back to C.T. – then back on ration fatigue (swear!) Up to firing line (trenches only 15 yds apart![150.4] – Saxons? [150.5] put up notice "If you don't fire we won't" – sensible? Carried back "empties"? (misnomer – d – d heavy) "Sing Song" at stand-to to keep us awake.

[152.1] Belgian Battery going strong – Belgian artillery unit firing nearby.

[152.2] Loophole – the purpose of a loophole was to enable a soldier to look out of a trench towards the enemy without exposing his head, a move that would otherwise risk his life, particularly from a German sniper. A loophole could be as simple as a small gap in the sandbags, or a larger opening fitted with a metal plate.

[152.3] Sir John French – Field Marshal Sir John French – See Annex A - People in the Diary

Monday 26th July - St Eloi Trenches (Whizz Bang Wood)

(Belgian Battery going strong)[152.1] Raining slightly in morning - refused to get to work too early after late ration fatigue. New 'brain waves' with regard to traverses (Begg along) Putting in loophole[152.2] - some dead enfilade sniping put wind up us. "Whizz bangs" started in wood (saw reason for its name).
Volunteers for ration fatigue. Got fighting kit out when 'mine' went up and rapid fire started. Notice fr Sir J French[152.3] - suspect Ger. attack in our qr - found us ready for anything. Gas sentries.
Had decent sleep. Heard the sector had been too quiet (Tommies not sufficiently "offensive") so we were sent to stir things up - we have.

Tuesday 27th July - St Eloi Trenches (Whizz Bang Wood)

Glorious day. Beginning to take pride in work on C.T. - hate to see traverse put up 'anyhow' - just completed one when told to put in loophole. Damn! Rotten job in afternoon 'humping' sandbags thro muddy C.T.s to suppt. line but troops cheery. Quite a difference in the general 'peace' of the wood - wonderful how we can't let "sleeping dogs" lie!
Relieved by Suffolks. Long wait before marched out but filled in time with "singsong" in "dugouts". (v cheery). Dickens of a roundabout way to Camp - think the piper didn't feel too sure of way!

[154.1] "hog" – here, to sleep deeply.

[154.2] Whole Coy (pract) at 'office' to explain 'deficiencies' – This was almost certainly a parade at the quartermaster's stores, where soldiers would declare all the items that they were deficient, compared to what they should have had if fully equipped. Whilst it may have been understandable to have equipment misplaced, damaged or destroyed during spells in the trenches, soldiers – and the quartermaster - still had to account for such losses.

[154.3] Jock Milne – See Annex A - People in the diary

[154.4] Saw spring mattress! – Many soldiers had not slept on a spring mattress since they arrived at Bedford in 1914 where many billets in Bedford were in very basic accommodation, no matter how luxurious that must have seemed compared to the trenches.

DON'T WORRY !
I'm Quite Comfortable at BEDFORD.

[154.5] 7yds by 3ft deep – The 4th Gordons War Diary tells us that these were trenches for telephone wire, linking the Gordons' 1st Battalion to Royal Artillery batteries farther to the rear.

Wednesday 28th July - Dickebusch - Rest Billets

Pouring in morning. Pract. whole "bivvy" (on slope of hill) flooded out. Covered up head with blankets & "let it rip" - small rivulet running through below me! Not allowed to "hog"[154.1] fr long. Crichty tickled up my bare feet with a stable broom till I got up (jealous because he was wet?) Soaking gt coat & blankets. Gt reformation. Complete toilet (+ sewing on of tunic buttons before parade!) - too good to last. Whole Coy (pract) at 'office' to explain 'deficiencies'[154.2] Gt sport over discarded 'lousy' shirts. Visited Jock Milne[154.3] in tr port lines with Silver (no longer Coy cook) & heard him murdering a tune on a violin - strings flying everywhere! Saw spring mattress!! [154.4] Promotions out, Crichty Sgt, McLag. Cpl, Gunn Cpl., Pete L/cpl. Letter fr W. Horne.

Thursday 29th July - Dickebush - Rest Billets → Trenches (fatigue)

Glorious day. Hectic rush for r&rm hadn't time to lace boots up properly! Usual parades - 'troops' getting very fed up. Lect on rifle & trajectory of bullet, eschelon & 'blob' formation in afternoon. Officers not too clear on it yet. Trench digging fatigue (fighting kit). Marched to Yser Canal (icl pipers) - signs of shelling all along rd. Crossed canal at barricade. Each given section 7yds by 3ft deep.[154.5] Got my section completed & hopped on to next.

[156.1] Finished work about 2am – it was necessary to finish the night's work this early to be able to return to camp in darkness. As Rule tells us, they made it just in time, even without taking a break for a rest on the way.

[156.2] Blair Atholl – a Scottish Horse depot was located here at this time.

Scottish Horse training in Perthshire in 1915

[156.3] Some more of 'U' Coy getting word of Coms (Low & J Forbes) – Ever since Bedford days, members of the former U Company were going through the commissioning process, unsurprising for a band of such bright young men. As it turned out, George Low was commissioned but J Forbes was not – See Annex A – People in the Diary.

[156.4] On way up – Rule tells us in his '*Students Under Arms*' that *"our rest, however, was in name only; the normal training and sports programme was subordinated to the work of trench digging, in the forward zone by night and in the reserve zone by day. It said much for our physical fitness that on two occasions, after putting in a whole day with pick and shovel near Dickebusch, we followed it up by digging trenches all night east of the Yser canal, after walking eight or nine miles."*

Friday 30th July – Trenches (fatigue) → Dickebusch

Glorious day. Finished work about 2am. [156.1] Right to camp without rest – just clear in time – Jerry started to chip 'em in quick & lively. Breakfast at 5am (arrd). Slept till dinner. Gt many Bns on move (full m order & shovels) Limbers at "double" with shells – 'dirty work' somewhere tonight. A & B Coys had a few casualties (shell fire) on way to trenches. Ch (brother) with unit at Blair Atholl. [156.2]

Saturday 31st July – Dickebusch (R. Billets) → Trenches (fatigue)

Glorious day. Country around looking very prosperous – golden stooks & swinging windmills. 'D' Coy on fatigue digging trench by side of main road. Hurt our dignity to be mistaken for 'travailleurs' (like the Belgians) instead of 'fighting troops'. Some more of 'U' Coy getting word of Coms. [156.3] (Low & J Forbes) Resting in afternoon for night fatigue. Ran into heavy shell fire at Kruisstraat on way up [156.4] but decided to carry on – magnificent view of bombardment – like fireworks on gigantic scale! Just skimmed the danger zone. Canal again – some bullets pretty close.

Sunday 1st August – Dickebusch – Trenches (fatigue)

Glorious day. Great fun coming home from Yser Canal. Troops in form (singing etc)

[158.1] Capt walked! – Captain walked! In the rear areas, all the more senior officers would normally ride. Presumably riding skills had improved somewhat from the early days at Bedford where there were significant numbers of injuries suffered, mainly due to officers' lack of horse-riding experience. Now at war, grooms brought horses up to a Rendezvous Point (RP), behind the trenches and not too exposed to the enemy.

[158.2] Hielan' – Highland – in nature and speech.

[158.3] had to clear off road for artillery limbers at full gallop – as Rule describes, when faced with six horses, galloping at full speed, towing a couple of tons of artillery, the sensible thing to do is to get out of their way. The Royal Artillery was often required to change position frequently and at short notice and to get set up quickly at a new location. Their success in doing so could mean the difference between life and death for the troops they were supporting.

An 18-pounder travelling at high speed. Given the healthy state of the ground and the trees, this is probably a training exercise.

[158.4] Monymusk – a village in Aberdeenshire.

Sunday 1st August - Dickebusch - Trenches (fatigue) (Continued)

Capt walked! [158.1] Slept? till dinner.
Church parade in afternoon - Sam McLintock
i/c - very amusing old Scotch parson. (very
Hielan').[158.2] Glorious sunset in evening but
rain in the "offing"

Monday 2nd August - Rest Billets - Trenches (fatigue)

Very hot during day - rain in evening. 'C' & 'D'
Coys on trench digging fatigue. Long wait at
Kruistraat - had to clear off road for
artillery limbers at full gallop[158.3] - "guns
going into action" - very inspiring sight (Pratt
mounted) Picks issued - no relation to nature
of soil! Digging trenches along from
Dickebusch Rd - shelling gradually got worse
- few shells right amongst bombing section
(few casualties). Knocked off work. Home at
abt. 5pm. Saw 7th / 9th Brigades (III Div)
marching past Liverpool Scottish - very thin
'red line' (136 rifles) - ragged them
thoroughly. Orders out for trenches.

Tuesday 3rd August - Rest Billets - Trenches

D - d cold at physical jerks. Baths at 9am. -
thro' part of Dickebusch ("wash"? pretty poor
affair) Circuitous march thro' pleasant fields
on way back - reminded me of
Monymusk![158.4] Inspections on return.

[160.1] swarms of flies – Huge numbers were to be found around the battlefield and they got into everything. Like the rats, flies had an abundant supply of food from the human and animal corpses that littered the battlefield and carried the potential for disease wherever they went. They would swarm inside dugouts and other shelters and would descend on food or drinks whenever they appeared. They would also settle on the faces and hands of sleeping soldiers.

[160.2] Very nice looking girl making lace – Lace making was a commonly-found craft that provided additional income for a family. Soldiers often bought items to send home as souvenirs.

A Belgian girl making lace

[160.3] "for 't a'" – "for it all".

[160.4] 1ˢᵗ Anniversary of Outbreak of War – These and many other headlines had signalled the start of what was felt could be a short war, but which turned into a four-year slog that killed millions.

159

Tuesday 3rd August - Rest Billets - Trenches (Continued)

Aftⁿ parade cancelled owing to rain. Visited farm with Silver - refugees in barn converted into dwelling house - swarms of flies[160.1] in everything - had to drink milk before flies got it.
Very nice looking girl making lace.[160.2] Fine old specimen of farmer. Left for trenches in evening (no opportunity to pursue acquaintance with m'selle). Rain & very heavy going. No shelling till past K'straat - evidently knocked about recently. Passed dugouts by canal & thro' grounds of chateau - long trek.

Wednesday 4th August - St Eloi - Trenches (Suppts)

Long "stand-to" - very feeding up. A little "stand-to" goes a long way. Long, but not a very sound sleep. Raining heavily. Met Belgian Artilleryman (while on fatigue) who spoke Eng. well. Long chat. Digging C.T. to firing line at night. Rotten digging my bit - hard packed shingle - had to use pick "for't a'" [160.3] 1st Anniversary of Outbreak of War[160.4] - Apparent Brit superiority of guns (in this sector)

Thursday 5th August - St Eloi - Trenches

Weather more pleasant after stand-to. On ration fatigue to HQrs - rotten track - almost broad daylight by time we got back (risky in open). Heavy fatigue duty in aftnoon.

[162.1] Pioneer Bn – pioneers, often simply labourers.

[162.2] How have our sponsors fallen! – For many units, it would be seen as a lessening of prestige to be used in a pioneer role. However, it was sometimes a little less dangerous.

[162.3] Dare-devil – crossing open ground was usually more dangerous, but the journey would probably be quicker than slogging through mud in the communication trench.

[162.4] 15 – another platoon in D Company.

[162.5] Sap – In trench warfare, 'sapping' was the practice of digging small 'sap' trenches at roughly ninety degrees out from existing lines and then digging a new trench line at the front of the saps. This was a slow, but relatively safe, way of moving forward.

[162.6] Sniper just missed me in sap at stand-to deafened me for a bit. – yet another close call for our diarist.

A German sniper and his spotter

Thursday 5th August - St Eloi Trenches (Continued)

Suffolks, in their role as pioneer Bn.[162.1] laying trench boards in C.T. How have our sponsors fallen! [162.2]
On fatigue again at dusk - putting bridge over new C.T. Very solid piece of work & done in record time - characteristic of Sandy Gunn!

Friday 6th August - St Eloi - Trenches

Heavy rain. Long sleep after "stand-to" - broken only by necessity to 'louse' (or 'delouse') Scorned muddy C.T. while on water fatigue - over 'the open' (dare-devil?)[162.3]
No sentry duty all day (mistake)
Relieved '15'[162.4] in firing line. Making 'sap'[162.5] during night - trying to get ahead of Sandy Gunn by flopping loads of full sandbags on top of him but couldn't (demon for work!)
Sentry duty in sap - bit of a thrill with the snipers bullets (very close). Rat caught in trip wires in front caused unnecessary "wind up". Heavy shelling in vicinity of "Crater" caused by mine.

Saturday 7th August - St Eloi - Fire Trench

Drizzling. Carrying full sandbags till further orders.
Sniper just missed me in sap[162.6] at stand-to deafened me for a bit.

[164.1] "Bluff" – The Bluff of St Eloi – an artificial mound formed when the River Yser was canalised, at a point about a mile south of Zillebeke.

[164.2] F.M. – Field Marshal.

[164.3] Attack on left – 6th Division were mounting an attack at Hooge.

[164.4] hair-raisers – shells passing just over the top of the trench on an almost-flat trajectory.

[164.5] Rifle grenades – Early rifle grenades were not always reliable and there was a risk that, if the blank cartridge designed to make the grenade fly towards the enemy did not function properly, the grenade, now primed, could 'drop short', close to the firer and explode in his own trench. The Hales Grenade was the solution to this problem of the unit exploding in front of the rifleman. In 1915, Frederick Marten Hale designed a fuse that could not explode until it was in the air and travelling at speed. It worked by a wind vane that, once it had turned over a 'safe' distance, would prime the grenade and trigger the fuse. This ensured that, if it fell out of the rifle without travelling at speed through the air, it could not explode. Manufacture of these grenades was difficult and expensive but, for the safety and confidence it gave the user, it was deemed to be worth the cost.

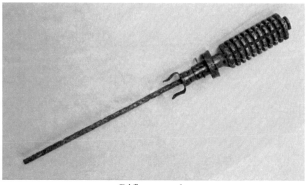

Rifle grenade

Saturday 7th August - St Eloi - Fire Trench (Continued)

Lot of shelling in region of the "Bluff" [164.1] & new C.T. on left.
Splinters & mud flying all over the place. New order out - no braziers to be lit for cooking purposes in fire trenches! - rotten.
Pipe & newspapers a great comfort during a trench day.

Sunday 8th August - St Eloi - Fire Trench

Warmer (sultry at times). Not much sleep - on water fatigue. Great discussion in trench as to feasible frontage for successful attack by British Army.
Sunny Jim in great form (ought to have been a F.M.!)[164.2]

Monday 9th August - St Eloi - Fire Trench

Attack on left[164.3] - commenced between 2am & 3am. Some 'hair-raisers'[164.4] over our trench. Long 'stand-to' - felt sleepy after heavy shelling & sultry atmosph.
Jerry plonking 'em into the "Bluff" all day - not much sleep.
Our bombers had temerity to 'let them have it' with TMs & got reply with interest. Firing rifle grenades[164.5] from our sap & rapid fire (with rifles) to encourage Belgian battery.
Few casualties in 'C' Coy.

[166.1] "3 pipper" – Watson had been promoted to Captain.

[166.2] Gooseberries – a further example of how mail from home was considered important enough to be fast-tracked to the front. In Rule's book he describes how the fresh fruit had been *'picked two or three days previously in a quiet home garden far removed from war's alarms, and here they were, delivered as a matter of course to a destination actually in No Man's Land!'*

[166.3] Rose – Another former pupil from The Gordon Schools, Huntly, commemorated on their memorial window (detail below).

[166.4] Henessey – the Hennessy cognac-producing family dynasty was founded by a soldier – an Irish officer who served with the French King Louis XV's army – in 1765.

[166.5] Brigade Reserve – accepted practice was to hold some troops in reserve, in anticipation of either bolstering a unit that was under heavy attack by the Germans or, less frequently in the early years of the war, adding momentum to a successful attack by the British. They had to be located far enough from the front to be out of immediate danger, yet close enough to be available at short notice.

Not to be confused with Reserve Brigades, formed from 1916 onwards when, with the introduction of conscription (compulsory military service), the existing regimental structure simply could not cope with the growing numbers. In order to train in excess of 200,000 recruits in 1916, 26 Reserve Brigades were formed.

Tuesday 10th August – St Eloi – Fire Trench → "White Chateau"

Watson "3 pipper".[166.1] Glorious day.
Mails up – eating gooseberries[166.2] (picked at home) in sap during misty "stand-to". 3 rounds rapid (for Kaiser's birthday or summat). Jerry shelling "Bluff" suppts. Lt Fred Rose[166.3] killed – & some other serious casualties.
Relieved at 9pm by 1st Jocks (Bombers & MGs preceded main body) Hellish congestion in C.T. & lot of sniping.
Billeted in Bedford House (White Chateau) – upstairs on 2nd storey. Sleeping on hard floor but wonderful how comfy a bed can be made with kilt folded under hips. Lofty rooms and fine grounds. 'WELCOME' & 'FAREWELL' (in English) on tiles at entrance. Belonged to Henessey[166.4] (3 star brandy)

Wednesday 11th August – Bedford House (Brigade Reserve[166.5])

Glorious day. Usual camp breakfast (cooker up!) Enjoyed thorough wash in ornamental pond in grounds. Visions of boating but punt a casualty.
Enjoying 'laze' in big "dormitory" – reading & smoking. Inspected the Chateau thoroughly.
Making emergency dugouts.
Mounted pukka guard at 5.30pm: Sentry. Got very quiet in grounds during night except for peculiar "bark" of hedgehogs.
Good few 'planes around during the day.

[168.1] "The Glorious Twelth" – *memories of heather clad moors at "Gairtly".* – The Glorious Twelfth (of August), the traditional start of the grouse-shooting season. Like many country teenagers, Rule would probably have had a few days working as a 'beater', walking in a line to drive the birds towards the waiting guns. "Gairtly" (Gartly) is a village near his native Huntly, near where large expanses of heather moorland provided excellent grouse shooting opportunities.

[168.2] 17" naval guns? – The Germans had purposely, to cause confusion, named the type of gun in question the '*Kurze Marine-Kanone' (short naval gun)*, but its intended use was always land-based bombardment.

The gun was of the mortar type, i.e. it could fire at a high angle – up to 75 degrees of elevation. The caliber was 42cm (16.6 inches) and could lob a high explosive round weighing 820kg (1,807lb) some 12.5km (7.8 miles). The name given to this type of weapon was 'Big Bertha'. The one that shelled Ypres was hidden in the Houthulst Forest to the north of the town.

Big Bertha

Thursday 12th August - Bedford Ho -
Brigade Reserve

"The Glorious Twelfth"[168.1] - memories of
heather clad moors at "Gairtly".
Some very big shells sailing overhead into
Ypres. Thought they were coming right on top
of us always. Could feel the vibration of the
shell landing - then hear the sound of the
explosion (20 secs afterwards) followed by the
roar of falling masonry in Ypres! (17" naval
guns?)[168.2]
Few small shells bursting in N pt of grounds.
NO "Allemand" planes around. Gt fun at
dismounting of guard - shower of plaster fr
roof right on top of us - followed by 2 dirty
hairy legs waving thro' ceiling (Silver
souveniring on top storey)
Lachie wild.

Friday 13th August - Bedford House -
Brigade Reserve

Glorious day - another dip in pond. Wood
cutting fatigue in forenoon on rd to
Vormezeele - traces of Fr troops occupation
in earlier days of war. Pratt working like a
demon.
One of our batteries near chateau getting high
explosive & percussion stuff fairly slung at it.
Fatigue in evening carrying hurdles.
Gt golf? tournament (got knocked out in 1st
round - handicap 100)
Silver trotted out the goods in form of vin
"blink".

[170.1] Maj Lyon – See Annex A - People in the Diary

[170.2] Vlamertinghe, Rheninghelst and Poperinghe –

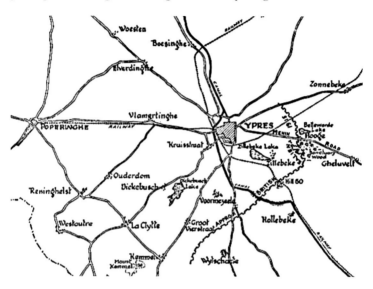

[170.3] Big "Straafe"on a/c of Hooge – likely to have been a retaliatory bombardment by the Germans on account of the attack by 6th Division on 9th August.

[170.4] touch of dysentery – as Rule suggests, this may have been as a result of drinking contaminated water, although strident efforts were made to ensure a clean supply. However, given the general state of filth and decay from human and animal remains in and around the front lines, the source could just as easily have come from his own hand-to-mouth actions without him realising he was doing so.

[170.5] Mason – See Annex A - People in the Diary

[170.6] unfrm – uniform. Mason obviously arrived for guard duty with a less than acceptable standard of uniform.

Saturday 14th August - Bedford Ho.

Glorious day. Sleepy after night fatigue –
excused till 9.30am. Washing person & clothes.
Maj. Lyon[170.1] & Sammy (McLintock) up –
rumours of gt Brit success? Vlamertinge razed
to ground? Few shells landed in Reninghelst!
Poperinghe[170.2] evidently got it too. Big
"Straafe" on a/c of Hooge.[170.3] Touch of
dysentery[170.4] (from water?) Working on
dugouts again. Singsong in evening – very
enjoyable then another night fatigue –
unloading heavy beams fr waggons.

Sunday 15th August

Showery at intervals (heavy too!) Easy day
after inspections. Held gt. golf tournament
(my handicap 4). Knocked out 4 & won the
'rubber'. Shelling – mostly long distance but
some heavy percussions sending splinters all
round chateau.
Could detect new Brit batteries firing. On
guard again (Pete Cpl) – wore glengarries.

Monday 16th August - Bedford Ho - Brigade Reserve

Glorious day – not much rain. Inspecting
pond while on guard – teeming with all sorts
of trout. (gt many minnows). Poor old
Mason[170.5] got it in the neck for his unfrm[170.6]
at guard mounting. Plenty of 'birds' all round
in fact.

[172.1] creosol – creosol, a clear to yellowish liquid disinfectant, would probably have been used undiluted around, for example, the latrines beside the trenches. It was not intended, as Rule painfully discovered, for direct application to the skin.

Diary page (enlarged)

[172.2] poultice walloper – slang for medical orderly. In some ways, it made sense for equipment from the dead to be reused. However, there were instances, like this involving Joe Reid, when wounded men had possessions stolen when in the care of the Royal Army Medical Corps. Thus their abbreviated name, the RAMC, was often corrupted to Rob All My Comrades. (However, see also *[102.3]*)

Monday 16th August - Bedford Ho - Brigade Reserve (Continued)

On fatigue after tea – carrying bricks fr chateau vineries to dugouts – vineries very well equipped – reminiscent of Bailleul Grapperies.[18.3] Tragic mishap with creosol.[172.1] Applied it neat for lice – along seams of kilt & felt as if I had furnace round my waist.

Tuesday 17th August - Bedford Ho.

Good sleep – tho' bit of straafe in night (chateau shaken a bit). Trench digging fatigue near canal (behind firing line).
Feeling effects of burn with creosol – no skin round middle – had to take kilt off!
Misty in evening. Sing song before leaving – relieved by 'C' Coy with 'wind up' about gas attack. One rest on way to rest billets at Dickebusch via Kruistraat but felt in great form. Quiet journey as regards shellfire.

Wednesday 18th August - Dickebusch - Rest Billets

Heavy rain in night – dripped onto head – kilt soaked. Baths at brewery in forenoon – 'grumpy' attendant (v. unusual). Traces of recent shelling in streets. Pay parade – Joe Reid in gt form after it (& as result of) – telling yarns about his trip home wounded – got new boots pinched by 'poultice walloper'[172.2] who thought him dead – so woke up bet. 2 corpses w 2 left boots on his feet!

[174.1] Rorie MacTavish – See Annex A - People in the Diary

[174.2] EW Brander – See Annex A - People in the Diary

[174.3] when we awoke – being caught stealing another soldier's food would result in severe punishment through official channels - or by those who had had food stolen if they got to the thief first.

[174.4] Hay – See Annex A - People in the Diary

[174.5] Old 'U' Coy (or what's left of them) grad. finding way to Commissioned ranks. – With a shortage of experienced officers, it was hardly surprising that these bright young students were being commissioned.

[174.6] 7th York & Lancs Regt. – Probably the 7th Battalion of the York and Lancaster Regiment. The regiment formed 22 battalions during WWI, including several 'Pals Battalions', deliberately keeping together young men who worked together or lived in the same community (and often both). The positive outcome of this type of recruitment was instant camaraderie and mutual support throughout their training and beyond. There was, however, a devastating drawback to this well-meant policy and that was amply illustrated in the case of the York & Lancs. Eight of their battalions went into battle on the first day of the Somme, on 1st July 1916, including their 3 Pals' Battalions - 12th (Sheffield City), 13th & 14th (Barnsley Pals) – who suffered particularly heavy casualties. Overall in WWI, the Yorks & Lancs suffered 48,650 casualties out of 57,000 men serving, with 8,814 killed or died of wounds (72 out of every 100 men being either wounded or killed). The regiment won four Victoria Crosses and 59 battle honours, the most of any English regiment during the war.

[174.7] Scot Horse off to east – Quick reporting! The Scottish Horse only received their Warning Order (by telegraph in NE England to move to Devonport for embarkation) on 11th August. They entrained on 16th August and embarked on ship for the Mediterranean (and to Gallipoli) on 17th August 1915.

[174.8] G.A.F. Henderson – See Annex A - People in the Diary

Wednesday 18th August - Dickebusch - Rest Billets (Continued)

He met Rorie MacTavish[174.1] on hosp ship going over! Officers playing cricket. EW Brander[174.2] bowling well (tennis ball)

Thursday 19th August - Dickebusch - Rest Billets

Pleasant weather.
Found bread & var other items of rations had disapp. (when we awoke)[174.3] Usual parades etc but dinner different. Salmon followed by pineapple (not army issue!)
Low, J Lamb & Hay[174.4] off for month's leave! Lucky beggars!
Isaac Maciver gazetted to 4th Seaforths. Old 'U' Coy (or what's left of them) grad. finding way to Commissioned ranks.[174.5]

Friday 20th August - Dickebusch - Rest Billets

Hot during day.
Usual parades & r. march thro' Ouderdom - Reninghelst, Rozenhill - passing old huts (like old friends) occup. by 7th York & Lancs Regt.[174.6]
News fr. home - Scot Horse off to east[174.7] - at last! Brit transport sunk at Dardanelles.
D.G. McLean & D.D. Booth gazetted to 6th Gordons, Macaulay to Seaforths,
G.A.F. Henderson[174.8] to 3rd Gordons - old 'U' Coy still disintegrating.

[176.1] Sports – although the opportunity for rest when away from the front line was important, so also were the fitness levels and morale boost created by sporting activity.

[176.2] "wrestling on horseback" – more accurately in this case "wrestling by piggyback".

[176.3] JB Ewen – See Annex A - People in the Diary

[176.4] Jimmie Fraser – See Annex A - People in the Diary

[176.5] Candidate to join church – for many men, their experience of war polarised their religious beliefs. Here we see Rule and others wanting to formalise their belief by joining the church. Rule wrote about this to his father who, as a proud father and an elder of the kirk, passed the letter to the Aberdeen Journal. An extract appeared in their edition of Saturday 4th September 1915. *"I joined the Church last Sunday (22nd inst). I think that next to taking my first communion under Dr Semple* (The Rev Dr Semple was a minister in Huntly for 39 years and had died in September 1914)*, which I would have liked most of all, it was the most memorable way of joining. A good many of D Company took communion for the first time. We had a sort of preparatory service on Saturday night at the chaplain's tent. We made a half-circle round the door, and the chaplain made a few remarks about the solemnity of communion and how it was instituted. It was a very nice service indeed. At the close the chaplain took down all our names and addresses, also church and minister. On Sunday we had the usual service in the forenoon, and the communion was at six pm at the door of the chaplain's tent. The service was attended by Major Lyon, commanding officer, Captain Hopkinson etc. A strange lull seemed to occur in the dull sound of the guns and the evening itself was an ideal summer night. The long slanting rays of the sun showed up, with their dying efforts, the golden harvest of man as it lay stooked in the fields around. Over the firing line the clouds were bathed in golden light. Away in the distance could be seen small mounds crowned with windmills. Nature was at peace, and men were locked in a life grapple. It was truly a memorable communion."*

[176.6] Coutts – See Annex A - People in the Diary

Saturday 21st August - Dickebusch - Rest Billets

Rain. Parades cancelled after r&rm & inspections. Getting bit wet in bivvies. Sports[176.1] in aftnoon. All in fr "wrestling on horseback"[176.2] - gt fun espec. JB Ewen[176.3] & Joe Reid. WR Kennedy, Jimmie Fraser[176.4], Low all gazetted. Entered name as candidate to join church[176.5] & attended prep. service at padre's tent - quite a big crowd there.

Sunday 22nd August - Dickebusch - Rest Billets

Lovely day. Inspections & church parade - Battn. looked bigger on parade (even without 'C' Coy) - gt contrast to our appearance after return from Menin Rd! Issue of "Balmoral" bonnets (16 ptn got outsizes ($7\frac{1}{2}$ - $7\frac{3}{4}$!)) Coy & ptn drill etc. Paraded for Holy Communion at 6pm (my first). Major Lyon, Capt Hopkinson, Coutts[176.6] & Pratt present. Lyon handed round the wine. Memorable ceremony - still summer evening - pleasant fields - with guns booming away in distance!
Blankets issued. 16 unlucky again - missed.

Monday 23rd August - Dickebusch - Rest Billets → Trenches (fatigue)

Cold in morning at r.&rm. Hard sprint at finish. Usual parades (Hoppy OC 'D' Coy) Silver very comical at Ptn drill. Easy afternoon in preparation for night fatigue.

[178.1] Digging in cables through a barley field – see *[154.6]*.

[178.2] "hogged it" – slept soundly.

[178.3] draft – a number of fresh recruits. Although Rule expressed strong feelings about 'non-varsity men' joining D Company, those who did join it generally felt welcome. G M Leys from Glen Tanar, near Aboyne, Aberdeenshire, who joined in early September, wrote, *"Awaiting us at Poperinghe were QM Hall, the pipe band and the transport of the 4th Battalion and we set out for the billets, which for the time formed the homes of Aberdeen's own battalion.*

The pipes announced our arrival and the whole battalion was out to welcome us. Shouts of recognition and handshakes were the order of the day and when we had halted and sat down to tea, we received a royal welcome.

We recognized old friends – some who had gone a year before upon mobilization and others who had trained with us and had left only a month or six weeks previously. These latter were in our midst in an instant, while the others who were members of the original 4th looked around in the hopes of meeting an old friend.

Tea over, we were assigned to units and it says much for the thought and sympathy of those in command that we were allowed as far as possible to go to those platoons and companies which we preferred or in which we had acquaintances. We were made to feel perfectly at home amongst the men of the 1st/4th and, although we were new to this rough life and unacquainted with the work of campaigning, they did not look down upon us with a sense of superiority.

It was the finest form of welcome, which any body of men could have received and I could not pass on without paying a tribute to the men who displayed such admirable qualities at a time when much that was human in man was being destroyed."

[178.4] Rennie – See Annex A - People in the Diary

[178.5] Teunon – See Annex A - People in the Diary

Monday 23rd August - Dickebusch - Rest Billets → Trenches (fatigue) (Continued)

Marched via corner of Zillebeke Lake then same track as for Hooge. Digging in cables through a barley field.[178.1] Allowed to smoke! Felt in great form but sleepy.

Tuesday 24th August - Dickebusch
Trenches → Rest Billets

Hit camp abt. 3am. 'Cookers' to "rescue" on arrival - hot tea & tucker - then sleep - dead to the world. Absolutely 'hogged it'[178.2] till roused for breakfast at 10am. Hadn't time to wash for inspections!
Camp fatigues in aftnoon - for all not taking part in Sports. 'D' Coy wiped 'A' hollow at cricket & footer. Brigade relieved. Had gramophone at door of 'bivvy' - great selections.
Another draft[178.3] arrived. Rennie[178.4] (S.M.) chucking his weight about. Not a bad looking lot (Teunon[178.5] with them) all round - made us feel very hardened & seasoned "veterans".

Wednesday 25th August - Dickebusch - Rest Billets

Glorious day. Usual parades & Coy practising attack on skeleton enemy (6 of us fr 16 Ptn) Our job to lie in ditch & smoke - very decent until I got stung by a wasp (d - d sore). Comforted by sight of main body making perspiring rushes at us.

[180.1] 'washed out' – fought off.

[180.2] knife rests – see [54.1]. In his book, Rule tells us, *"At Dickebusch we practised the art of crossing barbed wire entanglements by means of padded sheets – to the great detriment of our bare knees and to the unbounded amusement of the local lasses. One sergeant, demonstrating the simplicity of the feat, became suddenly unnerved by an over-inquisitive – not to say shameless – mademoiselle. He slipped, just when victory was in sight, losing at one fell swoop half his kilt and most of his self-respect."*

[180.3] Davy Scott – See Annex A - People in the diary

[180.4] "Brer Rabbit" principle – Brer Rabbit is a character that appears in the 'Uncle Remus' stories by American author and journalist Joel Chandler Harris (1848-1908). Brer Rabbit is portrayed as a trickster hero, forever using his guile to overcome adversity, avoid responsibility and shy away from hard work.

[180.5] Letter fr Charlie (brother) hellish fed up at his 'unit' being still in England. – Charles Rule served in the 2nd Line of The Scottish Horse. In the end, this unit did not go to Gallipoli. However, his brother John was in the 1st Line Brigade, which did go to Gallipoli, as evidenced in the Aberdeen Journal of 2nd October 1915. This article mentions Alexander Rule's wounding and his father, John, going on to say that another of Mr Rule's sons (John) was, by then, serving with the Scottish Horse in the Dardanelles.

179

Wednesday 25th August - Dickebusch - Rest Billets (Continued)

We 'washed out'[180.1] a flank attack with a mythical MG. 16 Ptn demonstrating in aftnoon how to cross barbed wire entanglement with aid of padded sheets. OK for knife rests[180.2] - but sheet tore badly on ordinary bare entanglements.

Thursday 26th August - Dickebusch - Rest Billets

Glorious day. No officers on morning parade. Pleasant "stroll" in fields then usual parades & bayonet practice. Sports in aftnoon - enthusiasm grad. worked up. Davy Scott[180.3] great at 100yds sprint. 'D' Coy gained most pts. - too light for tug-of-war. Escaped "boot race" on 'Brer Rabbit'[180.4] principle. Wrestling on horseback good fun.

Friday 27th August - Dickebusch - Rest Billets

Really hot. Too late for breakfast (glass of milk only). Usual parades.
Practising 'attack' through pleasant copses with hedgerows & "brambles" reminiscent of Bedford days. Musketry in aftnoon meant long lie on grass ('Hoppy' a gem). Idea of writing letters - failed under influence of Joe Innes. 4th v 1st GH at footer 3 - 0. Billy A played gt game. Heard Knockando gazetted to Seaforths. Letter fr Charlie (brother) hellish fed up at his 'unit' being still in England.[180.5]

[182.1] *Hefty British MPs* – Military Police. Rule expands on this incident in his book, *"Near Dickebusch I once witnessed the amusing sight of a little Belgian boy in tears being escorted between two hefty, mounted M.P.s. I failed to learn whether his crime was one of theft or of petty espionage; but, judging from the strength and solemnity of his escort, I judged that for all his tender years the lad must have been guilty of high treason at the very least."*

[182.2] *USA stuff* – By quite early in the war, it became clear that Britain did not have the manufacturing capability to supply all the materiel – arms, ammunition and other equipment – required to continue the war. Orders had to be placed with other countries, including the USA. Unfortunately, in many cases the American ammunition proved to be of inferior quality and was at best unreliable and often dangerous. In his book, Rule writes that *"Orders had been issued to scrap all SAA (Small Arms Ammunition – for pistols, rifles and machine guns) bearing the stamp of American manufacture. The brass cartridge case buckled easily and the contents also were by no means up to specification."*

Diary page (enlarged)

[182.3] *Addison* – See Annex A – People in the Diary

PREPARING FOR THE ATTACK

Saturday 28th August – Dickebusch – Rest Billets

Blazing heat. 6pm last on parade (as usual). D – d nuisance shaving every day (don't mind washing!) Very amusing scene – little Belgian boy being led crying between 2 hefty British MPs[182.1] (mounted). Practising attack – Pratt in great good humour. Lay down while he explained the 'scheme'. No doubling – sensible sort of attack!
9.2 gun in battery near camp blew up with round in breech (USA stuff)[182.2]
4th made clean sweep of tug of war & relay races in Brigade Sports. Steeple chase fine display.

Sunday 29th August – Dickebusche – Rest Billets

Dull. Good sleep. R. inspection with 5 mins warning – no time to waste! Ch parade immed. aftwds. Padre washout but brevity of sermon a pt. in his favour. Coy drill in "pleasant pastures" – all officers having a 'go'. Addison[182.3] good deal to learn (but decent fellow).
Bath parade w. gt coats decent tho long time to wait (big Coy). Saw good few ripe peaches in orchard on way to baths but none coming back!
Pleasant interlude in café – merry badinage with 'madame'. Raining heavily in evening. Rum very acceptable.

[184.1] Exhibition trenches – these would be used for training purposes. Built at a safe distance from the front line, they would be used to demonstrate to new arrivals how the system worked, the way it was built and the dangers involved.

[184.2] Poor instructor – there was sometimes a feeling that bomb instructors were selected for their enthusiasm over their knowledge and aptitude for imparting accurate information. Talk of "furmelite of mercury" was an example of this, quickly spotted by those who had studied chemistry at university. They realised the compound in question was actually fulminated mercury ($Hg(CNO)_2$), a primary explosive, mainly used in detonators, as well as percussion and detonator caps. When dry, it explodes violently if struck or heated.

[184.3] Hales R grenade – Hales rifle grenade - see [164.5].

[184.4] "tattie chapper" – or sometimes 'tattie masher'. A German stick grenade.

Monday 30th August - Dickebusch - Rest Billets

Dull weather. Rush to get on parade (9am!) – platoon getting slack in mornings. Making dugouts in exhibition trenches[184.1] – sleepers with 3 layers of sandbags for roof – everyone doing as little as possible!
Rumours of trenches. Detailed to go with bombers (with Mason & Shanks). No rum – damned cold night too.

Tuesday 31st August - Dickebusch - Rest Billets

Usual inspections & parades – got "bird" fr Sandy Gunn for being late (thoroughly deserved too).
Instruction in bombing – poor instructor.[184.2] Spoke about "furmelite of mercury", "Hales R grenade"[184.3] & German hand grenade ("tattie chapper")[184.4] 'lemon bomb' – all very interesting. Throwing in aftnoon: got some fair 'lengths' then firing r grenade with safety pin in. "Wind up" abt coming attack. Officers away seeing trenches. Lots of 'staff officers' around. Parcel fr home containing heather & brace of grouse (partly decomposed).

Wednesday 1st September - Dickebusch - Rest Billets

Cold – (chilly in evening) & rain. Got new 'smoke helmets' (sealed) – up to date pattern with tube for mouthpiece.

[186.1] Bethune bomb – In late 1914 and early 1915, Captain Battye of the Royal Engineers designed and put into production through the Bethune Ironworks his 'Battye' or 'Bethune' bomb. The Bethune bomb consisted of a cast iron mug-shaped container, diced for fragmentation, filled with high explosive. The top was sealed with a wood stopper and wax with a Bickford fuze. A Nobel safety device was used to light the fuze but, as a safety measure, the fuze was only inserted at the time of use.

[186.2] Gen Plumer – At 58, General Plumer must have seemed ancient to the 19-year old Rule. See Annex A - People in the Diary

[186.3] R.T. Donald – See Annex A - People in the Diary

[186.4] r inspection – rifle inspection.

[186.5] J Dewar – a bottle of John Dewar whisky. At that time the firm was run by John Dewar Jr., 1ˢᵗ Baron Forteviot. In addition to being the chairman of the family business (John Dewar and Sons), he was a director of The Distillers Company, was the MP for Inverness-shire for 17 years and was twice Lord Provost for Perth. In 1912, he was appointed as Chairman of the Dewar Commission that examined the provision of medical services throughout the Highlands and Islands. The result of his report was the establishment of the Highlands and Islands Medical Scheme. This state-funded health system served the whole community in an area that comprised half the landmass of Scotland and was directly run from Edinburgh, 35 years before the advent of the National Health Service.

As for the bottle in question, Rule expands in his book, *"The cork was removed – with becoming ceremony – and the bottle was handed round, first for a sniff only, in order to make the effects of the whisky spin out as long as possible. Then each of us had a tot, after the exact quantity had been carefully calculated beforehand. As the bottle travelled round the circle, the sigh of satisfaction from each participant in turn was followed by a look of fond farewell as he passed it on."*

Wednesday 1st September – Dickebusch – Rest Billets (Continued)

Bombing instructions interesting – discussions on bombs 'potato', 'pitchers', 'Bethune',[186.1] 'hair brush', 'knife hand grenade', 'Newton's pippin' (latest) & modes of attack.
Ceremonial parade in aftnoon. After long wait in rain – inspected by Gen Plumer[186.2] – repulsive, bloated looking beggar.
Hellish cold in bivvies overnight.

Thursday 2nd September – Dickebusch – Rest Billets → Ouderdom

Pouring in afternoon & evening. Usual parades. Watty Inkster getting really wild with Ptn for being late on parade.
Bombing instruction & practice in throwing. Bombing traverses in exhibition trench.
Shifted camp to Ouderdom and got everything thoroughly soaked in rain. Ground very sodden when lay down for night.
R.T. Donald[186.3] gazetted to B. Watch.

Friday 3rd September – Ouderdom – Rest Billets

Pouring most of day. Driven in from r. inspection[186.4] even – bivvies absolutely flooded – pools on floor. Crichty back fr. leave (with bottle of 'J Dewar')[186.5] – solemn ceremony inside bivvy. handed round 1st for a 'smell' only (to make it spin out to utmost) – then a 'wee houp' – carefully measured.

[188.1] Short r. mr in even w gt coats – Short route march in the evening with greatcoats.

[188.2] Reveille – Music played in the morning to wake troops. In the case of the Gordon Highlanders, it would be supplied by the Drums and Pipes. Usually, duty pipers would play 'Johnny Cope' but, on occasion, the whole band would turn out.

[188.3] Jehovah of the Thunders – From Rudyard Kipling's 'Hymn Before Action' –

> The earth is full of anger,
> The seas are dark with wrath,
> The Nations in their harness
> Go up against our path:
> Ere yet we loose the legions --
> Ere yet we draw the blade,
> Jehovah of the Thunders,
> Lord God of Battles, aid!

Diary page (enlarged)

Friday 3rd September – Ouderdom – Rest
Billets (Continued)

'Wind up' written on faces of last in order &
fond lingering farewell on those of others
whose turn has passed. Potent stuff.
Wretched day lying about bivvies. Writing on
letters (when attempted) washed out or blurred
by raindrops. Short r. mr in even w gt
coats[188.1] (roads awful) came back in dusk
with windows of cottages lit – wonderful
effect

Saturday 4th September – Ouderdom – Rest
Billets

Rotten night in bivvies – cold and damp.
Tried to dry kit in sun – usual parades – but
dodged all forenoon with Mason & Shanks
(cleaning amm)
Bath parade in afternoon (gt coats). Went to
bed pretty early.

Sunday 5th September – Ouderdom – Rest
Billets

Reveille[188.2] sounded hellish loud – just along
our lines (pipes, drums and all).
Ch parade abandoned at 10am & held at 11.30
(gt coats)
Padre put "wind up" us. "Jehovah of the
Thunders".[188.3]
Parade for aftnoon – "Creeping & crawling
over obstacles" cancelled. Coy r. march with
pipes & drummer. Rds in frightful state.

[190.1] Falconer – See Annex A - People in the Diary

[190.2] A R Henderson – See Annex A - People in the Diary

[190.3] Gibbon – See Annex A - People in the Diary

[190.4] 3rd line – of trenches.

[190.5] "an old hand at the game" – although not mentioned previously in the diary, Rule must have displayed some aptitude at erecting marquees, or perhaps just following orders and working as part of a team.

[190.6] G.S. Wagons – General Service Wagons – a widely-used type of horse-drawn wagon.

[190.7] Gow – See Annex A - People in the Diary

[190.8] (S&G tight!) – Silver and Gow were drunk.

Monday 6th September - Ouderdom - Rest
Billets → Trenches (fatigue)

Glorious day. Usual parades. Off's promotions
out. Capts - Falconer[190.1] & Down. 1st Lieuts -
A R Henderson,[190.2] 'Mons', Pratt, Gibbon[190.3]
etc.
Practising attack under Pratt - great fun.
Good few fell into ditch in excitement of the
'charge' - we could scarcely take 3rd line[190.4]
for laughing! Lectures - gen criticism of
attack. No afternoon parade. Putting up
marquee under Rennie C.S.M. - recognised me
to be "an old hand at the game". [190.5]
On trench digging fatigue at Hooge by night.
Travelling in G.S. wagons[190.6] over rough
roads - experience. Shaken to b - ry!

Tuesday 7th September - Ouderdom -
Trenches (fatigue) → Rest Billets

Another rough journey on homeward trip (&
very cold). Breakfast 3.30am. Long sleep but
still sleepy tired when got up.
Bath parade (clean water) in afternoon & Pay
(chat with 'Hoppy' - knew my father) (Note in
'dry' diary to effect that 'H' had bath -
implication quite unfair!) H allowed us to fall
out in Dickebusch on way home (always
thinking of his troops)
'Night out' with Gow,[190.7] Silver & Booth (vins
- rouge et blanc, champagne?; spuds, salmon
& pickles! (S. & G. tight!)[190.8] Silver lively on
way home & obstreperous in bivvy.

[192.1] Sgt (C.) – Sergeant Crichton – See Annex A - People in the Diary

[192.2] p jerks – physical jerks.

[192.3] barrack square style – formal drill, normally performed on the barracks parade square back in Britain. This would not have been at all welcome by Rule and his comrades, especially when they had been expecting a session on the rifle range.

[192.4] camp fatigue (punsh') – punishment, probably for having been caught yawning during exercise the previous morning.

[192.5] Dr. (Yank) trying to introduce baseball – although America did not, as a country, enter the war until 1917, many Americans felt the need, for ideological reasons or perhaps out of a sense of adventure, to fight for the Allies. Many did so by joining Canadian units.

[192.6] "Tommy's" speech – Rule was reading the account, in the Aberdeen Journal of Saturday 4th September, of Lt Col Tommy Ogilvie's speech at a recruiting drive in Aberdeen. The meeting, held in the Drill Hall at Woolmanhill, would have been like hundreds of such meetings held up and down the country, designed to persuade young men to sign up to the colours. Exactly which part of Ogilvie's speech Rule felt was 'childish' is unclear, but it may refer to his comments on professional footballers.

The Journal reported that Lt Col Ogilvie "*…hoped every man there would use his influence among his fellows and get them to think a little more seriously of the state of affairs at the front. It was rather a dreadful thing that professional football was going on. He had been a great lover of football all his life, but this was not a time for going to see professional football matches (Applause). If a man could play professional football he could fight for his country. He really ought to be ashamed of himself that he could go to a fine field here and play football while his fellows were out yonder in the trenches (Applause).*"

Wednesday 8th September – Ouderdom – Trenches (fatigue) – Rest Billets

Glorious day. Usual parades. Got 'bird' for yawning at r.&rm! Practising "attack" Silver gt fun – 'casualty' in 2nd charge. Sandy Gunn not much "gift of gab" as instructor (bayonet fighting). Watty very "chatty" with Ptn.
Discov. some nice look m'selles in Ouderdom!
R march (Coy) in aftnoon – 2 pipers. Saw Gen Plumer inspecting a brigade of III Div.
Whole Ptn 'tight' in evening incl Sgt (C.) [192.1] Crichty gave masterly 'review' of his troops at advanced stage of evening.
Low back as 2/Lt – posted to 'C' Coy. Letter fr. Miss Horne.

Thursday 9th September – Ouderdom – Rest Billets –>Trenches (fatigue) – (Sanct Wd)

Glorious day. Ptn had to coach Sandy Gunn good deal in 'p. jerks'.[192.2]
Paraded for range w. targets but found it held in force by 1st Jocks.
Coy drill (barrack square style)[192.3] instead – heartbreak – then camp fatigue (punsh') [192.4] did damn all.
Trench digging fatigue ("Sanctuary Wood") in afternoon under Capt C Reid (whose horse bolted with him) – full m. order! Pretty tired when got back & feet sore.
Dr. (Yank) trying to introduce baseball[192.5] amongst officers.
Saw "Tommy's" speech[192.6] in Abdn (in papers) – rather childish.
Spuds at fm. house again in evening.

[194.1] Brigade standing by – this indicated a level of preparation, to be ready to move at short notice.

[194.2] Meeting of "Johns" – See Annex C - The Society of Good Johns

[194.3] Varsity Y 'Gorra – A student song. In her book "*1915 – The Death of Innocence*", Lyn Macdonald quotes from Rule, "*Our source of inspiration was also augmented by a bottle of whisky and the 'Johns' rapidly got down to business. We opened up with a chorus of 'University Y'Gorra', then every member sang a song or told a story….Middlesex and Suffolk veterans afterwards assured us they would never forget the honour of being present as privileged spectators at a festive meeting of 'real students' as they put it!*"

[194.4] distance judging – this was an important skill for all soldiers to develop for two main reasons. Firstly, for example, if the enemy were spotted whilst a soldier was on sentry duty, it was important to be able to indicate to other soldiers where they should also look for those enemy. Secondly, in order to give effective fire, distance to the enemy had to be estimated to allow the sights of rifles and machine guns to be set at the correct range.

[194.5] W Troup – See Annex A - People in the Diary

[194.6] "Drummy" – friendly slang for the Drum Major.

[194.7] (D. Mjr' Wilson) – Drum Major Wilson – See Annex A - People in the Diary

[194.8] "Retreat" – the Beating of Retreat. This ceremony can be traced back to the days when the drum was widely used to broadcast messages across the battlefield, in much the same way as the bugle was in later years. The purpose of Beating Retreat was to summon all troops to return to their quarters if they had been out in the evening, usually just before sunset. Gradually other instruments were added and it became a band and social event.

[194.9] "sign of the Johns" – See Annex C - The Society of Good Johns

[194.10] 'neep park' – turnip field.

Friday 10th September - Ouderdom - Rest Billets

Glorious day. Usual parades & pract "attack".
Brigade "standing by"[194.1] - summat doing? No
afternoon parade.
Range at 5pm - no luck rifle kicking badly -
marking under 'Hoppy' who kept beating time
to music of band with his marking stick! - a
gt. "sport".

Saturday 11th September - Ouderdom - Rest Billets

(Meeting of "Johns".[194.2] Varsity Y' Gorra.
[194.3] Bivvy per C.T.)

Glorious day. Usual parades incl. distance
judging[194.4] in forenoon. With bombers in
afternoon - bombing trench - "bird" for
smoking.
New draft (met W Troup,[194.5] Rhynie) - rotten
physique.
"Drummy" [194.6] (D. Mjr' Wilson)[194.7] in gt form
leading band at "Retreat" [194.8] & big drummer
excelling himself.
Great Meeting of "Johns". Crichton, Gunn, C
Reid, Sunny Jim, Shanks, John Forbes, Booth,
Silver, Mason, Gow, Scott (Davie) & self.
Initiated "sign of the Johns".[194.9] (12 - both
hds extended fingers upwards & (2) thumbs up
= "12 bots vin rouge Madame.")
Gt concert on way back & in bivvies (Silver
wanted to sleep in 'neep park').[194.10]
R.S.M. round.

[196.1] "identity discs" – According to the Imperial War Museum – *"By 1915 the British Army requirement was to wear two official tags, both made of compressed fibre (more comfortable to wear in hot climates) and carrying identical details. These were stamped a letter at a time. The two tags required stringing in a particular way. An eight-sided green tag with two holes was strung through one hole and hung around the neck. Through the second hole another much shorter cord was strung, which had a round red tag on it.*

This method allowed the red tag to be retrieved simply by cutting its short string, leaving the green tag still in place on the body. It meant that others subsequently finding a body with only a green tag would know that the death was already being reported. They could use the details on the green tag to prepare a grave marker."

[196.2] Col Lyon – See Annex A - People in the Diary

[196.3] .... some non-varsity men – here, Rule is clearly expressing his disapproval of the Army not taking the opportunity to restore, at the very least, a university-only platoon (if not an entire company) within 4th Gordons.

[196.4] "displenish" sale – in Scotland, this would often be the disposal of machinery, hand tools and domestic items when a farmer retired or died with no-one else to take over his farm.

[196.5] listening post – situated in front of the fire trench, a listening post was, as the name suggests, used to try and gather information on the enemy's activities. Listening posts were usually shallow, narrow and inherently dangerous places to listen for noises of, for example, work parties digging, handling barbed wire or the metallic clanging that would go with connecting dozens of poison gas cylinders in preparation for an attack.

[196.6] "Sherwoods" – The Sherwood Foresters (Nottinghamshire and Derbyshire Regiment).

Sunday 12th September - Ouderdom - Rest Billets → Hooge (Trenches C2)

Glorious day. Breakfast in bed! Fairly free fr
bad effects of "night out" with 'Johns' (vin
rouge unless got rid of has v. curdling effect
on stomach).
Ch parade - padre improved "Prodigal Son"
"Business-like" inspections - incl "identity
discs"[196.1] (probably v necessary!)
Address by Col Lyon.[196.2] (all varsity men in
draft went to 13 Ptn - rotten principle when
we have some non-varsity men).[196.3] Packing
up & "displenish" [196.4] sale. Silver nobly
resigned position of offr's servt & S Jim took
over. (Inkster for course) Heather (lucky) fr
padre. Left after tea. Bn looking like ancient
crusaders in setting sun (on the march) Cd.
almost imagine pennants.

Monday 13th September - Hooge - Trenches

Felt in much better "nick" than usual. Went
right out to "listening post" [196.5] without
stopping in trench.
Lovely autumn day - if we kept our eyes on
the heavens. Difficult to realise it in C2
(hellish mess - blown to bugary - horrible
stench) German line a bit nearer - cd. hear w.
parties quite distinctly (our listening post on
crest). Back to main trench at 1am
(Sherwoods'[196.6] old lines) Fire position v.
confusing - nasty sharp salient. No sleep.
Trench cleared at 10am for Brit barrage
(practice?)

[198.1] R.G.A. gunner – Royal Garrison Artillery gunner, possibly a member of a Forward Observation Officer's party, spotting for the guns further back. This was yet another example of a very lucky escape for Rule.

[198.2] ("J.K.") – In his book, Rule recalls that *"Sgt. J.K. Forbes had a sort of roving commission in No Man's Land at all hours of the day or night studying the position of German snipers' loopholes and observation posts."* Forbes, through his observational skills, developed counter-sniping techniques that dramatically cut the Battalion's losses to German snipers. With his camouflage and covert movement expertise, he was also able to gain valuable intelligence through his ability to move across No Man's Land and get very close to the enemy trenches unobserved.

[198.3] S.B.s – Stretcher Bearers. The role these men undertook was often highly dangerous. Regularly undertaken under fire, it usually required four SBs to carry a wounded soldier over the extremely difficult ground. Thick mud, shell-holes, wire and other obstacles were, by themselves, a huge challenge, added to which such a group presented a target that many Germans found irresistible.

This was despite Germany having signed the Geneva Convention (fully the *'Convention for the Amelioration of the Condition of the Wounded and Sick in Armies in the Field. Geneva, 6 July 1906)*, designed to protect the wounded and those who dealt with them.

Although being clearly forbidden, the justification put forward by some for shooting at Stretcher Bearers was that, whilst a dead soldier is no longer a threat to his enemy, a wounded one is evacuated from the battlefield with the hope that he can be treated, recover and return to combat. In the eyes of some soldiers, that could make the wounded, as well as those helping them (such as the stretcher bearers) legitimate targets, despite the Geneva Convention.

[198.4] V. light – Verey light.

[198.5] 'wraith' – Scots for 'ghost'.

Monday 13th September (Continued)

Got pretty well shelled in suppts. too. R.G.A. gunner[198.1] killed beside me. Had to clear out of fire trench again in aftnoon (when trying to improve it - drainage etc) everybody gtly fed up.

Tuesday 14th September - Hooge - Trenches

Raining in forenoon. Collared one of 13 Ptns bivvies & had a great sleep after "stand-to" (went without breakfast & felt empty when awakened to go on sentry!) Brig Gen came along trench. Patrols out in front ("J.K.")[198.2] Cleared out of f. trench again at 3pm for Brit 'strafe'.

Working party on C2 (in front) during night. Sudden wind up & call for S.B.s. [198.3] Pratt hit badly (taking them to listening post) & left behind by his men (scattered by bombs & h. grenades).

Volunteered w. Crichty & C Reid to investigate. Got within 15yds of post - cd. hear the Gerry talking - very nearly caught by V. light[198.4] with stern in air (half over ditch immed. in front of post!) Luckily Jerry too busy! 'Hoppy' wandering abt in front like a 'wraith'.[198.5] C.O. out!

[200.1] t.m.s.& H. grenades – trench mortars and hand grenades.

[200.2] false alarms – Naturally anxious during their first experiences in the trenches, soldiers were quite likely to fire at unknown noises in No Man's Land, especially at night. Rats, finding an almost inexhaustible food supply amongst the dead, were abundant in and around the trenches. When they went foraging for food under cover of darkness – and sometimes in broad daylight too – they were responsible for many of the false alarms. As troops became accustomed to the many different sights and noises of the battlefield, they were better able to filter out the unimportant ones and concentrate on those that might herald real danger.

[200.3] Came in fr. listening post while "stand-to" was on! – As 'stand-to' took place during the time it was considered most likely that the enemy would attack, it made sense not to withdraw from an isolated listening post at that time, but beforehand or even after stand-to was over. Coming back to the fire trench, in the dark and at the very time when his comrades would be at their most 'trigger happy', was really quite dangerous. The fact that Rule marks this event in his diary with an exclamation mark shows his realisation of his mistake.

[200.4] Cleared trench again for practise 'strafe' – It was safer to clear the fire trench rather than risk the danger from 'friendly fire', especially when it was only a practice bombardment.

NB – The Battalion War Diary entry for 16th September mentions Sergeant JK Forbes –

"*During this tour in the trenches, Sgt Forbes did very useful work in crawling out in front of our trenches and reporting on wire, enemies lines and all kinds of useful information.*

At times he crawled in daylight to within 10 yards of the German trenches."

Wednesday 15th September - Hooge - Trenches

Dull weather. Got 'bird' from dugout - so very little sleep.
(Dugouts not considered good for effective work or vigilance)
In charge of listening post (no 2) - leadership qualities being recognised? Post in shell hole 50 yds in front of our wire.
Lively at first. 1st Jocks giving Jerry hell with t.m.s & H. grenades[200.1] (gt crowd - ideal offensive spirit) Slow aftwds.
Rats galore in front - but getting too 'old soldiers' to be led off on false alarms. [200.2]

Thursday 16th September - Hooge - Trenches

Dull. Came in fr. listening post while "stand-to" was on! [200.3] Tried hand at porridge & scored a complete success.
Cleared trench again for practise 'strafe'[200.4] & Fritz replied with whizz bangs fr. "Hill 60" - knocking hell out of Sanct Wd - trees crashing everywhere. Few casualties amongst us. Booth v narrow squeak. Still further back. Brit artillery had last word in argument (v. diff fr. former days) F. trench covered in earth, branches etc - our bivvy got direct hit. Tried to get something cooked (in dark) but interrupted by 'stand-to'.
Out working in front (L. post No 2). No 3 post again occup by Germans - cleared but leaving bombs etc!

[202.1] Shaved off 4 days growth – that Rule specifically mentions this indicates how unusual it was for him, as it was for most British soldiers for the majority of the time, not to be able to shave most days.

[202.2] Cleared trench for 'strafe' by our artillery – When, as in this case, British and German trenches were quite close together, it was safer to evacuate the first line trenches when an artillery bombardment was planned.

[202.3] Making sap right out from our traverse! – Digging a sap at right angles to the fire trench.

[202.4] (John (brother) at Dardanelles) – the 2nd Scottish Horse landed at Suvla Bay on 1st September 1915 and endured operations against the Turks until withdrawing from the Gallipoli Peninsula in mid-December that year.

[202.5] The Johns relieved the tedium towards sunset by singsong. – The same group of individuals who were the founder members of the Society of Good Johns (see Saturday 11th September).

[202.6] star shells – shells used to illuminate the battlefield at night. The shell would be fired at a high angle and would burst at a pre-determined height. A flare (often magnesium) would then ignite, suspended under a parachute that would slow its descent. This would provide enough light to observe activity and targets, usually in No Man's Land, that could include soldiers patrolling or erecting barbed wire.

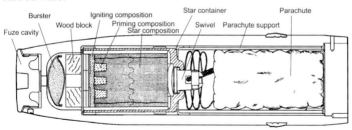

General features of a star shell

Friday 17th September - Hooge - Trenches

Bit sunnier.
Had to yank some of new draft out of 'bivvy'
to get sleep before "stand-to" (pretty wroth
about it!) Shaved off 4 days growth.[202.1]
'C' Coy finally attempt. to take possession of
our bivvy!
'Watty' back - offrs' courses cancelled.
Our snipers got some Germans at No 3 L Post.
Cleared trench for 'strafe' by our artillery[202.2]
- getting a bit of a nuisance 'spec as it means
no cooking! On sentry all night. Making 'sap'
right out from our traverse! [202.3]

Saturday 18th September - Hooge -
Trenches (Relieved by Lincs)

(John (brother) at Dardanelles)[202.4]
Glorious day. Arguments arising over "stand-
to" (troops getting fed up - I think). Had to
dash out in mid of prep breakfast to recall
Pete fr LP in front - C1 scarcely recognisable.
Cleared fire trench & got salvos of hair
raising shrapnel as we made for reserve
trenches. (nothing to eat all day practically).
The 'Johns' relieved the tedium towards sunset
by singsong.[202.5] "Somewhere a Voice is Calling"
- went very well.
Back to f. trench after dark then st. into LP
(still nothing to eat).
Lot of sniping & star shells[202.6] to begin with
(suspicious) then reassured by noise of Jerry
working parties.

[204.1] Lincs – The Lincolnshire Regiment.

Badge of the Lincolnshire Regiment

[204.2] Felt tired but enjoyed magnif sunrise – This march from the trenches at Hooge to the rest billets at Ouderdom was about 8 miles (nearly 13km).

[204.3] R Scot – A soldier of The Royal Scots (The Royal Regiment), the oldest – and most senior – infantry regiment of the line in the British Army.

[204.4] 'Deficiency' parade – It is likely that this particular parade would have had the specific purpose of ensuring that all the soldiers had all the equipment they would require for the coming attack. What Rule highlights in his diary entry is his fellows' reluctance to admit to the understandable – but, to the system, unacceptable – deliberate disposal of shirts on the basis of their being 'verminous', i.e. ridden with lice.

[204.5] Meeting of Johns – See Annex C – The Society of Good Johns

Sunday 19th September - Ouderdom -
Trenches → Rest Billets

Long march home after relief by Lincs[204.1] –
shells coming pretty close at 'dump'.
Avoided C.T. as if it were the devil – thro
Zillibeke – felt tired but enjoyed magnif
sunrise. [204.2]
Didn't feel refreshed with sleep when breakfast
called us for the Ch Parade – almost asleep.
(Padre not so "windy")
Gramophone music in bivvy – great – cricket
ball came thro hessian repeatedly but no
damage.

Monday 20th September - Ouderdom - Rest
Billets

Glorious day.
R&rm as usual.
Easy day on parade. Silver in gt. form at Ptn
drill after long spell as cook & offs' servant.

Musketry in aftnoon – lay on grass whole time
watching a R Scot[204.3] – putting in a good run
with a M'selle!
'Deficiency' parade[204.4] – very few seemed to
have courage to tell Hoppy why they had lost?
their shirts until Gow said "threw it away
because it was verminous".
Meeting of Johns. [204.5] 15 of us & whisky.
Broke up in disorder – stomach curdling stuff
red wine.

[206.1] so called "redoubt" – Rule is clearly unimpressed with this feature nominated by his instructors to be the focus of the day's mock engagement. A redoubt was normally a strong, stone-built defensive fortification, not at all replicable during a training session.

[206.2] English Channel reported to be 'closed'. – The Royal Navy constantly patrolled the Channel during the War, laying defensive minefields, clearing German mines, conducting anti-submarine and anti-surface vessel patrols. This was in addition to guarding the hundreds of ships that were required to sail back and forth across the channel to supply the army in France and Belgium. Sometimes the overall situation was deemed to be too dangerous for the merchant vessels and their daily crossings were suspended.

[206.3] Lord Kitchener, General Allenby and General Haldane – See Annex A - People in the Diary

[206.4] K of K – (Lord) Kitchener of Khartoum.

[206.5] Apparently we were to be sacrificed for the main attack to be staged elsewhere – We will probably never know the exact words Kitchener used on this occasion, but it seems unlikely that he would have directly told several battalions that they were to be 'sacrificed'. He may well have told them theirs was to be a diversionary attack to tie up German resources that might otherwise have been used to provide reinforcement against the main British attack at Loos. It could be that Rule wrote up this section of his diary some time after the battle when, having been badly wounded himself, as well as having lost quite a few of his friends, he might with some justification have thought of the action as a sacrifice.

[206.6] handing in to be stored – This would be the normal procedure at rest billets before a unit headed off to the trenches. Surplus kit and personal effects would be boxed up, labelled and put into storage to await the soldier's return.

[206.7] Letter writing ("just in case") – Before a major action, many soldiers wrote what might be their last letters home, often with the proviso that these would only be posted in the event of their death.

205

Tuesday 21st September – Ouderdom – Rest Billets

Warm & sunny: practising "attack" on so called "redoubt".[206.1] Felt lousy with the onset of a heavy cold in the head (Forgot it was my 20th birthday!) No mails. English Channel reported to be 'closed'.[206.2]

Wednesday 22nd September – Ouderdom – Rest Billets

Sunny & warm. On fatigue – filling in old trenches beyond Brandhoek – successfully dodged parade for inspection by Lord Kitchener accompanied by Gens. Allenby & Haldane.[206.3] We saw it as spectators later. A fine salute fr. K of K[206.4] as band played National Anthem and a very realistic speech. Apparently we were to be sacrificed for the main attack to be staged elsewhere. [206.5] 'Goodbye & Good Luck' said K of K.

Thursday 23rd September – Brandhoek → Sanctuary Wood Trenches (Hooge)

Sunny during day (pouring overnight). No parades. Packing kit, letters, etc and handing in to be stored.[206.6] Letter writing ("just in case").[206.7] Speech by Col. Lyon – pretty cheery. Officers & NCOs in solemn enclave.
As section leader of 16 Ptn bombers I received a sketch map of the German trenches.

[208.1] Appendix trench – British lines in blue, German in red

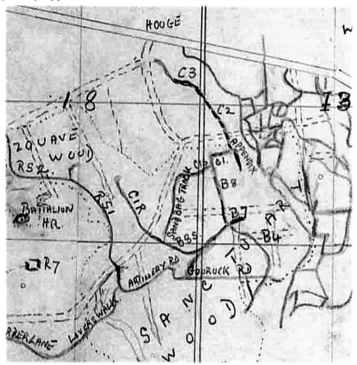

Appendix trench (right of centre), Sanctuary Wood

[208.2] OC Coy suicide squad – Rule had been put in charge of the Company bombers, the group he refers to as the 'suicide squad'.

[208.3] ...in the stillness – Rule commented a few lines earlier that there was a "*strange hush .. in evening*" and he tells us in his book that the Germans knew the attack was coming on the following day. "*The Germans had already placed placards on the wire, bearing the legend "Why not attack today, Jocks? Why wait for the 25th?"*

[208.4] Joe Reid's greeting – In his book, Rule tells us that Reid's greeting, seeing him with his supply of bombs, was "*Well, Cheerio. I dinna wish ye any ill-luck, mind ye, but if ye happen to get in the way of an explosive bullet with a' they boombs around ye, ye'll get blown to buggery.*"

207

Thursday 23rd September - Brandhoek →
Sanctuary Wood Trenches (Hooge) (Continued)

A long day sitting abt idle (except for a brief
lecture on common bombs and how to use
them) awaiting marching orders (and
discussing 'possibilities'). Finally set out after
dark under threatening sky and it rained
heavily before we reached Kruistraat, whence
we slipped & slithered to Sancty Wood. No 16
Ptn went straight out into "Appendix" trench
section[208.1] (in front).
On No.1 L Post. Cold as hell. CO & Adjt round.

Friday 24th September - Hooge Trenches

Heavy rain and 'whizz bangs" all day. Only
one meal and a d - d poor one at that.
Rather a nightmare of a day in fact.
Whizzbanged continuously. Withdrew to reserve
trench with Gunn. Too hungry & miserable to
sleep. Rain! Rain. OO in No. 1 L Post directing
a shoot by his battery only brightish spell in a
slow dreary day. Art. shooting - some good
some erratic. Wire cutters sounded sharply at
dusk. Brigadier made the round.
So the day wore on. Strange hush (not gloom)
in evening. Down to dump for supply of bombs
as O.C. Coy suicide squad.[208.2] Sneaked in a
snooze in old dugout & got a row for it.
Coffee? Wire cutters sounded very distinct in
the stillness.[208.3] Filed out into assembly
positions via Appendix. Silent handshakes Joe
Reid's greeting.[208.4]
My Section, Hay, Silver, Booth & self first into
"C2".

[210.1] Sent FS. pc home – Field Service postcard. Provided by the Army, this gave a few options, e.g. "*I am quite well*", or "*I have been admitted to hospital*", or "*I have* (or *have not*!) *received a letter from you recently*". The soldier could select the appropriate options, thus able to send something home – albeit brief - when there was no opportunity to write a longer letter (see *[76.7]*)

[210.2] <u>much</u> better re-echo – it was clear (see p207) that the Germans knew this attack was planned. They would therefore be ready to respond to the inevitable British artillery barrage with one of their own – in this case, a much heavier one.

[210.3] Wire not cut – there was a long-lasting belief that artillery-delivered shrapnel would easily cut through barbed wire defences and clear the way for attacking soldiers. This proved unfounded time after time, as seen again here.

[210.4] Charge of 1ˢᵗ Gordons on uncut wire magnificent. Bare knees and bayonets! – In his book, Rule elaborates, *"On our flank the 1ˢᵗ Gordons were sweeping forward against the German front line. In the half-light, with the visibility further obscured by a low haze of smoke from shell bursts, only their bayonets and bare knees were discernible, appeared in consequence as a race of terrifying giants. The wire ahead of them was intact, and as they charged into it, the German parapet was stabbed at intervals by the flashes of rifles and machine-guns in a withering deadly fire. Human bravery was as naught in the face of this."*

[210.5] H. explosive shell got me – "High explosive shell got me." With these few words, Rule's extraordinary luck shows yet again. Yes, he is badly wounded but, compared to so many round about him at that time, he is very fortunate.

[210.6] Our supply exhausted. – The defender has an advantage in a situation like this, as the attacker has to carry his ammunition, of whatever sort, with him. Rule and his fellow bombers could only bring so many bombs with them but the Germans would have had a generous stockpile to carry out their defence and initial counter-attack.

OVER THE TOP!

<u>Saturday 25th September</u> - Hooge - Trenches
(Sent FS. pc home).[210.1]

D - d long wait till 3am.

Then bombardment started with Bosche reply
as an immediate and <u>much</u> better re-echo. [210.2]

"Charge"!

Rain & pitch darkness. Rifles clogged.

Leapt parapet into an inferno of bursting
shells, bombs, grenades, rifle & M.G. bullets.

Mix up. Wire not cut.[210.3] Got through
somehow.
Into "Redoubt". Bombed out.

Charge of 1st Gordons on uncut wire
magnificent. Bare knees & bayonets! [210.4]

Trench blown in.

H. explosive shell got me.[210.5] Lay buried some
time.

Bosche bombed us into cul de sac. Our supply
exhausted.[210.6]

[212.1] Bolt for it. – As Rule and his bombers now have no bombs left, the only way to survive is to get back to the British front line.

[212.2] "Toes broken clean over" – Rule's left foot was badly wounded but, despite this injury, he makes his way back across No Man's Land into the temporary safety of the Royal Scots' fire trench.

[212.3] Crawled to dr. stn on hands and knees – With no-one available to help him, Rule then has to make his own way to the dressing station dugout in Sanctuary Wood by crawling on his hands and knees along the bottom of the trench. Here he waited to be taken back for medical treatment.

[212.4] Left in dugout – Whether Rule was just overlooked in the heat of the battle or, yet again, there was no-one to help him, he remained in the dugout when Sanctuary Wood was being evacuated due to the ferocity of the German counter-attack. Exhausted by battle and the effects of his wounds, he crawled into a corner and fell asleep.

[212.5] Medical Orderly digging for me – Once more, luck is with him. It appears a shell exploded close enough to the dugout to cause its partial collapse, but a medical orderly digs him out.

[212.6] Carried to Maypole Copse at midnight – Actually Maple Copse, this was a small plantation some 900 metres east of the village of Zillibeke and just west of Sanctuary Wood.

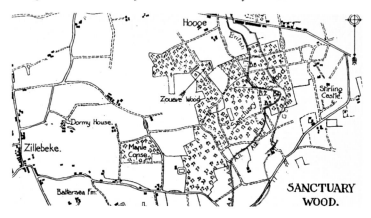

Saturday 25th September – Hooge – Trenches (Continued)

Bolt for it.[212.1] No Man's Land a h – l of a long stretch.

Toes broken clean over[212.2] – almost collapsed in R Scots trenches thro loss of blood.

Crawled to dr. stn on hands & knees.[212.3] Pretty ghastly sights.

Sanctuary Wd evacuated. Left in dugout.[212.4] Crawled into corner & fell asleep.

Woke up to find opp. corner blown in & Medical Orderly digging for me.[212.5]

Carried to Maypole Copse at midnight.[212.6] S.B.s slipping all over the place. Bullets.

Put me down right in front of horses.

ATTACKS AT LOOS AND HOOGE

In 1915, the Allies remained hopeful of breaking the stalemate of trench warfare on the Western Front by co-ordinated action that would punch through the German lines into the open country behind. Elsewhere, the Germans were fighting the Russians and the Italians and they had been forced to withdraw troops from the Western Front for these conflicts.

The French commander, General Joffre, was certain that there was an opportunity to mount successful attacks on the northern and southern flanks of the German positions, at Artois and at Loos, where their line formed a salient (similar to, but larger than, the one at Ypres). The British commander, Field Marshal Sir John French, agreed with Joffre that the way to win was to employ an intensive artillery bombardment to devastate the German front-line trenches. This would enable the infantry to occupy these positions, after which troops held in reserve would move forward and through the newly-captured trenches into the German rear areas and beyond. The British Minister for War, Lord Kitchener, told Field Marshal French, "*We must do our utmost to help the French, even though by so doing, we suffer very heavy losses indeed.*"

Preparations were made, training was undertaken, artillery was amassed and, for the first time, the British made plans for the use of poison gas. (Germany had set the precedent by using chlorine near Ypres on 22nd April 1915.)

Following four days of artillery bombardment, the assaults started on the 25th September 1915. The French were initially successful, fighting through the German front lines and taking large numbers of prisoners. However, the Germans had built a second line of trenches some 3 miles behind their front line and concealed concrete emplacements for machine guns in the zone between the two lines. In this zone, the French attack was halted under withering fire from these machine guns as well as from German artillery.

Due to lack of artillery ammunition, the British bombardment was not as intense as had been planned. Much of the wire defending the German trenches was not cut for the relatively small proportion of the attacking British who reached it, many having been cut down by machine gun and artillery fire on the way over the open fields. Yet superiority in numbers was on the British side and good progress was made. Unfortunately, the reserves arrived too late to capitalise on the initial progress and, within a few days, things were effectively back to where they were before the battle. The twelve attacking battalions suffered 8,000 casualties out of 10,000 men in four hours and there were 48,367 British casualties overall at Loos.

One of these casualties was writer Rudyard Kipling's 18-year old son Lt. John Kipling, who was reported as Missing In Action (MIA). Later, Kipling was asked to write an inscription for the gravestones of Unknown Soldiers and produced the famous "*Known unto God*". He also selected "*Their Name Liveth For Evermore*" for the Stone of Remembrance found in larger cemeteries and "*The Glorious Dead*" on the Cenotaph in London.

The action at Hooge on the 25th September, in which Alexander Rule and his fellow members of 4th Gordons were involved, was always meant to be a 'subsidiary' action, designed to prevent the Germans from moving troops south, from that area, to reinforce the Artois-Loos area. The Germans were aware of the British preparations, as witnessed by the entry in Rule's diary that describes the Germans hanging a sign in front of their trenches that read, "*Why not attack today, Jocks? Why wait for the 25th?*".

The Battalion War Diary describes events in detail:

22/09/15	*¾ mile E of Ouderdom*
	In rest bivouac. Field Marshal Lord Kitchener inspected 4th GH, 1st GH & 2nd R Scots. Addressed troops afterwards and said that 8th Brigade had done excellent work so far and he was sure they would do the same in the events which were to take place in the next few days. Bn warned for trenches tomorrow night. Fine. 3 men sick.
23/09/15	*¾ mile E of Ouderdom*
	Battalion left for the trenches, strength marching out 27 officers and 614 other ranks. Took over trenches

	C1 B8 C15 B8.5 CIR & R51 all in SANCTUARY WOOD from 1st Lincoln Regt.
24/09/15	**Sanctuary Wood**
	In trenches in SANCTUARY WOOD busy getting everything ready for attack. Copy of operation orders attached.
25/09/15	**Sanctuary Wood**
1.30am	*A small ration of coffee distributed in Dixies to men; immediately afterwards all ranks moved into their assembly positions, everyone in their correct positions by 3:40am.*
3.50am	*Our bombardment commenced; almost at once Germans started bombarding our trenches, causing some casualties mostly in C.15 and Half Moon Street*
4.5am	*Our bombardment lifted off German front line trenches.*
4.10am	*½ of B Coy crawled forward towards German line*
4.18am	*½ of D Coy and ½ of C Coy advanced and the other half advanced from our second line trenches.*
4.20am	*Our 1st and 2nd line got into German front line with little loss. Found many Germans in it most of whom bolted. 3rd line advanced over this trench and along with 2nd line, advanced to objective.* *Certain amount of confusion, Germans met with in considerable numbers in the open and in the trenches, and a good bit of rifle fire and hand-to-hand fighting but all were soon captured, killed or escaped.* *Reports gradually got back saying that objective had been gained.* *At the same time 1 off and 9 RE attached and 25 Battalion pioneers under 2Lt Waddell started to work on CT from Appendix to German line, but after a short time had to stop owing to heavy fire from artillery several of the Pioneers being killed.* *They then went forward to help consolidate the furthest line taken by us.*
4.50am	*Germans started heavy bombardment of captured trenches in redoubt, reports came back telling of this*

215

	and asking for shovels and sandbags to strengthen trenches, some were sent up but did not arrive owing to shelling.
	It was almost impossible to get up bombs etc. to the furthest line held by us as the German CTs were blocked by shell fire and anyone coming out into the open was fired at by rifle and machine gun fire from the North of the MENIN ROAD.
	*Reports came back from Capt Hopkinson that he was at point J13A 6 1. and that a field gun had been captured there. **Sgt Forbes*** *was killed at this point by a shell.*
	Lieut. Henderson now in command of C Coy (Capt Reed having been wounded in the middle of the redoubt and carried back to our own lines by his servant) reported that he was at point J13C 7 9 with 6 men he was afterwards driven back from this by shellfire.
4.50am – *12 noon*	*Heavy shelling from Germans all the time. Reinforcements were asked for by Coys in German 3rd line and half of B Coy under Capt Watson were sent up. Capt Watson was wounded in Appendix by a shell.*
5am – *5.30am*	*One half of A Coy in reserve in B 8 S was sent for to take the place of B Coy in C1 as supports. All our old trenches were being heavily shelled by Whizz bangs which made it very difficult to get up supplies of bombs etc even as far as the Appendix but it was done alright and a bomb reserve was made in German first line at point J13 C 3 9 but it was found almost impossible to take them further forward than there.*
About 11 *– 12 noon*	*Germans collected on North of the Menin road and at about 11:30am–12noon attacked from N and NE with bombing parties up the trenches and by others over the open.*
	Our bombers with some of the 1st G.H. who were isolated from their own battalion were driven back for want of bombs and the German bombers working along their old front line from the North forced our men to retire, but not before they had opened rapid fire on them killing a good many.

		*Our men retired to the Royal Scots trenches (**NB** Quite possibly including Alexander Rule – see p212) and across the open and through the wood to Appendix & B 8 where they were collected and lined the parapet of Appendix, C1 and B8. They were there well handled by 2Lt Bain. The Germans 4 times tried to advance from their own front line into C1 and Appendix but each time were stopped by accurate fire of these men. The men of C and D Coys who were in the German 3rd line were cut off and are missing. The remainder of A Coy were at once sent for, to reinforce and hold our old front line, all this time the Germans were accurately shelling our trenches with field guns, inflicting several casualties. The brigade was at once informed of the situation and asked to send up reinforcements.*
	1.pm	*1 Coy of the 4th Middlesex Regt was sent to relieve the men in Appendix, C1 & B8*
	1.30 – 2pm	*Men in C1 B8 were relieved and went back to Middlesex dugouts in SANCTUARY WOOD. One machine gun in New Trench not relieved till later, when it was relieved by 2 M.G. of the 2nd Suffolks.*
	9pm	*Battalion marched back to rest billets near **OUDERDOM***

Casualties as far as at present known:

Officers:

Killed	*Wounded & Missing*	*Wounded*	*Missing*
2nd Lt GP Dawson	*Lieut AR Henderson*	*Capt CD Peterkin*	*Capt J G Hopkinson*
		Capt C Reid	*Lt J Morrison*
		Capt LE Watson	*Lt RD Coutts*
		Lt C R Brander	*2LT WJC Sangster*
		2Lt ER Watts	*2Lt W Addison*
		2Lt W Inkster	*2Lt G Low*
		2Lt EM Tennant	

NCOs and Men	A Coy	B Coy	C Coy	D Coy	TOTAL
Killed	3	10	6	4	23
Died of Wounds	1	-	-	-	1
Wounded	23	43	36	46	148
Wounded & Missing	-	-	4	2	6
Missing	5	19	65	52	141
TOTALS	32	72	111	104	319

Total casualties and/or missing of all ranks – 334 out of 641 who took up positions in Sanctuary Wood on 23rd September.

The renowned military historian, Sir Cyril Falls, wrote in 1958, "*As a diversion, the operation had been of no avail because the Germans had been able to contain the attack with local reserves which would in no case have been moved down to the main battlefield (Loos).*"

However, he goes on to say, "*It may therefore not be surprising that, despite the sharp disappointment and the heavy loss, the majority of the surviving officers and men gained, rather than lost, confidence. They felt that such a chapter of errors and accidents could not recur and that they themselves had proved better men than even in their proudest moments they had claimed to be. In the last respect they were right, but accident and error are an eternal feature of war which only those who have never fought will mock.*"

* **Sgt Forbes** – it is a significant reflection of the high esteem in which JK Forbes was held that, especially as so many others of the battalion were dying at this time, he is the only non-officer named in this section of the Battalion War Diary, just as he was mentioned there on many other occasions.

[220.1] C.C.S. & Amb. Train – Casualty Clearing Station and Ambulance Train. The Casualty Clearing Station was the fourth stage rearwards from the area of fighting (see *[136.3]*). Ambulance trains, first used in the nineteenth century, were widely used in the First World War. They transported wounded soldiers, usually from the Casualty Clearing Stations, to hospitals and the Channel ports for transfer back to Britain. Each carriage could hold 36 beds in three tiers and had its own medical staff, mainly nurses. With the high numbers of casualties, these trains were a very effective means of moving large quantities of wounded soldiers.

[220.2] Rough spin – this would have been a very rough journey to the Menin Road, on a horse-drawn wagon, on roads and tracks that had been shelled and repaired over and over again.

[220.3] Brandhoek – a village about halfway between Ypres and Pop (Poperinge).

[220.4] Amb train splendidly apt – Ambulance train splendidly appointed. An example is shown below:

[220.5] Camiers – just over 62 miles (100 km) from Poperinge.

CASUALTY EVACUATION

Sunday 26th September - C.C.S & Amb. Train[220.1]

Some sun. Rain gone. Taken by G.S. wagon to Menin Rd. Rough spin.[220.2] My stretcher telescoped - bar rested on each back wound.

Motor amb to Ypres - shelled all the way. So sore I scarcely cared.

Brandhoek.[220.3] Oxo (hot). Anti-tetanus injection. Too sore gen. to feel addit pain. Clean shirt wonderful. Lay some time in peasant house then motor amb to 'Pop'. In marquee tent.

Dosed off & woke up between 2 dead uns! In amongst serious cases. Funked dressing stns. British nurse for first time in 8 mths! Magnif. women. M.O. (a Scot) abs. splendid & without nerves. Got new label & asked same questions (age, religion etc.)

Amb train splendidly apptd.[220.4] Saw old Doc (Grant). Sister a dear. Enjoyed meals. France looked at its best. Heard church bells (had forgotten it was Sund.) Civilisation once more.

Saw hosp boat on river. Felt thrilled as we neared the sea. Golf match in progress.

Stopped outside Camiers.[220.5]

[222.1] Canadian – Probably the best-known poem of the War – *In Flanders Fields* – was written in 1915 by a Canadian physician (Lt. Col John McCrae) when serving near Ypres –

> *In Flanders fields the poppies grow*
> *Between the crosses, row on row,*
> *That mark our place; and in the sky*
> *The larks, still bravely singing, fly*
> *Scarce heard amid the guns below.*
>
> *We are the Dead. Short days ago*
> *We lived, felt dawn, saw sunset glow,*
> *Loved and were loved, and now we lie*
> *In Flanders fields.*
>
> *Take up our quarrel with the foe:*
> *To you from failing hands we throw*
> *The torch; be yours to hold it high.*
> *If ye break faith with us who die*
> *We shall not sleep, though poppies grow*
> *In Flanders fields.*

[222.2] No. 2 Canadian General Hospital – Given the location, this suggests it is more likely to be No. 3 Canadian General Hospital.

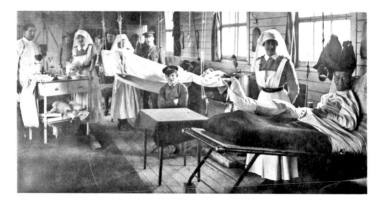

[222.3] Ether – First used in America in the 1840s, ether (properly diethyl ether) was widely employed as an anaesthetic during the war.

Monday 27th September - No. 2 Canadian[222.1] Gen Hosp[222.2] (McGill Univ Units)

Sunny day. MOs & Sisters very cheery and purposeful. Several of Scots ancestry & proud of it. Also of fighting reputation of the Highland Regts. Sisters in blue uniforms with 2 silver stars for rank. Matron sounded American.

After a bath I went straight to operating theatre as my foot looked gangrenous.

As I entered on marquee tent - 4 ops (incl 2 amputations) in progress - to cheer me up!

Ether[222.3] got me under quickly and I woke up back in my bed with cage over left foot and sensation of pain to tips of vanished middle toes - a common experience.

Tuesday 28th - Thursday 30th September - No. 2 Canadian Gen Hosp (McGill Univ Units)

Rain in buckets but double skinned marquee tents waterproof.

Orderlies 3rd year meds at McGill. hated to be called "Orderly".

Ration of stout incld with excellent meals.

[224.1] '*Brighton City*' – Properly *His Majesty's Hospital Ship (HMHS) Brighton.*

HMHS Brighton, by H Crane

[224.2] Whitworth Street Military Hospital – Whilst the 2nd Western General Hospital was headquartered at Whitworth Street, Manchester, there were 22 auxiliary hospitals designated for the treatment of war wounded across Manchester, Salford and Stockport. These were not all originally hospitals – some, as we see from Rule's description, were schools, or halls.

[224.3] Spectators – There was huge public interest as the network of centres for the treatment of war-wounded spread across Britain due to the ever-increasing quantity of casualties returning from France, Belgium, Gallipoli and other theatres of war. Much of this interest was from people, often with friends and relatives serving at the time, wanting to show genuine support and appreciation for these wounded soldiers – but some was simple curiosity.

[224.4] V.A.D.s – Voluntary Aid Detachment nurses. This voluntary unit, formed in 1909 by the Order of St John and the Red Cross, provided field nursing services in support of military medical services. Although not initially universally welcome (mainly through having less nursing skills and discipline than their military counterparts), they proved their worth and became much more valued as the war progressed. During four years of war 38,000 VADs worked in hospitals both at home and abroad, where they also served as ambulance drivers and cooks.

Friday 1st October - Camiers → Calais → Dover   Hosp. Train

Left early with ticket for Blighty attd to dressing gown. Col & Major of Unit on duty as extra stretcher bearers.

'Brighton City'[224.1] a hospital ship. Rough crossing but not quite seasick ('U' boat scare)

Unending & wearisome train journey with no inkling of destination. Finally reached Manchester Central Stn 3am.

Saturday 2nd October - Manchester Whitworth St Military Hospl.[224.2]

Crowds of people as spectators[224.3] even before daylight as we were carried to ambulances & taken into hospital. Burly "Cops" needed to keep free passageway. Big wards with umpteen beds (school rooms being used as hosp. wards) - not so comfy & snug as Camiers!

Sunday 3rd October - Manchester Whitworth St Military Hospl.

Pea soup sort of a fog.
Felt really off colour for first time since wounded. Food not nearly so appetising as from Regtl field cookers even! Boiled to blazes too - in case of chicken especially. Some of V.A.D.s[224.4] very charming and good-fun if not all expert nurses.

[226.1] Limbless Maori Prince – Whilst this one's identity is unknown, many soldiers from New Zealand and Australia, wounded in the Gallipoli campaign, were sent to the UK for treatment.

[226.2] Crowds of visitors – Crowds gathered to see the wounded arrive at hospital. Some came onto the wards to look at and, often, speak to soldiers. Some genuinely offered support to the often homesick teenagers, providing some normality after the horrors of the trenches, or perhaps just to listen when a soldier wanted to talk. Others wanted to hear the stories of derring-do, or of the horrors, the blood and gore, as if they were collecting these tales like trophies to be compared afterwards.

[226.3] She left me shortly afterwards – Rule seems to have felt this lady was one of the story collectors, who may have preferred an answer perhaps giving some philosophical insight into his experience of being wounded, rather than some light-hearted comment on his terpsichorean future.

Alexander Rule (with walking stick) in hospital in Manchester, 1916

Sunday 3rd October – Manchester Whitworth St Military Hospl. (Continued)

Given a glass of port wine but ruined big prospects by tossing it off at a gulp – instead of sipping it & making wry faces like a real invalid!
I hadn't tasted port for months and it felt like cream!

Manchester Monday 4th October – Manchester Whitworth St Military Hospl.

Fog and drizzle.

Limbless Maori prince? [226.1]

Crowds of visitors[226.2] – some activated by pure curiosity too I'm certain! One old dame asked me what were my first thoughts after I'd been hit and tempy buried. I told her I wondered "whether I'd ever be able to dance again!" She left me very shortly afterwards.[226.3]

I pretended to be asleep when others of her sort came along.

-------------ooOoo-----------

Alexander Rule's 1915 Diary entries end here. The following chapter gives more of his personal story.....

ALEXANDER RULE

Alexander Rule was born in Huntly, Aberdeenshire, Scotland, on 21st September 1895, the youngest of the four children of John Rule (born in South Uist in the Outer Hebrides in 1857) and his wife Jessie Forbes Rule (née Henderson, born in 1861 in Auchindoir, which lies between Rhynie and Lumsden in Aberdeenshire). Jessie died in 1912, aged 51, when Alexander was only 16 years old.

Alexander's father was Estate Forester (as had his father been before him at Monymusk) for Richmond and Gordon Estates and the family lived comfortably, along with other estate workers, in Huntly Lodge.

Alexander's siblings were Jane (born in 1888), John (born in 1891) and Charles (born in 1892).

Jane (Nettie) became a primary school teacher. She married William Philip at Huntly Lodge on Christmas Day in 1913. They had one son, John Rule Philip, who was the source of much of the material used by John McConachie in his book 'The Student Soldiers', including Alexander Rule's 1915 Diary upon which this book is based. Nettie died in 1978 aged 90.

John matriculated at Aberdeen University where he studied Science from 1912-1914, although there is no record of him having graduated. He served with 2nd Scottish Horse during the First World War, including a spell at Gallipoli. He married Elizabeth Chapman in Aberdeen in July 1928, at which time he was living at Cairnie in Aberdeenshire and his occupation was given as 'Farmer'. John died in March 1970 aged 79.

Charles trained to become a pharmacist. In 1918, aged 26, he married Annie Eddie, an engineer's clerk from Glasgow. His occupation was given as Pharmacist, although it was also noted on his entry in the 1918 Extract of Marriages that he was a 'Sergeant in the Cadet Corps, currently on active service'. The 1920 local valuation rolls show him as the owner of a shop at 37 Duke Street, Huntly, Aberdeenshire.

227

The doorstep of the Duke Street shop still shows a reminder of
Charles Rule's occupation there.

Whilst still living at Huntly Lodge, Charles also owned a house at 2
Church Street, Huntly, where his tenant was Robert Duffton, a
chemist and probably an employee in the Duke Street shop. Charles
died in 1968 aged 75.

Alexander Rule attended The Gordon Schools in Huntly and then,
in 1913 aged 17, followed in his elder brother John's footsteps to
Aberdeen University, almost certainly whilst John was still a
student there. He would have stayed in lodgings and the inside
cover of his 1915 diary shows his address to be 29 Mount Street,
Aberdeen.

He began his university career by studying geology and zoology and
passed exams in these subjects with good marks in July of 1913.

He enlisted in U Company, 4th Battalion, Gordon Highlanders
(Territorial Force), in November 1913 and took part in his first
Church Parade in February 1914.

Alexander continued to make good progress at university and more
examination passes followed in July 1914. Buoyed with the success
of another academic year behind them, Rule and his fellow student
members of U Company headed off, by rail, to their Annual Camp
at Tain, Ross-shire. The announcement of mobilisation came on the
30th of July and the relatively carefree days of camp came to an end
with everyone returning to the North East. Following local
preparation and a few days of concentrated training at Perth, a
sizeable contingent from the 4th Battalion headed south by rail,
bound for Bedford to join other units of the 51st Highland Division.

In '*Students Under Arms*', Rule's 1934 book, he describes how trainload after trainload of all-kilted Highland soldiers descended upon Bedford in August 1914 and how "*the quiet old country town was shaken to its foundations*", no small part of which was due to the Division being armed with twelve pipe bands. Yet Bedford made great efforts to make the soldiers welcome and the locals and the Division grew, for the most part, to understand and appreciate each other.

Although the military and physical training was hard, the things that Rule and his comrades found hardest were what they saw as the minutiae of military discipline – and the waiting for action. This led to some dissatisfaction and, despite the protestations of the Battalion Commanding Officer, Lieutenant Colonel Tommy Ogilvie, quite a few of the former U Company men successfully applied for commissions in other units. Rule, along with the majority, stuck it out and made the most of his training and his billets at 6 Shakespeare Road and 7 Woburn Road in Bedford.

At the turn of the year, the Bedford community made a particular effort for the troops, organising a large number of Hogmanay supper parties, with eighteen huts, marquees and public halls used to entertain seven thousand men that night and a further seven thousand on the evening of 1st January 1915.

Quite soon afterwards, the date for the move to France and Belgium was determined and, for the period between mid-February 1915 and mid-October that same year, Rule tells his own story in his diary, as transcribed in this book.

Alexander Rule's 1915 diary entries end when he is in hospital in Manchester in October after being wounded at Hooge on 25th September and, unfortunately, no more of his written material is now available.

John McConachie gives us a tantalising comment as to what might have been possible in terms of additional information for this book when he mentions Rule's nephew, John Rule Philip (Alexander's sister Nettie's son), in his acknowledgements.

He says he *"very generously gave me his uncle's papers and diaries and his copy of 'Students Under Arms' with the original dust cover which is reproduced in the text. My debt to Sandy Rule's writings is obvious."*

In 1916, towards the end of a long convalescence, Rule joined some of his fellow Aberdeen University student soldiers at the Gordon Highlanders Reserve Battalions at Ripon in Yorkshire. There, he received a 'Field Service Post Card' (see p.75) from Sandy Gunn, on which the second line of the address was '*LM of S of GJ*', standing for 'Life Member of the Society of Good Johns' (See Annex C), the short-lived but memorable secret society formed shortly before the action at Hooge.

On the 25th of January 1917 Rule was appointed, from officer cadet, to be a 2nd Lieutenant in the Gordon Highlanders and served again on the Western Front. In July 1918 he was promoted to Lieutenant and in August 1918 he was promoted to temporary Captain.

In October 1918, he was awarded the Military Cross. This medal is granted in order to recognize an act or acts of exemplary gallantry during active operations against the enemy. The citation reads, *"2nd Lt. Alexander Rule, Gord. Highrs. When all the officers of his company had become casualties this officer took command of the company, which he led with great courage and ability during continuous fighting for the remainder of the operations."*

The Military Cross

230

Following the end of the war, he returned to his studies at Aberdeen University, where he combined some subjects that would allow him to complete the M.A. degree course he had started before the war, with others that would lead to a B.Sc. In 1919 he completed studies in Botany and Latin towards his M.A. In 1920, towards his B.Sc., he undertook Forestry (for which he collected the Annual Prize and First Class Certificate), Forest Surveying and Forestry Economics, as well as 2nd Class Certificates of Merit in Practical Chemistry and in Systematic Chemistry.

He also passed the course in Natural Philosophy, which allowed him to graduate M.A. on 9th July 1920.

On 19th September 1920, he attended an Investiture Ceremony at Inverness where he was formally awarded his Military Cross. It was presented to him by Prince Albert, Duke of York, Earl of Inverness, who became King George VI following the 1936 abdication of his elder brother, King Edward VIII.

In November 1920, Rule was elected to the Students Representative Council at Aberdeen University and, in the following year, exam success continued with a 1st Class Certificate in Forest Botany and a 2nd Class Certificate in Forest Chemistry, as well as passes in Forest Management, Sylviculture and Forest Zoology.

These were sufficient to allow him to graduate B.Sc. (For.) on 15th July 1921.

During the following eighteen or so months, he spent much valuable time learning more about the practical business of forestry with guidance from his hugely experienced father. Together they attended events such as a visit in August 1921 to Countesswells Woods, organised by the Aberdeen Branch of the Royal Scottish Arboricultural Society, led by Mr S. J. Gammell of Countesswells, a 'well-regarded authority on forestry matters'.

Combined with a good academic record, this type of practical experience and background would have made him an attractive employment prospect. In February 1923, aged 27, he was appointed as Forest Officer in the West Australian Forest Service, based in Perth, Western Australia.

In 1927, he took up a new post as a Lecturer at the Australian Forestry School in Canberra in the Australian Capital Territory, where he was to be based for much of the remainder of his working life. 1928 saw him appointed to an important role as Australian Secretary to the Empire Forestry Conference held in Canberra.

In July 1929, he sailed to Montreal, 3rd class, for his first visit to Canada as a visiting lecturer, a sign of his developing status in the international forestry community. He was to stay with 'Peter Caverhill, Chief Forester, Victoria, British Columbia.' He gave his next of kin as 'Father, Thanesburn, Huntly', indicating that, aged 73, his father had retired and moved out of Huntly Lodge.

Alexander Rule in 1930

His father died in 1931, and it was noted in the Aberdeen Journal of 30th January 1931 that, for many years, he had been "*a valued member of the council of the Aberdeen branch of The Royal Scottish Forestry Society, a zealous elder of the Parish Church and a previous holder of high office in the St. John's Lodge of the Freemasons*".

In 1934, Rule's book, '*Students Under Arms - Being the War Adventures of the Aberdeen University Company of the Gordon Highlanders*' (Aberdeen University Press), was published and was highly praised in the Press and Journal's 'Book of the Week' review of 17th December that year.

In November 1937, now 42, Rule arrived at London on the 'Mongolia' from Brisbane. He travelled in Tourist Class – an improvement on 3rd Class - and his occupation remained 'Lecturer'.

Also aboard was Carmen Tovey, aged 30, whose given 'Proposed Address' in Bedfordshire was the same as Rule's.

The Sydney Morning Herald of 20th December 1939 gives details of a divorce case – *"Tovey v Tovey. Robert Mark Tovey v Carmen Beatrice Tovey (formerly Morris). Marriage April 1933 at Toorak, Victoria. Issue, adultery with Alexander Rule who was joined as co-respondent. Decree nisi."*

In June 1940, Rule joined the army once more, this time the Auxiliary Military Pioneer Corps, as a Lieutenant. (In September 1939, a number of infantry and cavalry reservists were formed into Works Labour Companies. These, in October 1939, became the Auxiliary Military Pioneer Corps (AMPC). On 22 November 1940 the name was changed from the AMPC to the Pioneer Corps.)

In the latter part of 1940, Alexander Rule and Carmen Tovey married in Uckfield, Sussex. The photograph (left) shows them in the garden of their home in East Grinstead during that year.

On 7th March 1941, Carmen Rule sailed on the 'Mantola' from Glasgow to Mombasa. She gave her last address in the UK as Thanesburn, Huntly. Disembarkation was to be at Cape Town, with 'Country of Intended Future Permanent Residence' given as South Africa.

Rule served as Technical Adviser, Timber Control, to the East African War Supplies Board from 1941-1944.

In November 1944, when Rule was aged 49, he and Carmen arrive at Liverpool on the 'Queen of Bermuda' from Port Said, Egypt. They travelled 1st Class and their 'Proposed Address' was Coombe Hill Rd., East Grinstead. He gives his occupation as Forest Engineer, with Carmen's being 'Housewife'. On the ship's passengers list, their 'Country of last Permanent Residence' was given as Kenya.

At some time in the 1940s, Rule chanced to meet up with Murdo Mackenzie (see Annex A), who had set up a very successful engineering business in London. Recognising the value of Rule's experience and contacts, Mackenzie employed him as a forestry consultant. Aberdeen University's Role of Graduates notes that, in the period immediately after the Second World War, Rule was employed as a Forestry and Timber consultant with assignments including advising the UK Food Corporation on a ground-nut scheme in Tanganyika and working with the U.N. in Pakistan. As McConachie writes, "this furthered Sandy's travels about the world by ocean liner and somewhat unreliable aircraft."

In June 1948, Mr and Mrs Rule arrived at London on the 'Llanstephan Castle' from Cape Town, South Africa. They travelled 1st Class, having embarked at Beira (Mozambique). Again, their 'Proposed Address' in the UK was 'The Spinney', Coombe Hill Rd, East Grinstead. Rule repeats his occupation as Forest Engineer.

For some years, Alexander and Carmen lived at 'The Spinney'. However, in the late 1950s, the telephone directory entry changed from 'A. Rule' to 'C. Rule', perhaps indicative of a breakdown in the relationship and Alexander going to live elsewhere whilst Carmen retained the marital home.

In any event, Alexander Rule returned to Australia where, from 1957-1960, he was Technical Assistant to the Director General of the Forestry and Timber Bureau in Canberra. He retired from that post, but spent much of the next few years – and travelled over 30,000 miles – researching a holistic study of Australian forestry.

In 1967, when aged 72, he published his second book, 'Forests of Australia', a "*comprehensive picture of Australia's forest regions and vegetation, outlining their topography and climatic conditions.*

Mr Rule has twenty years' experience in Australian Forestry, enabling him to gain a direct knowledge of phases of forest development, conservation and exploitation. He has also had extensive experience overseas, having acted as an advisor on forestry in Africa, Scandinavia, India and South-East Asia."

In a statement possibly even more relevant and valid today, Rule closes his forestry book by saying, "***If we want to be treated well by nature it is, in short, a golden rule to treat nature well***."

In 1981, he was living with his nephew at Thanesburn, Huntly, the house to which his father had retired in the 1920s.

Alexander Rule died on the 4th of July 1983, aged 87, at the Cottage Hospital, Meigle, Perthshire, having previously resided at the Hope Park Home, Rattray, Blairgowrie, in Perthshire. At his funeral, the congregation sang the University song *Gaudeamus* (see p112), a fitting link with the academic life that Rule and his fellow Aberdeen University students had voluntarily set aside – some for years, others for ever – in the service of their country.

Detail from the Rule family gravestone, Huntly Cemetery

POETRY IN WORLD WAR I

Thousands of poems have been written about the First World War. From famous authors such as John McCrae, Siegfried Sassoon, Wilfred Owen and Katherine Tynan, to lesser-known, or even to unknown writers, who wrote out of fear or friendship, pride or passion, relief or rancour, millions of words have been committed to paper about 'the war to end all wars'. One such lesser-known writer is Wilf Hastwell, a former boy-chorister at the 12th Century Temple Church in London, built as the English headquarters of the Knights Templar.

Wilf wrote this poem early in 1917 whilst at the Western Front and it mirrors many of the experiences found in Rule's diary.

A Phantasy

What a hole!
All holes; nothing whole;
Funkholes, shell holes, rat holes,
Unholy, unwholesome, Hell.

Much mess, megrims, melancholy,
Melancholy, immeasurable melancholy, tragic, weird;
Weird, odd, extraordinarily odd, rum.
(Rum, butter, biscuits, bully, tea,
More rum, no rum, nothing but petrol water.)

Arms,
Arms and equipment,
Arms and legs, corpses, bodies, Bosche;
Armless horrors, harmless, hideous haters, hideous, hardening Ha! Ha!
Huns hunted; helmet hunting, souvenir hunting,
Buttons and badges, badges of rank, rigid rankers.
Rank, bad, rotten, rancidity.

And the mud –
Paste mushy; slush and water, bloody water, chlorinated water,
Slime, slithery slough, bog, quagmire, beastly.
Puddles, pools and ponds
Wearing waders, weary waders; waders weak, wonky gone west,
'Ware wet feet. Where whale oil?
But where? Where? Where?

Cold, keen, cutting, excruciating fire.
Firing, fire flingers, firelights, flash, whiz, whistle, crump!
(where was it?)
Crumps, coalboxes, Jack Johnsons, whizzbangs – O jumping Jehosophat,
French mortars and aerial torpedoes; minenwerfer and machine guns,
Slingers and snipers, shots,
Good shots, bad shots, blighties, base buried or back again to billets,
Billets,
Bother, back again to billets,
Trudging trenches, trails and tracks; ruts and roads, real roads;
Tramping roads roaring with the nine point two.
Huts, heavy roads, habitations, houses – Heaven!
Billets, blankets and beds,
Blessed beds; bon, billowy beds; planks and straw,
Beds and bye-bye.

Wilf Hastwell was killed a few weeks afterwards.

Annex A – People in the Diary

NAME	NOTES	PAGE
ADDISON, William	Son of James Addison; born at Whitehills on 16th July 1886. Graduated from Aberdeen University M.A. in 1908 and B.Sc. in 1909. Commissioned into the 3rd Gordons, 10th April 1915, then transferred into 4th Gordons in July 1915. Served - Home, April-July 1915; France (4th Gordons), July-September 1915. Taken as Prisoner of War, Germany, 25th September 1915 until the end of the war. Final rank: Lieutenant.	182, 217.
ALLARDYCE, Alexander	Born on 22nd November 1884 at Rothiemay, Aberdeenshire, he was a son of the manse and a lifelong friend of J K Forbes. Attended Robert Gordon's College. Graduated M.A. from Aberdeen University in 1904. Undergraduate member of U Coy 1st Volunteer Battalion Gordon Highlanders. A solicitor with Hunter and Gordon in Aberdeen, he re-joined U Company 4th Gordons in 1914. Killed on 20th July 1915 aged 30, at Hooge whilst leading a bombing party. Cecil Sommers writes, in his book *'Temporary Heroes'*, *"When we arrived, the first sight that met us was my bombing sergeant, lying dead on top of the parapet. He had thrown all the bombs that he and his men had brought up and then, when they had run out and no more were to be had, he had climbed up on to the parapet and, in full sight of the German second line eighty yards away, had*	106, 144, 146.

NAME	NOTES	PAGE
	fired at their bombing parties as they tried to work up the front line trench towards them. He had kept them off like this for twenty minutes, standing up there amidst an ever-growing hail of bullets. Then he fell, shot through the heart." Mentioned in dispatches and recommended for the D.C.M. Final rank: Sergeant. Listed in the Robert Gordon's College Former Pupils' Magazine Roll of Honour in August 1915. **Burial Details**: Name inscribed on the Menin Gate Memorial, Ypres, Panel 38.	
ALLENBY, Edmund (From the 1917 journal 'The War'.)	A Major General in command of the single cavalry brigade in the British Expeditionary Force at the start of the war, Allenby proved his worth during the retreat from Mons. He was promoted to temporary Lieutenant General in October 1914 and given command of the Cavalry Corps. In May 1915, he left the Cavalry to take command of V Corps. Whilst this Corps was successful in holding the Germans at the Second Battle of Ypres, there was criticism of Allenby for the tactics he followed, which led to a high rate of casualties through his insistence on continued counter-attacks on the Germans. He was still in command of V Corps on 25th September 1915 when it made the diversionary attack at Hooge aimed at preventing German reinforcements being sent to counter the concurrent British Army offensive at Loos. Once again, as witnessed in this diary, V Corps under Allenby's direction	206.

NAME	NOTES	PAGE
	incurred substantial losses to its units that were involved in the action at Hooge. He became a substantive Lieutenant General on 1st January 1916 and a General on 3rd June 1917. He then moved to the Middle East as head of the Egyptian Expeditionary Force where, amongst much else, he 'commanded' Lawrence of Arabia. On 31st July 1919, Allenby was made a Field Marshal and became Viscount Allenby on 7th October 1919. He died in 1936 aged 75.	
ANDERSON, James	Born at Portknockie, 29th April 1892. Nicknamed 'Gamin'. His original nickname at Fordyce Academy had been 'Gammon', which had its origins in the smoke from the briar pipe that was his constant companion. When he arrived at Aberdeen University, his more sophisticated student companions soon changed it to 'Gamin', meaning 'urchin'. Arts at Aberdeen University 1911-14. Served in U Company 1913-14. Belgium Feb-Sep 1915. Member of the sniper section. Killed at Hooge 25th September 1915 aged 23. **Burial Details**: Name inscribed on the Menin Gate Memorial, Ypres, Panel 38, Column 5.	17, 44, 70, 132.
ANDERSON, William (Billy)	Son of William Anderson. Born in Peterhead on 6th January 1895. Studied medicine at Aberdeen University 1913-1914 and joined U Company in 1914. He was a very capable golfer, having won tournaments at Peterhead Golf Club.	14, 18, 20, 24, 28, 30, 38,

NAME	NOTES	PAGE
	He was mobilized in August 1914 and was sent to Belgium following a period of training at Bedford. He was wounded on 5th May 1915 and hospitalised. He returned to serve for the remainder of the war and was wounded again later in 1915. He graduated M.B. Ch.B. from Aberdeen University in 1919. Entered General Practice in Wollaston. Died in 1973 aged 78.	52, 54, 82, 86, 130, 136, 180.
ARCHIBALD, Alexander S	Company Quartermaster Sergeant. Son of Thomas Archibald, Architect, Huntly. He was, like Rule, a former pupil of The Gordon Schools in Huntly, Aberdeenshire. Killed whilst serving with 6th Gordons on 4th June 1915. He was awarded the Distinguished Conduct Medal (D.C.M.) and had been Mentioned In Despatches. (Detail from school's memorial window.) **Burial Details**: Name inscribed on Le Touret Memorial, Richebourg-L'avoue, Pas de Calais, France. Panel 39-41.	136.
ASHER, William Alexander	Son of Alexander Asher; born Elgin, 25th August 1893. Matriculated at Aberdeen University and studied Arts 1912-1914. Joined U Company Nov 1912. Mobilized August 1914. Commissioned to Highland Light Infantry Sept 1917. Final war rank: Lieutenant. Graduated M.A. from Aberdeen University in 1919.	74.

NAME	NOTES	PAGE
	Became Education Officer of 1st Gordons in 1919, then an Instructor at the Army School of Education in 1926. In 1932, he transferred to the Indian Military Academy, Dehra Dun. He served as Deputy Director of Military Education India from 1946-1948. Final rank: Colonel.	
BAIRD, Alexander Walker Frederic	Commanding Officer of 1st Gordons at this time. Born 1876. Son of Sir Alexander Baird of Ury, 1st Baronet, Lord Lieutenant of Kincardineshire 1889-1918. C.O. from 23rd April 1915 to 3rd July 1915. Died 1931.	88.
BANNATINE-ALLASON, Richard	Major General Sir Richard Bannatine-Allason. Born in 1855, he was commissioned in the Royal Artillery on 28th January 1875. He saw action in the Afghan War (1878–80), the Sudan (1885) and South Africa (1899–1902). He commanded 51st Highland Division from 27th August 1914 until 24th Sep 1915. The division suffered casualties even before it went abroad. Soldiers brought up in the healthy air of the Highlands were susceptible to the common diseases of urban England. Soon after the division's arrival at Bedford, many soldiers succumbed to these diseases and to measles in particular. Sir Richard died in 1940, aged 85.	8.
BARRON, Arthur Morrison	Son of George Barron; born at New Byth, Banffshire, 17th August 1894. Studied Arts at Aberdeen University, 1913-14. Enrolled in U Company in November 1913. Commissioned into	74.

NAME	NOTES	PAGE
	7th Gordons on 26th October 1915; transferred to R.A.F., February 1918. Served - Home, 2 years 3 months; France, Belgium, 2 years 2 months. Final rank: Lieutenant. Awarded Military Cross, August 1917. Graduated M.B. Ch.B. from Aberdeen University in 1924. Became Consultant Physician Poole General Hospital 1927. M.D. 1932. Died in 1979 aged 85.	
BEGG, J Henderson	See HENDERSON-BEGG, John.	64, 78, 80, 104, 106, 152.
BERRY, John	Son of William Berry, of The Royal Oak Hotel, Huntly, Aberdeenshire. A former pupil of The Gordon Schools, Huntly. Killed serving with 6th Gordons, 4th June 1915 aged 21. His brother George was wounded at Neuve Chapelle. (Detail from school's memorial window.) **Burial Details**: Name inscribed on Le Touret Memorial, Richebourg-L'avoue, Pas de Calais, France. Panel 39-41.	136.
BISSET, Robert Robertson	Son of James Bisset; born Macduff, 25th February 1894. Studied Science at Aberdeen University, 1911-12. Joined U Company, 1911. Mobilized August 1914. Commissioned in November 1914; attached to the 6th Gordon Highlanders. Served - Home,	50.

NAME	NOTES	PAGE
	1914-15; Abroad, January-March 1915; Home, 1915-16. Wounded at Neuve Chappelle when a Lieutenant with the 6th Gordons. Gazetted out on account of ill health.	
BOOTH, Douglas D	Agriculture, Aberdeen University from 1913-14. Joined U Company 1914. Served in France and Belgium February – September 1915. Wounded April 1915 and at Hooge, September 1915. Aberdeen Evening Express of the 29th September states *"Pte Douglas Booth, wounded by shrapnel, is a son of Mr Matthew Booth, Mastrick Dairy, Aberdeen. He was a student at the Agricultural College before enlisting, and about two months ago returned to the front after recovering from wounds. Pte Booth received a commission as second-lieutenant in the 2/6th Gordons on August 17, but had not been able to join his new regiment."*	17, 76, 174, 190, 194, 200, 208, Annex C.
BRANDER, Eric William Harcourt	Born in Aberdeen, 23rd August 1888. Graduated from Aberdeen University M.A. 1910; LL.B. 1911. 2nd Lieutenant, 4th Gordons, April 1910. Mobilized, 4th August 1914. Served - Home, 1914-16; France, 1916-19. Final rank: Brevet-Major. Given three Mentions in Dispatches, 1917 and twice in 1918. Awarded Ordre de Leopold (Insignia of Chevalier) (Belgium), 1921.	174.
CALDER, George Macbeth	Son of George Macbeth Calder and Isabella Calder, of Presley Cottage, Dunphail, Morayshire. Initially studied for an M.A. at Aberdeen	24.

NAME	NOTES	PAGE
	University, then became a medical student. Joined U Company in 1911. Soon promoted to Sergeant. Commissioned into 8th Seaforth Highlanders March 1915. Killed at Loos on the 25th Sep 1915, aged 24. (Therefore unlucky in the end – see p.24) One of two members of U Company to be awarded a posthumous M.A. by Aberdeen University. Listed in the Robert Gordon's College Former Pupils' Magazine Roll of Honour in August 1915. **Burial Details**: Dud Corner Cemetery, Loos, France. Grave Reference V.H.1.	
CLARKE, Ian Anderson	Son of John Clarke; born in Aberdeen, 23rd June 1890. Educated at Aberdeen Grammar School. Graduated M.A., 1911; B.Sc. (Agr.), 1912, both at Aberdeen University. Private, U Company, 1908-12; Wounded on 16th June 1915. Commissioned as a Second Lieutenant in the 4th Gordons on 1st September 1915. In 1916, he was seconded to the Machine Gun Corps where he served as an instructor at the Machine Gun Corps School at Grantham until returning to France in 1918. He was also attached for a spell to the Australian Imperial Force. As acting Major, he was wounded for the third time in July 1918 but survived to be demobilised in September 1919. Final rank: Major. Graduated BA (Oxon) 1919. Worked for the Forestry Commission 1920-1922. Headmaster of Stowe School,	4, 26, 38, 56, 72, 76, 78, 104, 134.

NAME	NOTES	PAGE
	Buckinghamshire, from 1923-1939. Died in 1939 aged 49.	
COOK, William Littlejohn	Son of George M. Cook; born in Aberdeen, 21st July 1883. Studied Law at Aberdeen University 1909-1910. Commissioned as a Second Lieutenant in the 4th Gordons 1st September 1914. Wounded 9th June 1915. Later attached to the Admiralty Transport Department, London. Also served in Archangel, Norway, Egypt. Final rank: Captain. Awarded the OBE (Military Division) and the Russian Order of St. Anne.	126.
CORNER, Harold Hartman	Son of William Corner; born in Inverness, 13th August 1896. Studied Agriculture at Aberdeen University 1913-1914. Joined U company in November 1913. Served - Home, 1914-15, France and Belgium, February-June 1915. Wounded (lost an eye when a sniper) and discharged. Final rank: Private. James Campbell Bursar in Agriculture, 1917-18 and graduated B.Sc. (Agr.) from Aberdeen University in 1919. PhD 1938. Agricultural Adviser, Roxburgh, 1941-1961. Awarded the OBE in 1957. Died in 1979 aged 82.	44.
COUTTS, Robert Disher	Lieutenant, 4th Gordons. Killed at Hooge between 25th and 27th September 1915, aged 27. **Burial Details**: Name inscribed on the Menin Gate Memorial, Ypres, Panel 38.	176, 217.
CRANSTON, Thomas (Tommy)	Son of William Cranston; born at Edinkillie, Morayshire, 9th February 1891. Graduated M.A. from	70, 100.

NAME	NOTES	PAGE
	Aberdeen University, 1912. Member of U Company from 1912-1914. Served - Home, 1914-15; Flanders, March-May 1915. Wounded on 17th May 1915. Commissioned Sept 1917. Final Rank: Lieutenant. Awarded the MBE (Military) in 1919. Listed in the Robert Gordon's College Former Pupils' Magazine Roll of Honour in August 1915. Became a Tax Inspector in Aberdeen, Glasgow and Galashiels. Died in 1966 aged 75.	
CRICHTON, Arthur ('Crichty')	Born in Alford, Aberdeenshire, 24th September 1894. Joined U Company in March 1912 following his matriculation at Aberdeen University. Graduated M.A. from Aberdeen University in 1914; commissioned, 24th February 1918 into the Labour Corps. Served - Home, 1914-15, 1916-18; Belgium, France, February-October 1915; Salonika, July 1918-January 1919. Final rank: Second Lieutenant. Graduated B.Sc. (Agric.) from Aberdeen University in 1920. Joined The Rowett Research Institute. Served as Commanding Officer of the infantry sub-unit, Aberdeen University OTC, from 1935-1940. He was appointed Deputy Principal at North of Scotland Agricultural College in 1948, then Manager of Weasenham Farm Complex in 1951. Died in 1972 aged 77.	18, 42, 58, 100, 104, 108, 142, 154, 186, 192, 194, 198, Annex C.
CRICHTON, David Wood	Son of Edward and Elizabeth Crichton, Rosebery Villa, Banchory, Kincardineshire. Born at Banchory,	88, 98.

NAME	NOTES	PAGE
	10th October 1896; educated there and matriculated at Aberdeen University in Agriculture, 1913. Joined U Company and was mobilized in August 1914. In February 1915 he went from Bedford to Belgium, one of the youngest students in D Company. Killed in action on 7th May 1915, aged just 18 years and 6 months, at Kemmel and lies along with other members of the former U Company. **Burial Details**: Buried at Wytschaete Military Cemetery, Belgium. Grave IV, C, 9	
CRUICKSHANK, James Orr	Son of Samuel and Agnes Cruickshank, of Schoolhouse, Craichie, Forfar. Native of Tarfside, Forfarshire, born in Brechin, 17th August 1895 and educated at the local school. Matriculated in Arts and Science at Aberdeen University, 1913. On the outbreak of war he was already a private in U Company and underwent training with his regiment at Bedford, before crossing to France in February 1915, where he 'actively and dutifully served' until he was killed, on 15th April 1915, aged 19, in the trenches near Wytschaete by a German sniper. He was the second of the ex-U Company contingent to be killed. **Burial Details**: Buried at La Clytte Military Cemetery, Reninghelst, West-Vlaanderen. Plot 1, Row B, Grave 3.	66, 72.
CUMMING, Marianus A	Lance Corporal. Son of Marianus Cumming, baker. Born in Strichen, Aberdeenshire, on 9th December	130, 132.

NAME	NOTES	PAGE
	1891; educated at Maud H.G. School and Robert Gordon's College in Aberdeen; took a high place in the Bursary competition; graduated M.A. from Aberdeen University in 1912. Schoolmaster at Kemnay before re-joining U Company. Then served with Machine Gun Section, 4th Gordons. Killed 13th June 1915, aged 23. Buried on 14th June 1915 but his grave was destroyed/lost in later fighting. Listed in the Robert Gordon's College Former Pupils' Magazine Roll of Honour in August 1915 as 'Killed in Action'. **Burial Details:** Named on Menin Gate Memorial, Ypres, Belgium. Panel 38, Column 5.	
DAVIDSON, Robert	Son of John Davidson; born in Ellon, Aberdeenshire, 20th October 1894. Aberdeen University, Arts, 1913-14. Joined U Company, 1913. Served - France, February 1915-July 1916. Wounded, July 1916. Commissioned, 1st Gordons, 26th June 1918. August 1918-April 1919. Final rank: Second Lieutenant. Aberdeen University M.B. Ch.B. 1923. General Practice in Nottingham.	17, 31.
DONALD, Charles (Chatty)	Son of George Donald. Born in Aberdeen, 14th February 1896. Studied Medicine at Aberdeen University, 1913-14, 1919-1922. Joined U Company as a private in 1913. Commissioned into 5th Gordon Highlanders in October 1915. Seconded to Royal Flying Corps, June 1917. Served - France, 13	64.

NAME	NOTES	PAGE
	months; Home, 3 years. Final rank: Lieutenant, and also Acting Flight-Commander. Services brought to notice of Secretary of State for Air, January 1919. Listed in the Robert Gordon's College Former Pupils' Magazine Roll of Honour in August 1915. Completed his medical studies at Aberdeen University after the war, graduating M.B. Ch.B. in 1922. F.R.C.S. 1925. Ch.M. 1930. Held posts at the London and Great Ormond Street Hospitals. During WWII he was Brigadier Consulting Surgeon Middle East Forces. Awarded O.B.E. in 1944. He was a recognised authority on Thyroid Surgery. Died in 1955 aged 59.	
DONALD, Robert T	Son of Charles Donald; born in Lumsden, Aberdeenshire, on 20th December 1892. Joined U Company, March 1912. Graduated M.A. from Aberdeen University, 1914. Mobilized, August 1914. Commissioned into the Black Watch August 1915. Served in India and Mesopotamia. Final rank: Captain. Head of the English Department at Inverurie Academy and originator of 'The Inverurie Players'. Died in 1936 aged 43.	186.
DONALD, William	Son of John Donald, carpenter, Rothiemay. Born at Marnoch, Banffshire, 2nd July 1893; educated at Rothiemay Public School and Robert Gordon's College, Aberdeen. Studied Arts, Aberdeen University, 1912-14. He joined the Gordon Highlanders in	108, 136, 138.

NAME	NOTES	PAGE
	1911, and became a member of U Company just prior to the war. He was mobilized with his unit in August 1914, volunteering at once for foreign service and went to France with the Battalion in February 1915. He was twice wounded during that spring and summer and was killed in action at Hooge on the 25th September 1915. Listed in the Robert Gordon's College Former Pupils' Magazine Roll of Honour in August 1915. **Burial Details:** Named on the Menin Gate Memorial, Ypres, Belgium. Panel 38	
DOWN, Norman Cecil Sommers	Captain, 4th Gordons. Author of *Temporary Heroes*, an at times irreverent account of his war, written under the name of Cecil Sommers. Down was commissioned into 4th Gordons in September 1914 and went with them to Belgium in 1915, sharing many of Alexander Rule's experiences; the issue of goatskins, the train journey to Bailleul and billeting in the 'cold Grapperies hothouses'. He was involved in the September 1915 action at Hooge. In July 1916 he was wounded on the Somme. Eventually deemed fit again for active service, he returned to France in November 1917, only to be sent to Palestine a week later. In April 1918 he was wounded again and evacuated to hospital in Cairo. He recovered quickly after surgery there and returned to France and the fighting around the Hindenburg Line. After the war, he became a Senior	52, 56, 190.

251

NAME	NOTES	PAGE
	Principal Inspector of Taxes, Board of Inland Revenue. He was later honoured by being made a Companion of The Order of St Michael and St George (CMG). Died in 1984 aged 90.	
DUTHIE, Andrew May	Son of John Duthie; born in Fraserburgh, 7th December 1895. Was in same Zoology class as Alexander Rule. Joined U Company, January 1914; Second Lieutenant, 11th Gordon Highlanders, July 1915. Attached to 4th London Regiment (R.F.). Served - Home, 1914-17, 1918-19; Abroad, January 1917-April 1918. Final rank: Acting Captain. Awarded the D.S.O. in November 1917 and the M.C. in March 1918. Mentioned in Despatches in February 1918. Graduated M.A. from Aberdeen University in 1920 and M.B. Ch.B. (Hons) in 1924. M.D. in 1929. Consultant Obstetrician at Chesterfield 1948. Died in 1981 aged 85.	66.
ERSKINE, T Barrie	Lieutenant (although shown as Captain elsewhere), 4th Argyll and Sutherland Highlanders, attached to 1st Gordons. Medical student at Glasgow University. Awarded the Military Cross for actions near Hill 60 in May 1915. Killed on the 20th July 1915 aged 25. At the Glasgow University Graduation Ceremony on Saturday 20th November 1915, Principal Sir Donald MacAlister announced that Erskine was entitled to an M.A. with honours in	144.

252

NAME	NOTES	PAGE
	Mathematics and Natural Philosophy due to work completed before his death.	
EWEN, John Birnie	Son of James and Helen Ewen, of 37, Hosefield Avenue, Aberdeen. Born in Aberdeen on 21st February 1893. Educated at Robert Gordon's College, Aberdeen. Graduated M.A. (Hons.) from Aberdeen University in 1914, where he had been Secretary of the University Athletic Association. In October 1914, after a previous medical rejection, he joined the 2nd/4th Battalion Gordon Highlanders and trained with them in Aberdeen until March 1915, when he had the hard experience of being drafted straight from his own home to the Battalion in France and then to Flanders. Killed, aged 22, on 25th September 1915 at Hooge. Listed in the Robert Gordon's College Former Pupils' Magazine Roll of Honour in August 1915. **Burial Details:** Named on the Menin Gate Memorial, Ypres, Belgium. Panel 38	176.
FALCONER	Captain. There were two Lieutenants Falconer in the Regiment around this time – Douglas and Robert – both of whom were promoted from Lieutenant to temporary Captain with effective dates of 4th and 11th June 1915 respectively. It is unclear which Captain is referred to in the diary.	190.
FALCONER, Robert	Son of James G. Falconer, commission agent; born in Aberdeen, 8th December 1890; educated at Aberdeen Grammar School and at	144.

253

NAME	NOTES	PAGE
	Robert Gordon's College. On leaving school he entered the firm of Messrs. Stephen & Smith, Advocates, Aberdeen, to whom he was later apprenticed as a law clerk. During his apprenticeship he studied Law at Aberdeen University, 1912 - 15. He joined the 4th Gordons as a Private in 1911. He was mobilized as a Lance-Sergeant, and crossed to France with the 4th Gordons in the spring of 1915; there he was soon promoted to Company Sergeant-Major. Early in 1916 he was home on leave. He rejoined the Battalion in May and returned to France with a draft in the beginning of July to take part in the Battle of the Somme. During this engagement he was reported wounded and missing on 23rd July 1916, and was later believed killed on that date. Listed in the Robert Gordon's College Former Pupils' Magazine Roll of Honour in August 1915. **Burial Details**: Caterpillar Valley Cemetery, Longueval, France. Grave Reference Plot 12, Row E, Grave 27.	
FERGUSSON, Charles	Major General. Commander, II Corps, at this time. He was the son of Sir James Ferguson, the sixth Governor of New Zealand. Commissioned into the Grenadier Guards in 1883, he served in the Sudan, Egypt and Ireland, where he was General Officer Commanding 5th Division. He took that unit to France in August 1914 and served throughout the war, latterly	24, 94, 108.

NAME	NOTES	PAGE
	commanding XVII Corps with the rank of General. He served as Military Governor of Cologne before leaving the army in 1922. He served as Governor of New Zealand from 1924 until 1930, as had his father before him and as did his son later. Died in 1951 aged 86.	
FORBES, John	Born 28th May 1894 at Fordyce. Graduated M.A. from Aberdeen University 1912. Private in $2^{nd}/4^{th}$ Gordons, January 1915. Served with $1^{st}/4^{th}$ Gordons March-September 1915. Final rank: A/CQMS (Acting Company Quartermaster Sergeant). Listed in the Robert Gordon's College Former Pupils' Magazine Roll of Honour in August 1915. Teacher at Fordyce, Dufftown and Fraserburgh. Headmaster at Kintore. Awarded MBE in 1931. Died 1956 aged 65.	142, 156, 194, Annex C.
FORBES, John Keith ('JK')	Son of Alexander Forbes, F.E.I.S., and Jessie Forbes (nee Keith), of Glenaden, Mintlaw Station, Aberdeenshire. Born in Aberdeen, 12th April 1883; he graduated M.A. at Aberdeen University in 1905; taught for seven years at Rathven Public School; in 1912 entered Aberdeen United Free (U.F.) College, taking the highest place in the examinations open to all the U.F. Colleges; gained Foote Scholarship in Hebrew and Eadie Prize in New Testament Greek. He enlisted in October 1914 as a Private in U Company and was sent to Belgium in February 1915.	106, 138, 198, 199, 216, 218.

NAME	NOTES	PAGE
	Although he could readily have obtained a commission, he contented himself with the rank of Sergeant, believing that as a N.C.O. he would be able to exercise a greater moral influence on his men. The invaluable services he rendered by organizing a corps of snipers, as well as by the accurate information he was able to gain regarding the German positions, were recognized in a letter addressed to him by the General commanding the Division. He was killed by a shell at Hooge on 25th September 1915 aged 32. It was said that *"a more versatile genius than Forbes never passed through Aberdeen U.F. College. A tireless walker, an intrepid mountaineer, a keen sportsman, a humourist, a skilled musician, a linguist, a scholar - no achievement seemed beyond his capacity. Even in the trenches he pursued his studies, and left behind him singularly able notes on the Book of Job, which to the last he studied in the Hebrew original, with the aid of the latest German commentary."* Final Rank: Sniper Sergeant. The book, *"Student & Sniper Sergeant, A Memoir of J K Forbes, M.A."* by William Taylor, M.A. & Peter Diack, M.A. (Hodder & Stoughton, London, 1916) is a tribute to him. **Burial Details:** Named on the Menin Gate Memorial, Ypres, Belgium. Panel 38	
FORREST, Robert Andrew Dermod	Son of Robert C Forrest; born in Leytonstone, 21st February 1893. M.A. from Aberdeen University,	108.

256

NAME	NOTES	PAGE
	1914. Private in U Company, 1910. Mobilized, Aug 1914. Commissioned as Second Lieutenant, 11th Gordons, January 1916; attached King's African Rifles. Served - Home, 1914-15, 1916-17, 1918-19; Flanders, February-December 1915; East Africa, July 1917-September 1918. Final rank: Lieutenant. Joined Hong Kong Civil Service 1919. Became Postmaster General, Chief Magistrate then Secretary for Chinese Affairs. Lecturer in Oriental Languages at London University. Author of a standard textbook on Chinese Language. Died in 1977 aged 83.	
FOWLIE, Andrew Thomson	Son of Patrick Fowlie, farmer, Auchentumb, Strichen. Born 9th July 1888; educated at Glasslaw and New Pitsligo Public Schools. Matriculated at Aberdeen University as a student in Agriculture, 1906. He took the University Diploma in Agriculture and the National Diploma in Agriculture, 1909, and the National Diploma in Dairying, 1910. He was appointed Assistant-Lecturer in Agriculture for the Counties of Inverness, Ross and Cromarty in 1909, a post he held until September 1912, when he was appointed County Organizer for Orkney. When war broke out Fowlie immediately asked the College to relieve him of his appointment, and in September 1914 he joined U Company as a Private. After training at Ripon he crossed with the 4th Battalion to France in February 1915. Killed on 16th June,	31, 106.

NAME	NOTES	PAGE
	aged 26, when the 4th Gordons were in action on the Bellewaarde Ridge, east of Ypres, and D Company took part in a bold assault on the German lines in a wood near Hooge. **Burial Details**: Name recorded on the Menin Gate Memorial, Ypres, Panel 38, Column 5.	
FRASER, James Fowler (Jimmy)	Youngest, and tenth surviving, child of Thomas Fraser; born at Clyne in Newmachar parish, Aberdeenshire, 14th March 1893. Educated at Rayne North Public School and Robert Gordon's College, Aberdeen. Joined 4th/7th Gordon Highlanders in 1910. Private in U Company, 1911. Graduated M.A. from Aberdeen University, 1914. Mobilized, August 1914, at which point Fraser held the rank of Colour Sergeant, a role which he described as *'one of the 'plums'*. Commissioned in August 1915; attached to 2nd Argyll and Sutherland Highlanders. Suffered a severe leg wound on 25th September 1915 at Loos. After a period of recuperation he re-joined the 3rd Battalion; administrative duties, S.O. training, August 1916-January 1917; Signal Officer, February 1917-Summer 1918. Served - France, February 1915 - October 1915; UK, August 1916 - October 1917; Ireland, November 1917 - Summer 1918. Final rank: Lieutenant. Graduated M.B., Ch.B. from Aberdeen University in 1922. Entered General Practice in Aberdeen in 1923. Joined Aberdeen University Officers Training Corps in 1926 and	103, 129, 139, 176.

NAME	NOTES	PAGE
	was appointed Officer Commanding of the Medical Unit from 1937-1939. Also served in WWII in the RAMC at Newbattle Abbey, Dalkeith and then in India where, from 1940-1945, he held several posts, including that of Medical Specialist in charge of the Medical Division of No. 60 British General Hospital as a Lieutenant Colonel. In 1945 he was posted, with the rank of Colonel, to Copthorne Hospital, Shrewsbury. Later in 1945, he was demobilized, returning to General Practice in Aberdeen. He remained in the TA until 1951, and held the Territorial Decoration with three clasps. He retired from the NHS in 1962 and from private practice in 1967. 'Dr Jimmy', as he was widely known, was persuaded by his family to record some of his reminiscences, a task that, sadly, was not completed before his death in 1979, aged 86. His family, however, had the available material transcribed and published the very enjoyable and interesting book - *'Dr Jimmy'* (Aberdeen University Press, 1980)	
FRENCH, Sir John	Field Marshal. Commander-in-Chief, British Expeditionary Force, until replaced by Haig after the Battle of Loos. French was reluctant to attack at Loos, aware that his supplies of artillery shells were inadequate for an effective pre-assault barrage. Pressure from France's commanders, Lord Kitchener and his own career aspirations overcame his reservations. The subsequent attack was deemed a	152, 213, Annex C.

259

NAME	NOTES	PAGE
	failure; under pressure he resigned and became Commander-in-Chief of Home Forces. After the War, French became President of the "Ypres League", a society for Veterans who served in the Ypres Salient. Awarded the Earldom of Ypres, 1922.	
GIBBON, Charles W	Second Lieutenant, 4th Gordons. Promoted to Lieutenant with effect from 19th June 1915 and to Captain on 26th September 1915.	140, 190.
GORDON, Charles James Donald Simpson	Son of Robert Gordon, farmer; born at Pitkerry, Fearn, Ross-shire, 29th January 1896. Tain Academy; matriculated in Medicine, Aberdeen University; joined U Company 1913. Went to Belgium, February 1915; wounded at Hooge on 23rd September 1915. After recuperation and further training in Ripon he returned to the front. During the heavy fighting round High Wood in the summer of 1916, he voluntarily attempted to get information about the enemy trenches and was reported missing on 23rd July 1916, aged 20, and later presumed killed. His C.O. wrote of him: "*He died the death of a hero. He 'played the game' in everything and finished with a stainless character.*" **Burial Details**: Buried at the Caterpillar Valley Cemetery, Longueval, Somme, France. Grave reference Plot 16, Row F, Grave 32.	Annex C.
GORDON, Robert Patrick	Son of James A. Gordon, farmer. Born at Kennethmont, 5th August 1895. Attended The Gordon Schools in Huntly. Matriculated in Arts at	136, 138, 147.

NAME	NOTES	PAGE
(Detail from school's memorial window.) **Burial Details:** Named on the Menin Gate Memorial, Ypres, Belgium. Panel 38	Aberdeen University in 1912, and joined U Company that year, where he *"applied himself to his training with such zeal and interest that he soon gained the complete N.C.O.'s Proficiency Certificate"*. After mobilization he trained in Bedford, arriving in France in February 1915. He was killed in action in the assault on the German lines in a wood near Hooge on 19th June 1915, aged 19.	
GOW, John	Born in Glasgow, 17th April 1890. M.A. at Aberdeen University, 1913. Private, 2nd/4th Gordon Highlanders, 1914. Wounded at Hooge on 25th September 1915. Teacher and Principal Teacher of Maths, Kirkwall Grammar School 1914-1951 (with break for military service).	190, 194, 204, Annex C.
GRASSICK, William James	Son of Charles Grassick; born in Aberdeen, 30th March 1892. Enlisted as Private, 4th Gordons, 30th October 1914; commissioned, 3rd Gordons, October 1917; attached to 2nd King's Liverpool Regiment. Served - France 1915-17; India, 1918-19. Final rank: Lieutenant. Listed in the Robert Gordon's College Former Pupils' Magazine Roll of Honour in August 1915. Graduated M.A. from Aberdeen University, 1919.	48, 62.

NAME	NOTES	PAGE
GRAY, Walter (Wattie)	Son of William Gray of 'Hazelwood', Queen Street, Huntly, Aberdeenshire. A former pupil of The Gordons Schools, Huntly. L/Cpl. 10709, H Company $1^{st}/6^{th}$ Gordons. (6th Battalion was Donside and Banff (TF) Battalion, recruiting in Huntly, Keith, Banff, etc.) Died 26th February 1915. Although not a member of U Company, Rule would have known Gray from his Huntly days. **WALTER GRAY** (Detail from school's memorial window.) **Burial Details:** Rue Petillon Military Cemetery, Fleurbaix, Pas de Calais, France. Grave reference I.D.36.	30.
GUNN, Alexander James (Sandy)	Son of Alexander Gunn, J.P., Achalone, Halkirk, Caithness; born at Halkirk, 5th February 1895. He matriculated in Medicine at Aberdeen University in October 1913, and in University Class Lists was invariably well placed. As a schoolboy he had become a Territorial, joining the 5th Seaforth Highlanders, and, on entering the University, transferred to U Company. Went to Flanders in February 1915 where he was recommended for decoration for bravery in the field on 16th June 1915. In the Hooge offensive he was seriously wounded but made a good recovery. Posted to France in June 1916, just in time for the Somme offensive. He was reported wounded and missing after a night attack on High Wood on 22nd July 1916, and	17, 106, 124, 140, 142, 154, 162, 184, 192, 194, 208, 230, Annex C.

NAME	NOTES	PAGE
	thereafter it was concluded that he was "killed in action", aged 21, on that date. Final rank: Lance Sergeant. **Burial Details:** Serre Road Cemetery No. 2. Grave Reference Section V Row F Grave 10.	
HAIG, Douglas (1st Earl Haig) 	At the start of the war in August 1914, Haig (at that time a Lieutenant General) helped plan for and organize the British Expeditionary Force (BEF), commanded by Field Marshal Sir John French. Haig initially commanded I Corps, which was heavily involved in the fighting withdrawal, in the face of vastly superior German numbers, that took place at the end of August 1914. Haig's I Corps was then ordered North in the 'race to the sea', the move, by both sides in the conflict, to secure access to the North Sea ports. This became the First Battle of Ypres, a success for the Allies. Haig's part in this, linked to concerns about Sir John French's health, saw Haig promoted to General on the 16th November 1914. In September 1915, the unsuccessful Battle of Loos (and the subsidiary action at Hooge) became sources of much criticism that compounded pressure on Sir John French, ultimately leading to his removal. This was followed by Haig's appointment as Commander-in-Chief of the British Expeditionary Force. (**His admission to the ancient Society of Good Johns, as explained in Annex C, was one of the most closely guarded secrets of the war**	93, Annex C.

263

NAME	NOTES	PAGE
	and has never before been included **in the long list of honours rightfully bestowed upon him – so secret, in fact, that he was probably not aware of it…**) On 1st January 1917, Haig was made a Field Marshal and, despite the considerable discord developing between him, politicians and the French, he remained in command until the ceasefire came into effect at 11am on the 11th day of the 11th month in 1918. After the end of the war Douglas Haig was created 1st Earl Haig and he left the army in January 1920. He spent much of the following years, as well as pursuing a wide range of non-military interests, working for the welfare of ex-servicemen. He persuaded various organisations to merge into the Royal British Legion in 1921 and set up the Haig Fund, which provides financial assistance to ex-service men and women. Died in 1928 aged 66.	
HAIG, William Stephen	Son of William Haig, permanent way inspector. Born in Lonmay, 6th November 1892; educated at Robert Gordon's College, Aberdeen, where he was a member of the original Robert Gordon's College section of the 4th Gordons, enlisting in 1910. He matriculated in Arts at Aberdeen University in 1911; graduated M.A. in 1914. On entering the University he transferred to U Company. After training at Bedford, he went abroad with his unit. He served with the 4th Battalion until 25th September 1915 when he was reported missing, and	106, Annex C.

NAME	NOTES	PAGE
	later was presumed killed on that date at Hooge, aged 22. Final rank: Corporal. Listed in the Robert Gordon's College Former Pupils' Magazine Roll of Honour in August 1915. **Burial Details:** Menin Gate Memorial, Ypres, Panel 38, Column 5.	
HALDANE, Sir James Aylmer Lowthorpe	General. Born on 17th November 1862 at Gleneagles, Perthshire. Commissioned into the Gordon Highlanders in 1882. He fought in the Second Boer War and was captured at about the same time as Winston Churchill. Haldane planned the escape that made Churchill famous, but failed to escape at the same time. His view was that Churchill might have had more consideration for his fellow prisoners, but he managed to make his own escape a short while later. Haldane earned some quite rapid promotions – Lieutenant to Captain in 1901, Captain to Major and Major to brevet (a former type of promotion often made for outstanding service - an officer was promoted to a higher rank without a corresponding rise in pay) Lieutenant Colonel in 1902; from brevet Lieutenant Colonel to brevet Colonel then to substantive Colonel all in 1906; from Colonel to temporary Brigadier General in 1909. Haldane fought in WWI, firstly as General Officer Commanding (GOC) 3rd Division and subsequently as commander of VI Corps with the rank of Lieutenant General. After the war, he was appointed as GOC	140, 206.

NAME	NOTES	PAGE
	Mesopotamia from 1922-1925 and retired in 1927. Died in London in 1950 aged 88.	
HAWES, Arthur Joseph	Son of William A. Hawes; born in Aberdeen, 9th May 1894. Joined U Company in 1911. Mobilized, 1914. Served - France, February-May 1915. Left Belgium in May 1915 to return to Aberdeen to complete his medical studies. Graduated M.B. Ch.B. at Aberdeen University, 1916. Was commissioned into the R.A.M.C. in June 1916; attached 1st Royal Irish Rifles in France, June 1916-October 1917. King George Hospital, Poona; 99 Squadron. R.A.F. India, October 1917-1919. Final rank: Captain. Awarded the M.C. 1917. Mentioned in Despatches, 1917. Went into General Practice in Cambridge, Norfolk and London. Died in 1974 aged 80.	40, 70.
HAY, George Robert	Born in Peterhead on 1st August 1892. Enlisted as a private, 4th Gordons, 24th October 1914; transferred to the Royal Engineers; commissioned, September 1917. Served - Home, 1914-15; France, Flanders, June 1915-March 1919; Germany, April-October 1919. Final rank: Acting Captain. Mentioned in Despatches, 1918. Graduated M.A. from Aberdeen University, 1919.	174, 208.
HENDERSON-BEGG, John	Son of Sherriff John Henderson-Begg; born in Greenock on 19th October 1890 and attended Greenock Academy. He later lived at 15 Albert Terrace, Aberdeen and attended	64, 78, 80, 104, 106,

NAME	NOTES	PAGE
	Aberdeen Grammar School and Robert Gordon's College. From there, he entered the Glasgow Technical College, later securing an appointment with the Luther Engineering Co., London, at their agency in Russia. He was commissioned into 4th Gordons in 1910, but resigned his commission when he went to Russia. On the outbreak of war, he returned to Aberdeen and was gazetted Lieutenant, 4th Gordons, on 12th September 1914. He went with his unit to Belgium in February 1915. He was killed on 23rd July 1916, aged 25. **Burial Details**: Bucquoy Road Cemetery, Ficheux, France. Grave Reference I.L.4	152.
HENDERSON, Alexander Rennie (Henny)	Lieutenant. Son of Alexander R. Henderson, teacher. Born in Aberdeen, 8th November 1888; educated Robert Gordon's College; graduated M.A. from Aberdeen University, 1911. After graduation he was appointed a teacher at Aboyne Higher Grade School. Henderson joined U Company in 1907 and became Colour-Sergeant in 1910. He resigned in 1912 but volunteered on the outbreak of war and in September 1914 was gazetted to the 4th Gordons with whom he went to France in February 1915. He led his platoon into action at Hooge on 25th September 1915 and had reached the third line of German trenches when he was wounded. He was later reported wounded and missing on	58, 190, 216, 217.

NAME	NOTES	PAGE
	that date, aged 26. His Commanding Officer wrote; "*The courage and pluck shown by him and his men that day are beyond words of mine.*" Listed in the Robert Gordon's College Former Pupils' Magazine Roll of Honour in August 1915. **Burial Details**: Name recorded on the Menin Gate Memorial, Ypres, Panel 38, Column 3.	
HENDERSON, George Andrew Falconer	Son of Rev. Richard Henderson, Longside, Aberdeenshire; born at Manse of Maryton, Forfarshire, 19th March 1895; educated at the Public School Longside, then Peterhead Academy, followed by Robert Gordon's College. He entered Aberdeen University in 1913 and joined U Company. On the outbreak of war he volunteered for foreign service, but owing to ill-health he was unable, to his great regret, to proceed with his Company to France. In August 1915 he was commissioned to the 3rd Gordons and, in July 1916, was attached to the 2nd Battalion. With this Battalion he served in France until November 1917, when he was transferred to the Royal Flying Corps. In February 1918 Henderson graduated as Pilot, and thereafter was appointed Flying Instructor. He received a commission in the Royal Air Force and attained the rank of Flight-Lieutenant. While acting as Flying Instructor he received fatal injuries in an aeroplane collision on 2nd July 1918. He died in the Military Hospital, Grantham, on	174.

NAME	NOTES	PAGE
	4th July 1918, aged 23. Listed in the Robert Gordon's College Former Pupils' Magazine Roll of Honour in August 1915. **Burial Details**: Buried at Longside New Parish Churchyard, Aberdeenshire, Grave 508.	
HOPKINSON, Andrew Douglas	Son of James Hopkinson; born in St. Leonards-on-Sea, 30th November 1888. Graduated B.Sc. (Agr.) from Aberdeen University, 1911. Private, U Company in 1911. Commissioned, 4th Gordon Highlanders, August 1914. Served - Home, 1914-15, 1915-17; France, February - June 1915, July 1917 - January 1919. Final rank: Captain. Lecturer at the Royal Agricultural College, Cirencester. Forestry Commission from 1919. Awarded O.B.E. Died in 1969 aged 80.	120, 176.
HOPKINSON, James Garland (Hoppy)	Captain, 4th Gordons. Replaced Lachlan (Lachie) McKinnon as C.O., D Company, June 1915. Well liked and respected by his men. Killed at Hooge early on the morning of 25th September 1915 after reporting good progress and the capture of a German field gun. **Burial Details**: Name inscribed on the Menin Gate Memorial, Ypres, Panel 38.	48,176, 180, 190, 194, 198, 204, 216, 217, Annex C.
INKSTER, Walter (Wattie)	Son of James Inkster, shipmaster. Born in Aberdeen, 27th February 1890; educated at Ashley Road School and Aberdeen Grammar School. In 1908 he matriculated at Aberdeen University and graduated M.A., 1911 and B.Sc. (Agr.) 1912, after which he went to work for the	140, 144, 186, 192, 196, 202, 217, Annex

269

NAME	NOTES	PAGE
	Potash Syndicate in Germany. In December 1913 he accepted an appointment in Australia and the outbreak of war found him beginning his career there. By 8th March 1915 he was back in Scotland and a Private in the 4th Gordons; in April he received a commission in the same Battalion and in May crossed to France. A few months later he came home on leave, but a week after rejoining his Battalion, he was killed at Hooge on 25th September 1915. At first reported "wounded and missing", it became obvious that he had died of wounds received in action on or about the 25th, aged 25. Final rank: 2Lt. **Burial Details**: Name recorded on the Menin Gate Memorial, Ypres, Panel 38.	C.
INNES, Joe	There is no mention of this name on the Aberdeen University 'In Memoriam' website, nor in John McConachie's book '*The Student Soldiers*'. The Commonwealth War Graves Commission offers a choice of candidates, but there is insufficient evidence to say which of these is the correct Innes if, indeed, he is any of them.	128, 132, 180.
JOHNSTONE, Henry Watt (Lairdie)	Son of James Johnston; born in Aberdeen. Graduated M.A. at Aberdeen University, 1911. Enlisted in U Company in 1909. Wounded 24th April 1915. Commissioned, 4th Gordons, August 1915; attached to C Company 3rd Battalion Tank Corps, 22nd Light Battalion Tank Corps.	74.

NAME	NOTES	PAGE
	Served - France, March-April 1915; Home, 1915-16; France, 1917-September 1918; Home, 1918-19. Final rank: Acting Major. Awarded the Military Cross, February 1918. Head of Modern Languages at Alloa Academy 1924-1944. Headmaster of Clackmannan School until 1955. WWII Colonel Commanding Army Cadet Force. Died in 1974 aged 83.	
KENNEDY, William Robert	Son of Dr. John R. Kennedy; Born at Carradale, Argyllshire, 8th March 1896; educated at Dunbeath Public School, Tain Royal Academy, and Wick High School. Matriculated in Medicine at Aberdeen University in the summer session of 1914 and enlisted at once in U Company. He was mobilized on 4th August 1914, immediately volunteering for foreign service, and left Bedford with the Battalion for France in February 1915. Whilst there he displayed such conspicuous bravery in carrying dispatches across a shell-swept zone, that he was complimented by the Major-General commanding the third Division (Haldane) for his distinguished conduct in the field, was recommended for the D.C.M., and singled out for promotion. After a course of training at St. Omer he was gazetted to the 2nd Argyll and Sutherland Highlanders in August 1915, and was serving with them as a 2nd Lieutenant when he was killed in action leading his men at the Battle of Loos on 25th September 1915, aged 19. **Burial Details**: Buried at	17, 176.

NAME	NOTES	PAGE
	Cambrin Churchyard Extension, Pas de Calais, France. Grave reference Plot 1, Row B, Grave 20.	
KITCHENER, Horatio Herbert	Field Marshal, 1st Earl Kitchener. He was appointed Secretary of State for War in 1914. He spearheaded the national drive to recruit the huge additional number of soldiers needed to sustain the war, part of which was the use of his picture on recruiting posters, one of the iconic and best remembered images of World War 1. Unsurprisingly, Kitchener was a very determined individual with his own views on how the war should be waged and this led to tensions with politicians as well as army commanders. In June 1916, Kitchener set out from Scapa Flow in Orkney in HMS Hampshire on a diplomatic mission to Russia. At 7:30 pm on the 5th June, Hampshire struck a mine laid by a German U-Boat and sank west of the Orkney Isles. Kitchener and his staff were amongst more than 600 who perished. He was aged 65.	68, 118, 206, 213, 214, Annex C.
KNOWLES, John Forbes	Son of George Knowles, Aberdeen; born in Aberdeen, 26th February 1891; educated at the Grammar School; graduated MA from Aberdeen University 1912. Went to the United Free College to train for the ministry. He had been a U Company member when a student and rejoined U Company in October 1914. His health was not robust and he rejoined the unit from hospital only one day before a sniper killed	86.

272

NAME	NOTES	PAGE
	him on 5th May 1915, aged 24. (He was the first U.F. College student to join up and the first such student to be killed.) **Burial Details**: Wytschaete Military Cemetery, West-Vlaanderen, Belgium. Grave reference IV.D.1.	
KNOX, Edward Wilson (Eddie, or Knoxie)	Son of Joseph Knox; born in Aberdeen, 22nd April 1890. He studied Medicine at Aberdeen University for one year, 1910-11, then Arts from 1911-14. He joined U Company in 1911 and was mobilized in August 1914. Commissioned, 29th August 1915. Served - Home, 1914-15, 1915-16, 1917-18; Abroad, February-June 1915, October 1916-March 1917, March-August 1918. Wounded, June 1915. Final rank: Lieutenant. Returned to Aberdeen University to study medicine after the War, yet, according to McConachie's '*The Student Soldiers*', gained an M.A. there in 1925. Head of History Department at Kelso High School. Died in 1962 aged 72.	12, 20, 31, 40, 44, 56, 62, 72, 78, 92, 136, 138.
LAMB, John Gordon	Born in Peterhead, 16th July 1892. Aberdeen University M.A., 1913, B.Sc. (Agric.) 1914; Arnott Prize. Private in U Company, 1910. Mobilized, 4th August 1914. Commissioned, Meteorological Section, Royal Engineers, 9th February 1916. Served - Home, 1914-15, 1915-16; Western Front, February-October 1915, February 1916-June 1919. Mentioned in Despatches, May 1917. Final rank:	103, 106, 118, 120, 128, 174.

NAME	NOTES	PAGE
	Acting Captain. Teacher of Maths, Science and Agriculture, 1921-1937. Inspector of Schools until 1957. Died in 1978 aged 86.	
LAWSON, Donald Boyd Cameron	Son of J. C. Lawson; born at Rathen, Aberdeenshire, 7th February 1895. Matriculated in Arts at Aberdeen University, 1913-14. Joined U Company 1914; commissioned, 18th April 1915; served with 4th Cameronians, Royal Flying Corps, Royal Naval Air Service. Served - Home service, 4 years 3 months. Final rank: Captain.	80.
LESLIE, James Dawson	Born 2nd July 1894 in Macduff. Matriculated in Arts at Aberdeen University 1912-1914. Joined U Company in 1914. Served in France from February - September 1915. Wounded April 1915. Commissioned 6th Gordons 1916. Awarded M.C. 1919. Final rank: Captain.	66.
LOW, George	Son of William Low, baker. Born Dyce, Aberdeen, on 20th January 1892; educated at Robert Gordon's College; entered Aberdeen University in 1910 as Eleventh Bursar; graduated M.A. in 1914, with First Class Honours in Classics, gaining the Dr. Black Prize in Latin. At the outbreak of war he was a Sergeant in 'U' Company, and did much valuable work at Bedford as a musketry instructor. He was promoted to Company Sergeant Major shortly after the Battalion arrived in Belgium. In August 1915 he received his commission and came home for a	44, 156, 174, 176, 192, 217.

NAME	NOTES	PAGE
	short spell of leave. He was recalled to take part in the attack at Hooge, 25th September 1915, where he died aged 23. He was last seen surrounded by enemy soldiers, but kept fighting with the utmost determination until he was killed. **Burial Details**: Name recorded on the Menin Gate Memorial, Ypres, Panel 38, Column 3.	
LYON, Alexander	Officer in 4th Gordons. Captain at the outbreak of war, he was promoted to Major, then Lieutenant Colonel, replacing Tommy Ogilvie in the summer of 1915 as Commanding Officer of the 4th Battalion.	170, 176, 196, 206, 208.
MACAULAY, Alexander	Son of George Macaulay. Born in Uig, 31st July 1890. Joined the Ross Mountain Battery in 1909. Joined U Company 1911. Matriculated in Arts at Aberdeen University 1913-14. Wounded April 1915. Commissioned into 4th Seaforths 17th August 1915. Mentioned in Despatches April 1917. Awarded Military Cross May 1918. Final rank: Captain. After the war, graduated M.A. from Aberdeen University in 1922. Teacher at Cowdenbeath and St. Andrews 1923-1957. Died in 1962 aged 72.	70, 174.
MACIVER, Isaac Hunter	Son of John MacIver. Born in Lochcarron, Wester Ross on 22nd February 1893. Private in the Ross Mountain Battery in 1912. Studied science at Aberdeen University, 1913-14. Transferred to U Company August 1914. Commissioned into 4th Seaforths 12th August 1915. Served -	74, 174.

NAME	NOTES	PAGE
	France, February-May 1915; wounded; Home, August 1915-19. Mentioned in Despatches. Final rank: Captain.	
MACIVER, Murdo	Son of Alexander MacIver, fisherman. Born at Coll, Stornoway, 3rd June 1890; educated at Back Public School and The Nicolson Institute, Stornoway; student in Arts at Aberdeen University, 1911-1914, combining his attendance at the University with his training for the teaching profession, until war broke off his studies. He trained with the Ross Mountain Battery whilst at school and, on going to Aberdeen University in 1911, joined U Company. With the 4th Gordons, he went to Flanders, where his Battalion took part in the very heavy fighting near Ypres through the early months of 1915. He was killed there on 16th June 1915, aged 25. Final rank: Corporal. **Burial Details**: Buried at Birr Cross Roads Cemetery, Zillebeke, Belgium. Grave reference Plot 2, Row E, Grave 10.	106, 134.
MACKAY, Keith	Son of George M. Mackay, schoolmaster; born in Aberdeen, 3rd March 1895; educated at Robert Gordon's College, Aberdeen; student in Arts and Medicine at Aberdeen University, 1912 – 1914. Mackay joined D Company 4th Gordons while still a pupil at Robert Gordon's College, then joined U Company when he went to Aberdeen University, where he became a	30, 78.

NAME	NOTES	PAGE
	Corporal. He went to France and Belgium with the Battalion in February 1915, but was wounded in the trenches near Kemmel only a few weeks later. He died in hospital at Bailleul from the effects of the wound on 28th April 1915, aged 20. He was, most unusually, granted a posthumous M.A. by Aberdeen University. **Burial Details**: Buried at Bailleul Communal Cemetery Extension, Nord, France. Grave reference Plot 1, Row B, Grave 23.	
MACKENZIE, Murdo	Son of Roderick MacKenzie; born at Aultbea, Ross-shire, 27th August 1894. Joined U Company in 1912. Mobilized, 4th August 1914. Commissioned, 22nd October 1915. Served with 8th Cameron Highlanders, 4th Field Survey Company Royal Engineers, 1st Army Calibration Section. France, two and a half years. Final rank: Major. M.A. from Aberdeen University 1917. Awarded M.B.E. in 1918. Chairman of MacKenzie Engineering Limited, London. Died in 1959 aged 64.	124, 234.
MACKINNON, Lachlan (Lachie)	Son of Lachlan Mackinnon; born in Aberdeen, 9th September 1886. Lawyer from a long line of Aberdeen lawyers. Aberdeen University M.A., 1906; B.L. (dist.), 1908; LL.B., 1910. Enlisted in U Company, 1903 (then part of 1st Volunteer Battalion Gordon Highlanders (became 4th Gordon Highlanders (Territorial Force) 1st April 1908); commissioned on 1st August 1905. Promoted to	8, 10, 18, 26, 52, 54, 60, 70, 168, Annex C.

277

NAME	NOTES	PAGE
	Captain on 15th April 1910. (He is quoted as saying that being a private was much more fun that being the Captain.) He took over the Company from Edward Watt, who took over 4th Battalion from U Coy founder William Duncan in 1913. Mobilized, 4th August 1914. Promoted to temporary Major on 10th July 1915. Attached No. 19, Officer Cadet Battalion; Senior Officers School, Aldershot; 14th (Service) Battalion Argyll and Sutherland Highlanders. Served - Home, 1914-15, 1915, 1917-18; France, February-June 1915, September 1915-December 1916, April 1918-May 1919. Final rank: Temporary Lieutenant-Colonel. Awarded Distinguished Service Order (June 1919), Croix de Guerre. Twice Mentioned in Despatches, March 1918 and June 1919. Order of Leopold (Insignia of Chevalier) in recognition of his role as Honorary Consul of Belgium at Aberdeen, 1st March 1956. Made Commander of the British Empire (C.B.E.) in 1956. Appointed Deputy Lieutenant of the City of Aberdeen as '*Lieutenant Colonel and Brevet Colonel Lachlan Mackinnon, C.B.E., D.S.O., T.D.*' Died in 1973 aged 86.	
MACLEOD, John Angus	Son of Malcolm MacLeod; born at Barvas, Isle of Lewis, Western Isles 23rd December 1888. M.A. at Aberdeen University, 1910. Private, 4th Gordons 2nd Oct 1914. Served - Home, 1914-15; France, Belgium, February-August 1915. Wounded;	142.

NAME	NOTES	PAGE
	discharged, September 1916. Final rank: Lance Corporal. Teacher at Whithorn School 1913. History Master Ryhope Grammar School, Co Durham 1917-1950. Retired to Sutherland in 1950.	
MACRAE, Victor Charles James	Son of Donald MacRae, stationmaster; born in Inverness, 12th October 1892; educated at Plockton Higher Grade Public School, and Aberdeen Grammar School; entered Aberdeen University as Eighth Bursar in 1910, graduated M.A., 1914, with First Class Honours in Classics, a remarkable performance as, by a chain of unforeseen circumstances, he had to undertake the necessary work within one year. His Professor wrote: "*he was a strikingly able student*". While still at the Grammar School, he had joined "D" (the then School) Company of the 4th Gordons. With it he was mobilized in August 1914, and crossed to France and Belgium in 1915. A few weeks later, on 21st April 1915, aged 22, he was shot by a sniper while attempting to remove a wounded comrade from a shell hole. **Burial Details**: Buried at Wytschaete Military Cemetery, West-Vlaanderen, Belgium. Grave reference Plot 2, Row F, Grave 4.	30, 70.
MACSWEEN, George	Son of Mr. & Mrs. John MacSween, of 1, Upper Garrabost, Stornoway, Western Isles. Born near Stornoway. He was a student at Aberdeen Training Centre and joined U	134.

NAME	NOTES	PAGE
	Company in 1914. Killed in an attack on Y Wood, just north of the Menin Road, 16th June 1915, aged 23. **Burial Details**: Name recorded on Le Touret Memorial, Pas de Calais, France. Panel 39-41.	
MACTAVISH, Roderick M (Rorie)	Son of William T. MacTavish; born in Tain, Ross-shire, 29th April 1892. Studied Medicine at Aberdeen University, 1911-13. Joined U Company in 1911. Mobilized, August 1914. Wounded and discharged as unfit, September 1915. Rejoined, Royal Army Service Corps, April 1916. Served - France, Belgium, 6 months. Final rank: Sergeant-Major.	174.
MASON, John Hampton Strachan	Son of John Mason, painter. Born in Aberdeen, 17th December 1891; educated at Robert Gordon's College. He entered Aberdeen University in 1909; graduated M.A. (Hons. Eng.), 1913, and in the same year secured a literary post in London. As an undergraduate at Aberdeen he was editor of "Alma Mater" (1911-12), and later president of the Literary Society. He joined U Company in 1914 and, after training in Bedford, he crossed to France with the 4th Gordons in February 1915. He was killed on 25th September 1915 at Hooge, aged 22. Final rank: Private. **Burial Details**: Name recorded on the Menin Gate Memorial, Ypres, Panel 38, Column 8.	170, 184, 188, 194, Annex C.
MCLAGGAN, John Douglas	Sergeant. Son of James McLaggan; born at Kincardine O'Neil, Aberdeenshire, 18th June 1893.	70, 72, 90,

NAME	NOTES	PAGE
	Graduated from Aberdeen University M.A., 1914; Lance Corporal, U Company, 1914 and mobilized in August of that year. Wounded at Hooge 25th September 1915. Commissioned 4th Gordons 1916. Graduated M.B. Ch.B. (dist.) from Aberdeen University in 1920. FRCS (Edin.) 1924. F.R.C.S. 1926. Member of Staff Royal Free Hospital 1931-1958. Aural Surgeon to four generations of the Royal Family. Awarded C.V.O. 1950, K.C.V.O. 1958. Capped for Scotland at hockey. Died in 1967 aged 73.	154.
MCLEAN, Colin	Lieutenant Colonel. Son of Neil McLean, of Breda, Aberdeenshire. Commanding Officer of 6th Gordons. Killed at Neuve Chapelle on 13th March 1915.	50.
MCLEAN, Douglas Gordon	Son of William G. G. McLean; born in Boddam, Aberdeenshire, 19th December 1893. M.A. at Aberdeen University, 1920. Private in U Company, 1912. Mobilized August 1914. Returned to the front 17th June 1915 having been hospitalised, only to be wounded again two days later. Commissioned, 6th Gordons, August 1915. Served - Home, France, 1915-19. Final rank: Captain. Parish minister of Innellan (near Dunoon) 1928 and Earlston (Berwick) 1953. Author *'History of Fordyce Academy'*. Died in 1985 aged 91.	136, 138, 174.
MCLELLAN, Duncan Tait Hutchinson	Son of Robert McLellan; born in Brechin, 29th November 1893. Enlisted in U Company, 1912.	54, 58, 138,

NAME	NOTES	PAGE
(Sunny Jim)	Wounded 3rd June 1915; again at Hooge, 25th September 1915. M.A., Aberdeen University, 1916 whilst unfit to serve. Commissioned into 5th Seaforth Highlanders, January 1917. Served - France, February-September 1915; German East Africa, April 1917-May 1918. Discharged as medically unfit, March 1919. Final rank: Lieutenant. Graduated M.A. (Hons.) from Aberdeen University in 1919. Professor of Church History, Calcutta, 1920. Part of an Afridi Expedition for which he earned an Indian Frontier Medal. Author of *'A Short History of The Royal Scots'*. Minister at Boar's Hill, Oxford. Died in 1957 aged 63.	164, 194, 196, Annex C.
MCLEOD, M	No mention with this spelling in *'The Student Soldiers'* or in the University of Aberdeen Roll of Honour. Most likely to be MACLEOD, Malcolm; son of Kenneth MacLeod; born in Uig, Ross-shire, 15th August 1877. Graduated M.A. from Aberdeen University, 1900. Private in U Company, 1914 and mobilized in that year; commissioned into the R.A.M.C. in 1916.	106
MCLINTOCK, Stanley Robert (Sam)	Captain, Adjutant 4th Gordons. Promoted to Brevet Major, then to Lieutenant Colonel in July 1916. Awarded a DSO in June 1917 and a bar to his DSO in July 1918. He was further promoted to Colonel.	146, 150, 158, 170, Annex C.
MIDDLETON, Robert Hugh	Son of David Middleton. Born in Liverpool, 5th December 1892; educated at Robert Gordon's College,	4, 44, 78,

NAME	NOTES	PAGE
	Aberdeen; matriculated in Arts at Aberdeen University, 1912. He was a frequent contributor of prose and verse to 'Alma Mater'. Joined U Company in 1913, trained with them at Bedford and served with his unit in Flanders, till he was killed in action at Hooge, 1st June 1915, aged 22. **Burial Details**: Name recorded on the Menin Gate Memorial, Ypres, Panel 38, Column 8.	122, 132.
MILNE, John (Jock)	Son of Alexander Milne; born Turriff, Aberdeenshire, 24th February 1895. Joined U Company, January 1914. Mobilized, 5 August 1914. Attached 6th Yorkshire; transferred to Royal Army Service Corps, Served - Home, 1914-15, 1918-19; France, February 1915-January 1918. Final rank: Corporal. Awarded Military Medal, December 1917. Graduated M.A., 1919, B.Sc. (Agr.) 1921, from Aberdeen University. Emigrated to farm in New Zealand.	154.
MIRRLEES, Stewart Turnbull Alexander	Born in Lonmay, Aberdeenshire, on 22nd February 1892. Joined U Company, 23rd April 1912. Graduated M.A. from Aberdeen University 1914. Mobilized, August 1914. Wounded 30th May 1915. Transferred to Royal Engineers, Meteorology Section; commissioned, 26th July 1918. Served - Home, 2 years 2 months; France, 3 years. Final rank: Second Lieutenant. After the war was Principal Scientific Officer in the Air Ministry 1920-1953. Died in 1970 aged 78.	64, 70, 106, 120.

NAME	NOTES	PAGE
MITCHELL, Alexander	Son of the late Gilbert Mitchell and of Mrs Mitchell, Westburn Drive, Aberdeen. Born in Aberdeen, on 5th February 1890. Schooled at Robert Gordon's College, Aberdeen. Matriculated in Arts in 1912 at Aberdeen University. He was nearly finished his university course with a view to entering the teaching profession, when war was declared. He promptly volunteered, and left for Bedford with the 4th Gordons. He was sent out to France, then on to Belgium. Whilst digging a communication trench near Kemmel, he was hit by a stray bullet. He died from his wound on the following day – 28th April 1915, aged 25 - in a Field Hospital. Condolences were sent to his mother in a letter sent by Sergeant Dan Walker, his "Platoon Officer". **Burial Details**: Buried at La Clytte Military Cemetery, Reninghelst, Belgium. Grave reference Plot 1, Row C, Grave 8.	78.
MURRAY, Herbert (Bert)	Son of Peter Murray, builder; born at Newhills in Aberdeenshire, on 11th December 1885; educated at Robert Gordon's College, Aberdeen. Graduated M.A. from Aberdeen University in 1908, and joined the teaching staff of Robert Gordon's College. He was a member of U Company from 1906-1908 and rejoined in 1914. Early in 1915 he enlisted in the 4th Gordons and, after a short spell of training, was sent out to France. He was severely wounded on 16th June 1915 and sent to hospital	64, 120.

284

NAME	NOTES	PAGE
	in England. In August of the same year he received his commission, and spent about eight months as a musketry instructor at home. In April 1917 he was again at the Front. For his brilliant and courageous actions during March 1918, he was awarded the Military Cross. On 20th July 1918 he was killed, aged 32, at the Bois de Courton north of Epernay. Final rank: Captain. **Burial Details**: Buried at Marfaux British Cemetery, Marne, France. Grave reference Plot 1, Row B, Grave 7.	
MURRAY, Murdo	Son of Roderick Murray; born in Stornoway, 2nd March 1890. M.A. at Aberdeen University, 1913. Joined North Scottish Royal Garrison Artillery; transferred to U Company, 1909. Mobilized, August 1914. Commissioned into 4th Seaforth Highlanders, 18th December 1915. Served - Home, 1914-15; Belgium, February-September 1915; France, Belgium, April-August 1917. Wounded three times. Final rank: Lieutenant. HM Inspector of Schools at Edinburgh, Aberdeen, Inverness, and Ross-shire 1928-1954. Died in 1964 aged 74.	142.
NIVEN	There is only one mention of 'Niven' in Rule's diary. He does not appear in McConachie's '*The Student Soldiers*' nor in the Aberdeen University Roll of Honour. However, he is likely to be Private Alan Niven of Aberdeen. In the Aberdeen Weekly Journal's notes on war wounded, of 4th June	120.

NAME	NOTES	PAGE
	1915, it states, *"News has been received that Pte Alan G Niven of the $1^{st}/4^{th}$ Gordon Highlanders, has been wounded in Flanders. He was a member of the 4th Gordons as a Territorial, and up to the outbreak of war was employed in the office of Messrs. James Meston and Company, chartered accountant, Golden Square, Aberdeen."* Later, the Aberdeen Journal of 25th June 1915 reported the wounding of a now L/Cpl A G Niven (1740) of 4th Gordons. Alan Niven was commissioned in August 1915 at the same time as Eddie Knox. By December 1917 he was promoted to Lieutenant and the London Gazette shows him relinquishing his commission in December 1921.	
OGILVIE, Thomas (Tommy)	Lieutenant Colonel Thomas Ogilvie, Commanding Officer of the 4th Gordons for much of 1915, was a former pupil of Aberdeen Grammar School. Tommy (as he was usually known) joined the 4th Battalion as a Second Lieutenant in 1899 and began the First World War as a Major with that unit. One of his roles as a former pupil of Aberdeen Grammar School was to recruit senior pupils into the school's own detachment of the Gordons - D Company, 4th Gordons (Territorial Force). He attended the pre-war camp at Tain – the last camp of U Company - in the summer of 1914. The Commanding Officer of the 4th Battalion at the time was Lt Col DBD Stewart and, when he	72, 84, 92, 100, 132, 136, 139, 192, 229.

NAME	NOTES	PAGE
	relinquished command in November 1914, Tommy was promoted to Lieutenant Colonel in charge of the Battalion. In his book '*The Grammar At War, 1914-1918*', Richard Lewis Campbell Dargie tells us, "*He served in Britain and Belgium until 1916, when his talents brought promotion to the key post of Administrative Commandant of the 6th Army Railhead. Responsible for organisation of all railheads in sectors occupied by the 4th & 5th Armies until February 1918, when he was appointed 4th Army labour commandant. Colonel Ogilvie was awarded the C.M.G. in 1915, the C.B. in 1919 and was mentioned five times in despatches.*" Tommy was promoted to Colonel in November 1918. He served as a J.P. and was a Deputy Lieutenant. He died at home at Fernbank, Banchory, on 17th April 1944, aged 72.	
PATERSON, John McLellan Stewart	Son of the Reverend Robert and Mrs. Paterson, of "Thornwood," Lenzie Road, Stepps, Glasgow. He was born in Savoch in Aberdeenshire on 13th December 1890. Graduated M.A. (Hons) from Edinburgh University. Jimmy Fraser recounts in his diary that Paterson had been a pupil at Robert Gordon's College and joined U Company so he could serve with his old pals. Killed near Ypres 22nd April 1915, aged 24. **Burial Details**: Wytschaete Military Cemetery, West-Vlaanderen, Belgium. Special Memorial B.5.	72.

NAME	NOTES	PAGE
PETERKIN, James Harold Stuart (Pete)	Son of John Peterkin; born in Portsoy, Aberdeenshire, on 3rd March 1895. Studied Arts at Aberdeen University, 1913-14. Enlisted as a Private in U Company in 1913. Mobilized, 4th August 1914; commissioned, D Company, 15th Battalion Machine Gun Corps, 25th October 1916. Served - Home, 1914-15, 1916-17; France, February 1915-August 1916, June 1917-February 1919. Final rank: Lieutenant. Awarded the Military Cross in March 1918. Graduated M.A. in 1920 and M.B. Ch.B. in 1924. Was in General Practice in Hornsea in Yorkshire. Died in 1960 aged 65.	24, 42, 52, 82, 108, 122, 132, 140, 148, 154, 170, 202, 217, Annex C.
PLUMER, Herbert Charles Onslow	General. Born in Torquay in 1857. Educated at Eton and the Royal Military Academy, Sandhurst. Commissioned into the 65th Regiment of Foot as a Lieutenant in 1876. Promoted Captain 1882; Major 1893; Lieutenant Colonel 1900; Major General 1902; Lieutenant General in 1908. Plumer commanded V Corps at the Second Battle of Ypres in April 1915. He was made Commander of the Second Army in May 1915 and was promoted to full General in June 1915. He won a famous victory over the Germans at the Battle of Messines in June 1917, which started with the near simultaneous explosion of nineteen mines under German defensive positions, the sound from which was said to have been heard in London. He was promoted to Field Marshal in 1919, the same year in which he was	186, 192.

NAME	NOTES	PAGE
	created Baron Plumer of Messines and of Bilton. It has been said he was one of the few WWI generals who came through the conflict with his reputation enhanced. In 1927 he conducted the inauguration ceremony for the Menin Gate Memorial at Ypres. In 1929 he was created Viscount Plumer for his "long and distinguished public services". He died in 1932, aged 75, and was buried in Westminster Abbey.	
PRATT, James D	Born in Drumoak on 13th August 1891. Graduated M.A. (Hons.) in 1912 and B.Sc. (Hons.) in 1913 from Aberdeen University, where he subsequently became an assistant lecturer in Chemistry. Joined U Company in 1908 and became Company Sergeant Major. Mobilised in 1914 and went, via Bedford, to France and Belgium with D Company, 4th Gordons in 1915. He was commissioned on 18th March 1915 as Second Lieutenant. He was wounded three times in 1915. The Aberdeen Journal of the 4th of September 1915, announcing his promotion to Lieutenant, noted that he belonged to Glenbervie and that he was wounded in Flanders on the 16th of June. Another of his woundings was reported in the Aberdeen Journal of 23rd September 1915. Ended up in Ministry of Munitions as Staff Captain. Awarded O.B.E. in June 1919. He was chairman of the British Road Tar Association for 30 years and was Secretary and a Director of	5, 24, 44, 52, 60, 76, 122, 126, 130, 134, 140, 144, 158, 168, 176, 182, 190, 198, Annex C.

NAME	NOTES	PAGE
	the Association of British Chemical Manufacturers. He served as Controller of the Chemical Defence Board in the Second World War, for which service he was awarded a C.B.E. In later life, he was interviewed by the Imperial War Museum, which has made available on its website six audiotapes from these interviews. These cover pre-war U Company life, mobilisation, training at Bedford, deployment to France and Belgium, life in the trenches, casualties and much more. Died in 1978 aged 86.	
REID, Charles	Captain. Son of Walter A Reid; born Aberdeen 16th December 1889. Enlisted in U Company 1907. Graduated M.A. from Aberdeen University 1909. Commissioned into 4th Gordons, 1909. The Aberdeen Weekly Journal of October 1915 reports, "*Captain Charles Reid of Aberdeen, who has been severely wounded on the right arm and chest, is a son of Walter A Reid, C.A., Aberdeen, and has three brothers on active service. His father left for the south on Monday and Mrs Reid, on receipt of the information, left to join her husband with the intention of proceeding to France to visit their son.*" Captain Reid's commanding officer, Lieutenant Colonel Lyon, wrote to Walter Reid about his son, "*I am sorry to have to write you to say that Charlie has been wounded…… Charlie, with his men, had been instructed to capture portions of the*	192, 217.

NAME	NOTES	PAGE
	enemy trenches, when he was shot in the chest by a German officer with a revolver. Charlie's servant, McLean, at once killed this man and carried Charlie back to our trenches, where he received immediate treatment from our medical officer, Dr Hughes. I saw and spoke to Charlie when he was brought in and admired the pluck and endurance he was displaying. I need not hide from you the fact that his wound is very serious, as a bullet penetrated the lung, but I am very hopeful that, with his splendid strength, he will in time recover from his injury." (Private Duncan McLean was awarded the Distinguished Conduct Medal for his bravery that day.) The Aberdeen Journal of 18th December 1915 reports that, *"Captain Charles Reid, of the 4th Gordon Highlanders, who was severely wounded at the advance at Loos, is at home on sick leave to recuperate after being in hospital in the south of England."* The Aberdeen Journal of 28th July 1916 reports the now Major Charles Reid being injured again a few days previously with shrapnel wounds to the leg, but reassures readers that Major Reid treats the injury lightly and 'is quite comfortable'. He recovered and married Marjorie Mellor in London in January 1918 but, for a third time, on 27th April 1918, the Journal announces that Major Reid has been 'severely wounded'. By 24th October 1918, he was well enough to receive	

NAME	NOTES	PAGE
	his D.S.O. from King George V. Mentioned in Despatches, once in 1917 and twice in 1918.	
REID, Charles (Charlie)	Son of Charles Reid; born in Cove, Kincardineshire, on 9th May 1892. Served in U Company from 1912-1914. Graduated from Aberdeen University, M.A. 1914; B.Sc. (with special distinction), 1916; M.B. Ch.B. (Honours), 1917. Served with Aberdeen University O.T.C. Commissioned as a Lieutenant, Royal Army Medical Corps, August 1917. Served - Home, 1917; France, September 1917 - November 1919. Final rank: Captain. D.Ph. (Cantab) 1921. M.D. (Hons) 1926. D.Sc. 1927. Professor of Physiology, India, 1929-1932. Reader in Physiology at London University 1936-1948. World Health Organisation Professor of Physiology in Karachi, 1952-1957. Died in 1961 aged 69.	4, 17, 132, 194, 198, Annex C.
REID, George (Joe)	Son of George Reid, who was a timber merchant; born in Banff, 3rd June 1891; educated at Banff and Fordyce Academies; entered Aberdeen University in 1910; student in Arts, 1910-12, student in Medicine, 1912-14. He joined U Company in 1910, and was mobilized in August 1914. He went to France and then Belgium in February 1915; twice wounded, first in April 1915 at Hill 60 whilst bringing in a wounded comrade after Victor MacRae had been killed in the attempt, and again at Hooge, 25th September 1915. On	70, 172, 176, 208.

NAME	NOTES	PAGE
	his return to the Battalion he acted as Medical Orderly until gazetted to the 6th Gordons (he was a Banff man), on 22nd February 1917. His career as an officer was very brief, for he was killed in action at Arras, 9th April 1917 aged 25. Final rank: Second Lieutenant. **Burial Details:** Roclincourt Military Cemetery, Pas de Calais, France. Grave Reference I.B.3	
RENNIE, Hugh	Company Sergeant Major (C.S.M.), D Company, 4th Gordons. Became Regimental Sergeant Major (R.S.M.) of the Gordon Highlanders in 1920, the most senior Warrant Officer in the regiment.	178, 190.
ROBERTS, Lord (Frederick Sleigh)	Field Marshal Earl 'Bobs' Roberts. One of the most successful commanders of the 19th Century. He served in the Indian Rebellion, the Expedition to Abyssinia and the Second Anglo-Afghan War before leading the British forces to victory in the Second Boer War. Died 14th November 1914 aged 82 at St Omer whilst visiting Indian troops.	16.
ROSE, Frederick Alexander	Son of Hugh Rose, builder. Born in Huntly, 18th September 1890; educated at The Gordon Schools, Huntly; entered Aberdeen University in 1907 as Second Bursar. Graduated M.A., 1911 (with a First in English). After a short spell as an English assistant, he entered Christ Church, Oxford, in 1911, winning the Douglas Jerrold Scholarship. There, he won the Charles Oldham	140, 166.

NAME	NOTES	PAGE
	University Scholarship for a paper on Shakespeare. He graduated at Oxford with First Class Honours in 1913. He gained a post-graduate Scholarship and was beginning to prepare a thesis on Fulke Greville, Lord Brooke, when war broke out. Rose at once joined the Officers Training Corps and was soon gazetted to the 3rd Gordons. In the early Summer of 1915 he joined the 4th Gordons in France. On 10th August 1915, as the line was being heavily shelled and he was steadying and encouraging his men, he was struck and killed by a bursting shell. He was aged 24. **Burial details:** Chester Farm Cemetery, Zillebeke, Belgium. Grave reference I.F.4	
RULE, Charles	An elder brother of Alexander's – see chapter on 'ALEXANDER RULE'.	2, 56, 78, 156, 180.
RULE, Jane Elizabeth (Nettie or Jeannie)	Elder sister of Alexander's - see chapter on 'ALEXANDER RULE'.	3, 52.
RULE, John	Alexander's father - see chapter on 'ALEXANDER RULE'.	22.
RULE, John (Jnr)	An elder brother of Alexander's – see chapter on 'ALEXANDER RULE'.	52, 96, 202.
SANGSTER, William John Campbell	Son of William Sangster, draper. Born in Aberdeen, 1st January 1896; educated at Aberdeen Grammar School; Christ's College, Blackheath, and Aberdeen University; graduated M.A., 1914, and was studying for a medical career. He was a member of the University Officers Training Corps and when war broke out he	140, 217.

NAME	NOTES	PAGE
	immediately joined the Army, receiving his commission as a 2nd Lieutenant in the 4th Gordons on 3rd October 1914. After training at Aberdeen and Bedford, he crossed to France on 24th June 1915. He was killed on 25th September 1915 aged 19, having been detailed to lead a platoon to capture a portion of German trenches, which he did successfully. With great courage he and his men held on to the position, only to lose it later when it was re-captured by the Germans with the loss of most of these Gordons' lives, Sangster's included. Following his death, his father published a Memorial Book, now in the Imperial War Museum in London, in which he collected letters and other memorabilia relating to his son's short life. In one letter from young William to his parents, he talks about '*dressing Pratt's fingers*' (see diary for 19th July) and he mentions having a '*drum-up, i.e. tea*'. In one exchange of letters following William's death, his father had written to the Aberdeen University Principal, Sir George Adam Smith, enclosing a copy of a letter received from a 4th Gordons' soldier describing his son's death. The Principal, who himself had lost a son to the war by this time, replied, "*My own boy's photograph is here before me as I write and it is out of a full heart, as a fellow-sufferer with you, that I assure you of my deep sympathy with you. The days do not*	

NAME	NOTES	PAGE
	and will not lessen the pain of our loss in these brave sons of ours. But neither can any lapse of time subtract from the value of the high sacrifice which they have offered in so righteous a cause.... Your son has *gallantly served his country and the sacred cause committed to her and we of the University are proud of him – proud and grateful. Yours very sincerely, George Adam Smith*" **Burial details:** Name recorded on the Menin Gate Memorial, Ypres, Panel 38.	
SCOTT, Colonel	Padre at Bedford.	106.
SCOTT, David (Davy or Davie)	A private in the Suffolk Regiment, one of the 4th Gordons' 'sponsoring' units when they first arrived in the trenches.	34, 36, 94, 180, 194.
SCOTT, William D H (L C)	Lance Corporal. Membership of U Company was not restricted to students and graduates of Aberdeen University. L.C. Scott (actually William D.H. Scott – L.C. was probably a nickname with reference to his rank) transferred to 4th Gordons from the Lothian and Borders Horse when the unit was at Bedford, having graduated from the University of Edinburgh. Scott was killed on 17th March 1915, the first soldier of the former U Company to die in the fighting. **Burial details:** Wytschaete Military Cemetery, Belgium. Grave Reference IV.D.8	42.
SHANKS, John	Son of John Shanks, inspector of collectors; born in Aberdeen, 4th June 1893. He matriculated in Arts at	4, 40, 44,

NAME	NOTES	PAGE
	Aberdeen University in 1912, with a reputation as an English scholar. He was a regular contributor (as 'Jus') of vivid prose, as well as verse of real merit, to "Alma Mater". Joined U Company in March 1914, mobilized in August and, after Bedford, crossed with the Battalion to France and on to Belgium in February 1915. He was wounded on 3rd June 1915, during the long spell in the trenches beside the Menin Road. He was reported missing at Hooge on 25th September 1915 and was afterwards presumed killed, aged 22. **Burial details:** Name recorded on the Menin Gate Memorial, Ypres, Panel 38.	132, 184, 188, 194, Annex C.
SILVER, Alexander (Sandy)	Born in Kinneff, Aberdeenshire, on 14th September 1894. Educated at Robert Gordon's College, Aberdeen. Matriculated at Aberdeen University in 1912 to study Agriculture. Deployed with D Company. Early on was a company cook but soon volunteered for a rifle platoon. Posted as missing, presumed dead, aged 21, after the action at Hooge on 25th September 1915. **Burial details:** Name recorded on the Menin Gate Memorial, Ypres, Panel 38.	8, 102, 154, 160, 168, 176, 190, 192, 194, 196, 204, 208, Annex C.
SIMPSON, James	Eldest son of Mr James Simpson, 13 Jackson Terrace, Aberdeen. Former pupil of Aberdeen Grammar School. Second Lieutenant in 4th Gordons. Wounded in the leg at Hill 60 on 9th June 1915 and had to have his leg amputated. Died 21st June 1915, aged 25. **Burial details:** Le Treport	126.

NAME	NOTES	PAGE
	Military Cemetery, France. Grave reference Plot 1, Row D, Grave 2.	
SKINNER, Alexander (Sandy)	Sergeant. Son of John Skinner, roadman; born in Dingwall, Ross-shire, 21st July 1889. Educated at Dingwall Academy, Glasgow Technical College, Aberdeen Provincial Training College and Aberdeen University (Arts and Science, 1909-11). Joined U Company, 1909. After graduating, appointed assistant teacher and manual instructor, the Supplementary School, Dumbarton. Continued with U Company. Mobilized in August 1914 and proceeded to Bedford, from where he went to Belgium in February 1915. He was killed in the trenches near Kemmel on 22nd April 1915, aged 25, by a rifle bullet fired from an enfilading flank 900 yards (825 metres) away. **Burial details:** Wytschaete Military Cemetery, Belgium. Grave Reference IV.C.7.	4, 38, 44, 54, 58, 72.
SMITH-DORRIEN, Sir Horace Lockwood	General. Commander of the Second Army at this time. One of the few survivors of the Battle of Isandhlwana against the Zulus in 1879. He also fought in the Second Boer War. Although he was well-respected by many soldiers of all ranks, his relationship with Field Marshal Sir John French, the Commander-in-Chief of the British Expeditionary Force (B.E.F.), was not good. Lord Kitchener, the Minister of State for War, appointed Smith-Dorrien as commander of the	24.

NAME	NOTES	PAGE
	B.E.F.'s II Corps, whereas French would have preferred Douglas Haig. The relationship deteriorated further until, in May 1915, French sacked Smith-Dorrien from his command of the Second Army. He held several other posts including that of General Officer Commanding East Africa, Lieutenant of The Tower of London and Governor of Gibraltar. He died in 1930, aged 72, after a car accident.	
SMITH, George (of Pittodrie)	Captain, 6th Gordons. Son of George and Mary Workman Smith, of Glenmorag, Dunoon, Argyllshire. Husband of Kathleen Marion Smith, of Pittodrie, Aberdeenshire. Killed during the action at Neuve Chapelle on 13th March 1915, aged 44. A poem in tribute appeared in the Aberdeen Evening Express on Friday 19th March 1915: *He sleeps now in a soldier's grave upon a foreign strand,* *No more he'll roam the heather hills of his native land,* *He fell fighting like a hero – fearless, strong and brave –* *But now, alas, they've laid him in a British soldier's grave.* *In many a little homestead at the foot of Bennachie,* *Along the valleys of the Don, the Deveron and the Dee,* *In humble ha' and cottage where leal-hearted Scotsmen dwell,* *They are sorrowing for the Captain who so nobly fought and fell.*	50.

NAME	NOTES	PAGE
	We will miss his cheery welcome, we will miss his sunny smile; *Before we meet his equal we will travel many a mile,* *He was one of "Nature's gentlemen" a true and trusty friend;* *To his loved ones in their darksome hour our sympathies extend.* **Burial Details**: Name inscribed on Le Touret Memorial, Richebourg-L'avoue, Pas de Calais, France. Panel 39-41.	
SMITH, George Alexander	Lieutenant Colonel. Son of Robert Smith J.P.; born at Auchmar, Leslie, Aberdeenshire on 21st November 1874. Educated at Aberdeen Grammar School; graduated in Law from Aberdeen University in 1897. Advocate in Aberdeen, 1913. For many years Smith was an enthusiastic Volunteer and Territorial, being commissioned 2nd Lieutenant in the Gordons in 1900 and reaching the rank of Major in 1913. On the outbreak of war he was mobilized with the 4th Battalion Gordon Highlanders and went out with them to France in February 1915 as second-in-command. He was wounded at Y Wood, Hooge in June 1915 (where his pocket book slowed what would have otherwise been a fatal hit from a shrapnel bullet) and for a second time in August 1916. From December 1915 till October 1916 he commanded the 8th King's Own Royal Lancasters, and saw service at the Bluff, St. Eloi, and the	46, 132, 134.

NAME	NOTES	PAGE
	Somme battles of Delville Wood, Guillemont, etc. For his services at the front he was created a Companion of the Distinguished Service Order in March 1916. From October 1916 till October 1917 he was in charge of the Territorial Records at Rouen. Preferring to go in the line again, he joined the 5th Gordon Highlanders and took part in the big retreat at St. Quentin. Following the loss of Lieut. Colonel McTaggart and most of the Battalion's officers in March 1918, Smith was promoted to Lieutenant Colonel and appointed to the position of Commanding Officer of the 5th Battalion. He was killed by a shell on 28th July 1918, aged 43, whilst leading his men at Buzancy in France. Colonel Smith was four times mentioned in Dispatches, 13th June 1916; 4th August 1917; 21st December 1917; 28th August 1918. **Burial Details**: Buried at Raperie British Cemetery, Villemontoire, France. Grave Reference Plot 3A, Row D., Grave 10.	
SMITH, Robert J (Knockando)	Son of John Smith, East Mains, Knockando; born at Knockando, Morayshire, 11th October 1889. He received his early education at the local Public School and afterwards matriculated at Aberdeen University where he studied Agriculture from 1910-14. Joined U Company in 1910. He obtained the University Diploma in Agriculture in 1913, as well as the National Diploma in Dairying. In 1914 he gained the National Diploma	14, 180.

NAME	NOTES	PAGE
	in Agriculture, with distinction. He was appointed to a post in the Inland Revenue Lands Valuation Department, but had only been there three months when, as a member of U Company, he was mobilised. After training he crossed to France in February 1915, but in May was severely wounded and sent home. Smith was recommended for a commission and gazetted to the 6th Seaforths in August 1915. On 1st September 1916 he returned to France and in autumn of that year he was killed by a shell when leading his company on the third enemy line on 13th November 1916 aged 27. Final rank: Second Lieutenant. **Burial Details**: Buried at Mailly Wood Cemetery, Mailly-Maillet, Somme, France. Grave Reference Plot 1, Row F, Grave 29.	
SOMMERS, Cecil	See – DOWN, Norman	
SPARK, Arthur Percy	Son of Robert Spark; born at Durris on 4th June 1894. Private, D Company, 4th Gordon Highlanders, 1909, later U Company. Mobilized, 4th August 1914. Commissioned, 7th Gordons, 20th July 1915. Served - Home, 1914-15; France, February-May 1915. Severely wounded. Resumed studies and graduated M.B., Ch.B. from Aberdeen University in 1917. Commissioned, Royal Navy, 24th April 1917. Served - Belgian Coast Patrol; Royal Navy Hospital, Corfu; Constantinople; Gallipoli;	17, 52, 82, 84.

NAME	NOTES	PAGE
	served with the Dardanelles Commission on H.M.S. Triad, June 1917-August 1919. Final rank: Surgeon-Lieutenant. Played for Scotland in wartime rugby international. Represented Great Britain in 1924 Paris Olympics. Represented British Empire in USA 1928 (Hammer, Shot and Discus.) Lord Mayor of Stoke-on-Trent from 1945-1950. Died in 1953 aged 59.	
STEPHEN, Frederick Charles	Lieutenant. Son of John Stephen, farmer. Born at Fordyce on 4th December 1886; educated at Fordyce Academy; entered Aberdeen University as Seventh Bursar; graduated M.A. (I Math.), 1909; Simpson Mathematical Prize, Greig Prize in Natural Philosophy, and David Rennet Gold Medal. In October 1909 he went up to Emmanuel College, Cambridge, and in June 1910 was elected to a College Scholarship, holding at the same time both the Fullerton and Ferguson Scholarships in Mathematics. He left Cambridge with a First Class in both parts of the Mathematical Tripos, joined the staff of Merchant Taylor's School, London, and was doing very successful work in preparing boys for Sandhurst and the Universities. Although never a member of U Company, in August 1914 he enlisted in the 4th Gordons and, soon afterwards, went to the Front having been commissioned into the 6th Gordons. He was killed at Loos on 25th September 1915, aged 28, as a	76.

303

NAME	NOTES	PAGE
	Lieutenant of bomb-throwers. **Burial Details**: Name recorded on the Loos Memorial, Pas de Calais, France, Panel 115, Column 1.	
STEVENSON	A soldier in 1st Gordons who, like Rule, came from Huntly.	98.
TAYLOR, John William	Born in Aberdeen on 1st March 1895. Graduated M.A. from Aberdeen University, 1916. Enlisted as a Trooper in the Scottish Horse in 1911 (after U Troop disbanded in 1908). Transferred to U Company, 4th Gordons, in 1913. Mobilized, August 1914. Commissioned, 3rd March 1915; attached to 11th Gordon Highlanders (training battalion). Served - Home, France, Germany, 1914-19. Final rank: Captain.	28.
TENNANT, Edward Martin Cookes	Lieutenant. Son of Edward Tennant, insurance secretary; born in Aberdeen on 30th August, 1896. Educated at Aberdeen Grammar School where he joined D Company, the Grammar School Company of the 4th Gordon Highlanders in 1913. He had completed his first year of study in science at Aberdeen University when war broke out and he was mobilised. He was, unlike most of the former soldiers of U Company, in training at Bedford until May 1915, when he received his commission in the 4th Battalion, the Gordon Highlanders. On 25th September 1915 he was wounded at Hooge, and spent some months in hospital in England, returning to France in May of 1916. His death, on 16th September 1916,	140, 217.

NAME	NOTES	PAGE
	aged 20, was due to wounds received in action at Serre, while he was in charge of a party covering a raid on German trenches. **Burial Details**: Buried at Bertrancourt Military Cemetery, Somme, France. Grave Reference Plot 1, Row F, Grave 19.	
TEUNON, James MacAndrew	Son of James Teunon, Turriff; born in Turriff on 22nd September 1895. Educated at Turriff Higher Grade School and Robert Gordon's College, Aberdeen. Matriculated 1913 in Arts at Aberdeen University. Enlisted in the 2nd/4th Gordons in November 1914; drafted to D Company, 4th Gordons, September 1915; wounded at Hooge and invalided home. Listed in the Robert Gordon's College Former Pupils' Magazine Roll of Honour in August 1915. In March 1916 he transferred to the Royal Engineers and went to France. For eighteen months he served with the Special Brigade, Royal Engineers (formed in 1916 to develop the use of poison gas). Commissioned in June 1918 as Second Lieutenant in the Royal Garrison Artillery, but transferred in the following October to the Royal Air Force. He had just completed his pilot's course at Reading when he took ill with appendicitis and died in Queen Alexandra Military Hospital, London, on 30th December 1918, aged 23. **Burial Details**: Buried at Turriff Cemetery, Aberdeenshire. Grave Reference C. 549.	178.

NAME	NOTES	PAGE
THOMSON, 'Spud'	D Company cook.	8, 10, 44.
THOMSON, James George (Jimmie)	Son of James Thomson, cabinet maker in Fochabers, Moray; born in Fochabers on 20th December 1893; younger brother of J M (Jock) Thomson. Educated at Milne's Institution, Fochabers. Matriculated at Aberdeen University in Arts, 1913. Joined U Company that year, was mobilized at the outbreak of war and saw service in France and Belgium with the 4th Gordons, rising to the rank of Sergeant. He was wounded in 1915 and later transferred to the Royal Field Artillery. He was killed on 19th October 1917 aged 23. **Burial Details**: Name recorded on Tyne Cot Memorial, Passchendaele, Belgium, Panel 6, Column 1.	56, 92, 100.
THOMSON, John MacLean (Jock)	Sergeant. Born in Fochabers on 2nd September 1889. Elder brother of James George Thomson. Graduated M.A. from Aberdeen University in 1911. He studied at Aberdeen United Free College from 1911-14. At the outbreak of war he was in charge of a Mission in Canada. He was serving with A Company, 4th Gordons when he was killed by a sniper in the trenches near Ypres on 22nd July 1915 aged 25. **Burial Details**: Name recorded on the Menin Gate Memorial, Ypres, Panel 38, Column 5.	64, 92, 148.
TOPPING, Robert Bayne (Roy)	Son of Robert Topping; born in Aberdeen on 28th August 1894. Studied Science at Aberdeen	12, 17, 20,

NAME	NOTES	PAGE
	University, 1911-12, 1919. Joined U Company, 1910. Served as Colour Sergeant in 1913. Mobilized, August 1914. Wounded in June 1915 at which time he was, according to the Aberdeen Weekly Journal of 25th June, 1915, serving as a Corporal. Commissioned, 16th October 1915; attached to 5th and 9th Gordons. Served - Home, 1914-15; France, February-June 1915; France, Germany, January 1917-August 1919. Final rank: Acting Captain. He resumed his studies after the war but did not graduate.	46, 54, 58, 62, 68, 76, 80, 100, 102, 104, 106, 108, 132.
TROUP, William	Son of Robert Troup; born at Rhynie, Aberdeenshire on 26th September 1895. Joined U Company April 1915. Served - Home, 1915; Belgium, 4-25 September 1915 (wounded and taken Prisoner of War). Graduated M.A. from Aberdeen University, 1919.	194.
WADDELL	Lieutenant. A Coy, 4th Gordons.	30, 215
WALKER, Daniel Ironside (Dan)	Son of James Walker, farmer, New Deer; born in New Deer, 11th January 1892. Enlisted in U Company, 1910; mobilized August 1914. Served in Belgium, February-May 1915. Wounded 4th May 1915 and hospitalized. M.A. Aberdeen University, 1916. Member, Aberdeen University O.T.C., Nov 1916-Oct 1919. Commissioned (unattached list), 26th August 1917. Graduated M.B. Ch.B. from Aberdeen in 1920. DPH 1921. Appointed Medical Officer of Health for Banffshire in 1939. Member of the North East	31, 46, 48, 52, 64, 84, 280.

NAME	NOTES	PAGE
	Scotland Regional Health Board. Died in 1951 aged 59.	
WATSON, James Innes (Jimmie)	Son of John Watson; born at Banchory-Devenick, Aberdeenshire, 27th April 1891. Joined U Company, 1909. M.A., 1912 Aberdeen University. Commissioned March 1914. Mobilized, August 1914, sent to Bedford and then Belgium during 1915. Wounded at Hooge on 25th September 1915 and returned to his studies at Aberdeen University from where he graduated M.B. Ch.B. in 1917. Transferred to the R.A.M.C. Served in Italy and France, August 1918-January 1919. Final rank: Captain. He was in General Practice in Dufftown and Nairn from 1920 until 1958. Died in 1970 aged 79.	10, 108, 166.
WATT, Lachlan McLean	Padre. Reverend L McLean Watt of Edinburgh.	12.
WELCH, William B	Captain in A Company, 6th Gordons (Science master, The Gordons Schools, Huntly). Wounded on 14th March 1915 at Neuve Chapelle. He was admitted to the General Hospital at Versailles with gunshot injuries to the face and arm. Towards the end of April 1915, he was in Aberdeenshire, supporting the drive to recruit volunteers for the army.	50.
WHYTE, James	Son of James Whyte, crofter. Born in Tarves on 3rd May 1894. After a highly successful school record at Tarves Public School, he matriculated as an Arts student at Aberdeen University in October 1912, with a view to becoming a	136.

NAME	NOTES	PAGE
	teacher. Concurrently with his University course he became a student at the Training Centre and took a very active part in the social side of the College, and in 1913-14 was vice-president of its Debating Society. Enlisted in U Company in June 1913, and in August 1914 was mobilized with his unit. Became a Lance-Corporal whilst at Bedford and went to France with the Battalion in February 1915. He received a fatal wound during an attack in which his Battalion took part near Ypres and died on 18th June 1915, aged 21. **Burial Details**: Buried at Aeroplane Cemetery, Ypres Grave Reference Plot 2, Row B, Grave 1.	
WILSON, Drummy	Drum-Major. In civilian life, he was a butcher with premises in South Mount Street, Aberdeen.	194.
WILSON, Robert	Son of W. W. Wilson; born in Auchnagatt on 20th August 1892. Private, U Company, 4th Gordon Highlanders, 1911. Mobilized, August 1914. Served - Home, 1914-15; Belgium, February-September 1915. Prisoner of War. Final rank: Private. Graduated M.A. from Aberdeen University 1919. B.D. in 1921, following which he became Assistant Minister at the West Parish Church, Aberdeen. He also served as parish minister at Udny, Perth, Eskdalemuir and Dumfries between 1922 and 1955. He then served at the East Church, Forfar, between 1955 and 1962. Died in 1967 aged 75.	132.

Annex B – Diary Data

Weather and Wet Conditions

There was considerable variety in the weather experienced by Alexander Rule during the eight months of 1915 covered by his diary entries. From snow in late February and early March, to experiencing sunburn in late May, Rule and his fellow students met conditions that were not too different to what could be encountered in the North East of Scotland.

Rule helpfully says a few words about the weather in many of his diary entries. A summary of these notes gives a good picture of what the days were like:

WEATHER	DAYS
Cloudy	15
Cold	20
Foggy	9
Frosty	11
Glorious Day	**55**
Hot	12
Mixed	26
Rain	33
Snow	9
Sunny	37

Unfortunately, the frequent good weather was not reflected in the state of the trenches. A combination of heavy clay soil, field drainage that had been destroyed and frequent digging below the water table meant that most of the trenches in Flanders permanently held water. It was often just a question of how deep it was, as well as how deep was the soft mud below the water.

Time in the Trenches

A considerable portion of the material written about life in the trenches on the Western Front can give the impression that soldiers spent months on end in the trenches.

The longest continuous period that Rule spent in the trenches was 24 days in May/June and that was considered a very long time. The fire trenches were not pleasant places to live and soldiers, often wet, cold and exposed to the enemy, would quickly become demoralised if they spent too much time in the trenches. Because of this, the British Army rotated men in and out continuously. Between battles, a unit spent perhaps 10 days a month in the trench system and, of those, rarely more than three days right up on the front line. It was not unusual to be out of the line for a month.

D Company spent a greater proportion of time in the trenches than many units, but still only 103 days in them, compared to 124 days out of the trenches – 45%. However, being out of the trenches did not often mean at rest, as there were fatigues to be undertaken, such as trench digging, laying communications cables and carrying ammunition, food and water to those soldiers in the trenches, as well as training in tactics, marksmanship and new equipment.

Alexander Rule's Close Encounters

Rule was by no means unusual in having many close encounters with injury or even death. The following list of those incidents that he notes in his diary gives some idea of what most soldiers faced every single day in an active sector of the Western Front:

Fri 5th March 1915 – First impression of verey lights & rattle of 'angry' musketry at close qrs (just like at rifle butts). Heard 1st bullet as left main road. Some felt much closer after that.

Mon 8th March 1915 – Exciting going across the open (hail of bullets) – didn't quite appreciate gravity of situation I 'spose. Man hit right in front of me.

Tuesday 9th March 1915 – Bullets whistling & cracking overhead by night. Sunny day – tempted out to back of 'grouse-butt' – driven in by shrapnel & 'coal boxes' – didn't realise danger at first. Got breakfast spoiled by snipers (showers of muck from sandbags).

Friday 12th March 1915 – Left with Suffolks at dusk but had d - d long wait on the road – bullets flying around.

Thursday 18th March 1915 – *Shower of bullets made us all lie flat in mud at back of trench.*

Sunday 21st March 1915 – *Shock when (after a "flop" to dodge rifle bullets) I told a dead Ger. to move on.*

Thursday 1st April 1915 – *Narrow squeak from falling shrapnel.*

Sunday 4th April 1915 – *Close shave 5th shot (the closest) luckily the last. Heavy showers of mud falling on everything and everybody. Don't think I quite realised the danger. Topping seemed aghast at my pleasantries when barbed wire was deposited practically on top of us.*

Sunday 25th April 1915 – *Some bullets pretty close.*

Friday 7th May 1915 – *Badly shelled in forenoon (small stuff) – some very close.*

Wednesday 26th May 1915 – *Big 'crump' just missed us – spaces bet. platoons.*

Friday 28th May 1915 – *Trench in front being heavily shelled; shrapnel bullet just missed me.*

Sunday 30th May 1915 – *Dodging trench mortar bombs – good fun!*

Wednesday 9th June 1915 – *On b. wire (knife rest) fatigue in front of new trench. Shrapnel right amongst us.*

Saturday 12th June 1915 – *Went to work on C.T. at dusk – narrow squeaks from set snipers rifles – while working in trench.*

Monday 14th June 1915 – *Back to dump – shelled off it – narrow squeaks – back again for amn.*

Wednesday 16th June 1915 – *Sniped at continually (attack disturbed hornets' nest). Pure hell on l. of Midsex trench. Dead & dying everywhere – moaning as we accidentally trod on them. Whizz bang shrapnel – marvellous escapes. Over the top into C.T.*

312

2ft deep. McSween & MacIver hesitated & got killed stone dead just behind me. Buried twice, relieved at midnight.

Tuesday 20th July 1915 – *H.E. in wood behind us but our suppt. line escaped. My traverse blown in but no casualties*

Thursday 22nd July 1915 – *Got it thick & heavy – shelled all the way. Could feel the vicious hot breath of the closer shell explosions.*

Sunday 25th July 1915 – *Few bullets singing around (mostly richochets) tended to mar sylvan solitudes*

Monday 26th July 1915 – *Putting in loophole – some dead enfilade sniping put wind up us.*

Friday 30th July 1915 – *Right to camp without rest – just clear in time – Jerry started to chip 'em in quick & lively.*

Sat 31st July 1915 – *Ran into heavy shell fire at Kruisstraat on way up but decided to carry on – magnificent view of bombardment – like fireworks on gigantic scale! Just skimmed the danger zone. Canal again – some bullets pretty close.*

Friday 6th August 1915 – *Sentry duty in sap – bit of a thrill with the snipers bullets (very close).*

Saturday 7th August 1915 – *Sniper just missed me in sap at stand-to deafened me for a bit. Lot of shelling in region of the "Bluff" & new C.T. on left. Splinters & mud flying all over the place.*

Monday 9th August 1915 – *Some 'hair-raisers' over our trench.*

Monday 13th September 1915 – *Got pretty well shelled in suppts. too. R.G.A. gunner killed beside me.*

Tuesday 14th September 1915 – *very nearly caught by V. light with stern in air (half over ditch immed. in front of post!)*

Thursday 16th September 1915 – *Fritz replied with whizz bangs fr. "Hill 60" – knocking hell out of Sanct Wd – trees crashing everywhere. Few casualties amongst us.*

Saturday 18th September 1915 – Cleared fire trench & got salvos of hair raising shrapnel as we made for reserve trenches.

Saturday 25th September 1915 – H. explosive shell got me. Lay buried some time..... Toes broken clean over – almost collapsed in R Scots trenches thro loss of blood.

Yet Alexander Rule survived, badly wounded but alive, going on to live for another sixty-seven years.

Overall, of 5,397,00 British men and women who served during World War I, 703,000* were killed and 1,663,000 were wounded; a total of 2,366,000 casualties, 44% of those mobilized.

* With this figure added to those from the (then) British Empire who died, each of the 888,246 fatalities was represented by a ceramic poppy during the 'Blood Swept Land and Seas of Red' art installation at the Tower of London during the autumn of 2014.

'Disposal' – and Dispersal – of U Company Members

Formally, U Company of the 4th Battalion, Gordon Highlanders, had ceased to exist – renamed D Company - at the time the 51st Highland Division 'invaded' Bedford. That most of the former U Company were not best pleased about the loss of identity is equally true. What might be less accurate is the interpretation that U Company was wiped out at Hooge on the 25th September 1915.

As we see from his diary entries, Alexander Rule was one of the staunch believers in maintaining a company of University men, yet even he had accepted the change of name as we can see from the inside front cover of his diary showing 'D' Company, not 'U'.

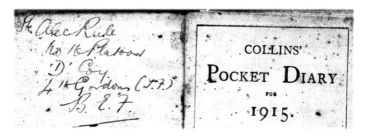

The Army certainly did not seem to be anxious to maintain the previous concentration of students and university staff that had existed in U Company. For example, Rule notes, on the 12th September that, when the latest draft of replacements arrived, "*all (the) varsity men in (the) draft went to 13 Ptn – rotten principle when we (16 Platoon) have some non-varsity men.*"

There were two main reasons for the need to bring in replacements – commissions and casualties.

It was hardly surprising that these bright university students and staff would be candidates for commissions, although the War Office did not take any sort of holistic view on this. There was a small number commissioned whilst still at Bedford, but at least sixteen former U Company soldiers were commissioned to other units between D Company's arrival in Belgium and the action at Hooge on 25th September 1915.

Turning to casualties, twenty-four former U Company men were killed in Belgium prior to the Hooge action. A further fifteen were so seriously wounded that they took no further part in the fighting before Hooge. There were almost certainly others who were sick or on leave or, for other reasons, did not fight on the 25th September.

There is clear evidence of thirteen former U Company men dying that day or shortly afterwards from wounds sustained that day. That is no small number, but compared to the one hundred and thirty or so students and academics from Aberdeen University who went to the Western Front with the 4th Battalion Gordon Highlanders in early spring that year, it hardly constitutes the mass demise that has been suggested elsewhere. It is also worth remembering that overall, on that day, the Gordon Highlanders lost seven hundred and twenty seven men killed.

The high rate of survival is also evidenced by the attendance of thirty-eight former members of U Company, who had gone to Flanders with D Company in 1915, at a reunion dinner in the Constitutional Club in London in March 1939. They also provided a strong contingent at 4th Gordons' reunions through to the 1960s and, with true grit, some even into the 1970s.

Annex C – The Society of Good Johns

It is somehow in the nature of many people, especially the young, to join with others of like minds to form an informal group that has a distinct identity. The catalyst might be music, or sport, or a hobby, or, as is the case here, shared experiences of the most demanding type.

Alexander Rule describes the birth of The Society of Good Johns in his book '*Students Under Arms*', as well as in his diary. It took place early in September 1915, drawing mainly for members on a few of D Company 4th Gordons who had originally been in U Company of that battalion. They "*met together as a secret and newly-born sect, called 'The Society of Good Johns', to promote the spirit of good fellowship. Full membership was rigidly restricted to 'good fellows' who had proved themselves by real comradeship in arms, but no more than three of the twelve foundation members bore the apostolic patronymic 'John'.*

The name and the birth of the Society had been entirely fortuitous, and at the first meeting our wine order – twelve bottles of vin rouge (tres ordinaire) – gave us an idea for a secret countersign. Madame, our hostess, was obviously puzzled at the magnitude of our initial order, and our chairman, doubting his pronunciation of the word douze, resorted to sign language. He held up both hands, palms inwards and finger extended, signifying ten; then, clenching the fingers of either hand, he left the thumbs projecting, in an attitude vulgarly known as 'Thumbs Up', to denote an additional two, and so supplied our countersign".

In his diary, Rule writes,

<u>Monday 20th September – Meeting of "Johns"</u>
(1st meeting held on Saturday 11th September)

(15 present)

The 2nd full meeting (and as it happened also the last) was held in fm house near Ouderdom.

The meeting was properly constituted (Crichty in the Chair) and the Honourable if not 'Ancient' Society was put on a proper footing with Pres, Vice Presidents, Life Members (Haig, French, Kitchener, "Hoppy", McLintock, Watty Inkster, Pratt etc admitted.) 'Lachie' was blackballed nem.com (*NOTE – "With no-one dissenting"!*) & a "Secret Sign" – a mystic no '12' (the no. present at inaugural meeting) given by
(1) holding both hands upwards (palms towards face) fingers & thumbs extended - & in rapid sequence
(2) "thumbs up"! This was the original "wine order" signifying "douze boteilles vin rouge Madame".

Each member contributed a song & story in turn amid Varsity choruses 'Varsity Y 'Gorra, 'U' Coy Y Gorra! (some unprintable) were sandwiched in to gt. delight of old Suffolks & Midsex "Regulars" who were "permitted" to be present.

Complete harmony prevailed with exc of one fleeting interruption by Silver who spoiled a gt speech by objecting to doing "ph jerks" under that neck-shooting ----t Pete - order restored & retreat in "fair" order.

Silver with difficulty prevented fr. sleeping it off in "neep park".
Choruses enlived journey & bivvies were carried in irreg. frontal attack & one flanking movement secured C.T. - really a drain.

In bivvies, the disturbance was so great – (one of Johns so far forgetting himself as to piss up against 13 Ptn's bivvy) that RSM came round on war path & order was at length restored.

The mixture of whisky & red wine was very potent & several of more cautious spirits judged discretion (in form of a 'peuk') the better part of valour – although realising the tragedy of wasting whisky!

Of the (12) original (foundation) Johns who attended inaugural meeting –
– Mason, Shanks, Silver – killed 25/9/1915
– Haig (2nd & last meeting) – killed 25/9/1915
– Gunn & Scott – wounded 25/9/1915 & killed on the 'Somme' 1916
– C Gordon killed on the 'Somme' 1916
– Self, C Reid, J Forbes, Booth, Gow – wounded 25/9/1915

Sole John remaining with 'U' Coy after 25/9/1915 – Crichty – wounded later. Pete attended 2nd meeting & also survived Hooge.

Another former U Company soldier, Robert Stewart, who attended the meeting and describes how there was an alternative name for the society – the Jocks' Society - described the evening in an article written for *Alma Mater* in 1917.

"The memorable day, September 22nd 1915, with all its bustle and preparation passed. Evening fell, and the distant guns beat a muffled tattoo, as, our day's drill over, we left our humble bivouacs and sought the unpretentious precincts of a neighbouring farmhouse, the rendez-vous of the Jocks' Society.

This, though we refused to believe it, was to be our last meeting, for on the morrow we were to be moving up to the trenches, preparatory to the September push in the Hooge Salient.

But the spirit of U Company rose above sinister premonition for the future, and laughter and song ran around the rough deal table of the farm kitchen.

It had been the custom of University men in the Battalion to meet here, and over a frugal dish of potatoes and sauce (erypels – in the patois of the district) to discuss subjects of common interest, and Alma Mater figured largely in the conversation. Those of us who were privileged to attend will recall the scene – Sergeant Crichton in the presidential chair maintained order with zest in debates.

The speeches of such as Privates Mason and Surtees were received with keen relish, and appreciated as literary delicacies by their hearers, while Peterkin's caustic humour, usually directed against some members of the Society, and Sunny's (McLellan) subtlety added greatly to the enjoyment of the evening.

Supper over, we gathered round the heart of the open fireplace and the past occupied our thoughts. Marischal College, with all its joys and associations, was discussed, and many a wish expressed that soon, notebook in hand, we would again cross the quadrangle. No mention of the morrow was made.

Soon we heard the first post blown and before departing, the strains of Gaudeamus – sung with great fervour – echoed far and wide."

Annex D – Sources & Background Reading

Alexander Rule – 1915 personal diary

Alexander Rule – '*Students Under Arms - Being the War Adventures of the Aberdeen University Company of the Gordon Highlanders'*. Aberdeen University Press, 1934

Alexander Rule – '*Forests Of Australia'*. Angus and Robertson, 1967

John McConachie – '*The Student Soldiers'*. Moravian Press, 1995

J B Duffus – '*Town, Gown And Gun – A Centennial History of Aberdeen Universities Officers Training Corps 1912-2012'*. J B Duffus, 2012

Lyn Macdonald – '*1914*'. Michael Joseph Ltd., 1987

Lyn Macdonald – '*1915 – The Death Of Innocence'*. Headline Book Publishing, 1993

Richard Lewis Campbell Dargie – '*The Grammar At War, 1914-1918*'. The Aberdeen Grammar School Former Pupils Club, 2014

William Taylor & Peter Diack – '*Student and Sniper-Sergeant – A Memoir of J. K. Forbes, M.A.'*. Hodder and Stoughton, 1916

Cecil Sommers – '*Temporary Heroes'*. The Bodley Head, 1917

James Fraser – *War Diary 1915*. Aberdeen University Review

James Fraser and Family – 'Dr Jimmy'. Aberdeen University Press, 1980

University of Aberdeen – Special Collections – 'In Memoriam' website. (www.abdn.ac.uk/library/roll-of-honour/)

The Gordon Highlanders Museum (www.gordonhighlanders.com)

Aberdeen Universities Officers Training Corps: Photo archive

The Old Boars: Photo archive (www.theoldboars.smugmug.com)

The Memorial Window, The Gordon Schools, Huntly, Aberdeenshire

Ancestry.co.uk

The British Newspaper Archive

Trove – the Australian Newspaper Archive

The London Gazette

Robert Gordon's College, Aberdeen – WWI Roll of Honour

The Commonwealth War Graves Commission

The Imperial War Museum

National Records of Scotland

1915 War Diary – 4th Battalion, The Gordon Highlanders

Lt Col John McCrae – '*In Flanders Fields*'

Alma Mater 1914-1917. Aberdeen University Press

'*Great War Tommy – The British Soldier 1914-1918 (All models).*' Haynes

www.4thgordons.com

www.firstworldwar.com

Wilf Hastwell '*A Phantasy*' 1917 (Incorporated into David Lewer's '*A Spiritual Song*' (London, 1961), pages 295-6.) Courtesy of The Temple Church, Temple, London

Annex E – Acknowledgements

The Commonwealth War Graves Commission for their kind permission to use images from their site.

Jenny Musker BA(Hons) R.M.S. W.F.M. M.A.S.F., Natural History Illustrator, for permission to use her painting *When The Day Ends – Remember Me*' on the cover of this book.

Valerie Ross, teacher at The Gordon Schools, Huntly, for explaining and caring about the history of that school's stunning, unique WWI memorial window.

Alison Allan and Neil Harrison at the Gatehouse Design and Print Consultancy, Robert Gordon University, Aberdeen, for their advice on the production process.

Andrew MacGregor and Paul Logie at The Library and Historic Collections, Aberdeen University, for their knowledge, advice and willingness to help.

At The Gordon Highlanders Museum, Aberdeen, much thanks is due to several individuals: Anne Park (who freely gave of her considerable knowledge on WWI – particularly of memorials in and beyond the North East of Scotland – as well as lending items from her personal collection); Bob Donald (who I met as an Officer Cadet at AUOTC, who also has an excellent store of military knowledge equalled only by a moustache of similarly admirable breadth and depth); Royan Yule (a fellow pupil at The Grammar School in Aberdeen, who also helps bring the excellent museum to life); Curator Ruth Duncan who patiently and effectively answered a long list of very diverse queries.

Mike Taitt for the very generous and thoughtful gift of his copy of '*Student and Sniper-Sergeant – A Memoir of J.K. Forbes M.A.*'

Aileen Shanks, my sister, for useful comment on the draft from the viewpoint of a non-military background.

Jim Duffus, a fellow pupil, member of the Combined Cadet Force and friend at Aberdeen Grammar School and beyond, for providing a huge amount of support, both practical and personal, during the writing of this book. It is a better work for the time and experience he so freely gave.

Dr. Ros Shanks, my wife, for an incredible amount of help, time, patience, advice, proofreading and coffee. Seldom has a red pen been able to convey such clarity of approval – or otherwise – and I am so very grateful for her never-faltering encouragement.

To the soldiers mentioned in this book and to so many others, is acknowledged a debt that we can never express, never repay, but will never forget.

Annex F – Author

Graham Shanks has lived in the North East of Scotland most of his life. He attended Aberdeen Grammar School, Mackie Academy in Stonehaven and Aberdeen University.

His great-grandfather, William Gourlay Shanks, served with the 78th Highlanders, including a spell in Canada and as part of the Royal Guard at Ballater, looking after Queen Victoria (and taking the train into Aberdeen on nights off, thereby meeting the young lady who later became his wife). When he left the army in 1874, he was serving at Fort George, N.B. (North Britain).

His grandfather, David T Shanks, served with 1st Battalion, The Seaforth Highlanders and, upon the outbreak of war in 1914, he and his family (including Graham's father, William) returned to Scotland from their posting in India. Service in Mesopotamia and the Western Front was followed at the end of the war by a spell with the Royal Air Force's Number One Flying School. There, as a Company Sergeant Major, he endured the thankless task of teaching drill to the 'boys in blue'.

With war looming once more in 1939, Graham's father was strongly advised by the aforementioned CSM Shanks to avoid any prospect of serving with the infantry in trenches. He therefore voluntarily joined up before being conscripted and opted for the Royal Artillery Battery based in Arbroath, where he was a bank clerk.

Unfortunately, that went hand-in-hand with a visit to France with the British Expeditionary Force; a trip to the seaside at Dunkirk; a cruise on a splendid paddle steamer called the "Gracie Fields" that was cut short by a Stuka; his hair and scalp exchanged for bomb splinters; a bumpy trip in a small boat back to Blighty and a free hospital stay in Bath; easy to describe, awful to have experienced.

Like many, Graham's father opted not to talk about the war to his children, thus engendering Graham's interest. Fed initially only by snippets such as those from the lamented original "Victor' comic and the BBC's 'The Valiant Years', he had to wait until second year at the Grammar to join the Combined Cadet Force to learn more.

Five years with the CCF followed, which included a trip to 1st Gordons whilst they were training at Sennelager, near Paderborn in Germany. That was a visit that provided tremendous opportunities to see and participate in the live firing of a number of different weapons that would have been impossible in the UK and would nowadays freak a small army of overly protective risk-stoppers.

Next for Graham came University and the opportunity to join the Officers' Training Corps. However, unlike Alexander Rule and his cronies who leaned more to 'studenting rather than soldiering', Graham's enthusiasm for the OTC contributed greatly to his passage through university without being called to a graduation ceremony.

The world of work followed, a significant part of which was spent with Post Office Telecommunications, latterly British Telecom and BT. That brought Graham into contact with Royal Engineers (Postal and Courier) TA, with whom he spent many happy years and rose to the rank of Major. By way of coincidence, one of Graham's roles, when a civilian employed by Grampian Police, was to give instruction to soldiers of the Royal Guard at Victoria Barracks, Ballater, just as his great-grandfather would have done some 140 years previously.

He remained in touch with Aberdeen Universities Officers Training Corps and, through that connection, became aware of Alexander Rule's 1915 diary languishing in a safe there. Graham's initial attempt at a transcript some years ago was foiled by Rule's 'foul handwriting'. It was only by employing a range of photographic techniques during the second attempt that the diary became tolerably readable and made possible the publication of this book.

Now retired, Graham is considering other projects.